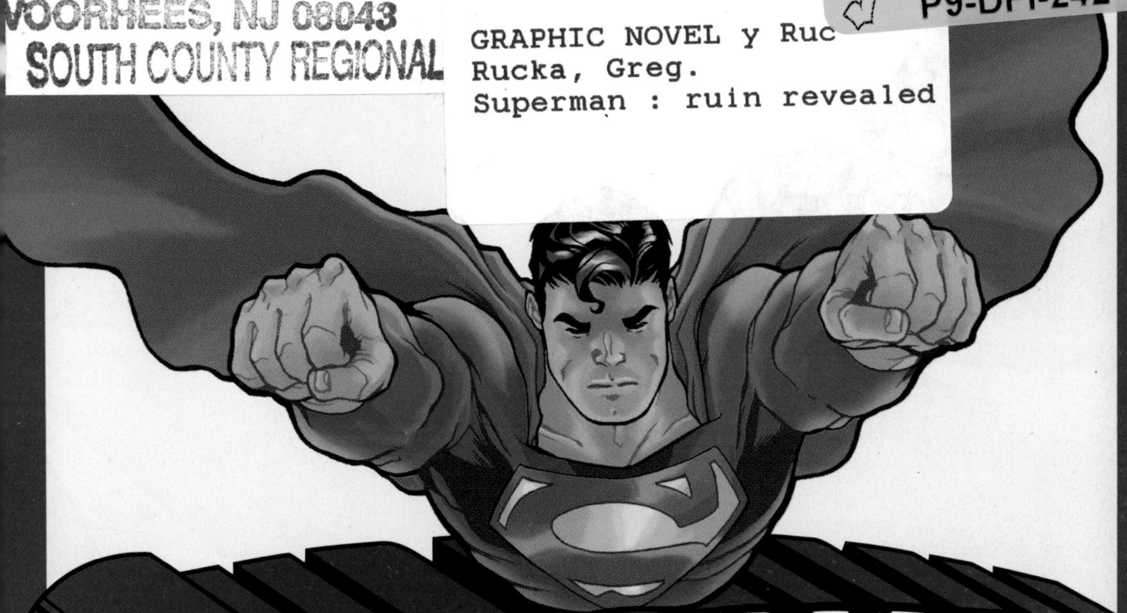

SUPERMAN
RUIN REVEALED

WRITERS GREG RUCKA
NUNZIO DEFILIPPIS & CHRISTINA WEIR

PENCILLERS KARL KERSCHL
RENATO GUEDES
DARRYL BANKS
ADAM DEKRAKER

INKERS KARL KERSCHL
RENATO GUEDES
WAYNE FAUCHER
CAM SMITH
ROBIN RIGGS

COLORISTS TANYA & RICHARD HORIE
RENATO GUEDES

LETTERERS PAT BROSSEAU
ROB LEIGH
NICK J. NAPOLITANO

ORIGINAL COVERS KARL KERSCHL

SUPERMAN CREATED BY JERRY SIEGEL & JOE SHUSTER

Dan Didio Senior VP-Executive Editor   **Eddie Berganza** Editor-original series   **Tom Palmer, Jr.** Associate Editor-original series
Jeanine Schaefer Assistant Editor-original series   **Robert Greenberger** Senior Editor-collected edition   **Anton Kawasaki**
Associate Editor-collected edition   **Robbin Brosterman** Senior Art Director   **Paul Levitz** President & Publisher   **Georg Brewer**
VP-Design & DC Direct Creative   **Richard Bruning** Senior VP-Creative Director   **Patrick Caldon** Executive VP-Finance & Operations
Chris Caramalis VP-Finance   **John Cunningham** VP-Marketing   **Terri Cunningham** VP-Managing Editor   **Alison Gill**
VP-Manufacturing   **Rich Johnson** VP-Book Trade Sales   **Hank Kanalz** VP-General Manager, WildStorm   **Lillian Laserson**
Senior VP & General Counsel   **Jim Lee** Editorial Director-WildStorm   **Paula Lowitt** Senior VP-Business & Legal Affairs
David McKillips VP-Advertising & Custom Publishing   **John Nee** VP-Business Development   **Gregory Noveck** Senior VP-Creative
Affairs   **Cheryl Rubin** Senior VP-Brand Management   **Jeff Trojan** VP-Business Development, DC Direct   **Bob Wayne** VP-Sales

SUPERMAN: RUIN REVEALED Published by DC Comics. Cover, introduction and compilation copyright © 2006 DC Comics.
All Rights Reserved. Originally published in single magazine form in ADVENTURES OF SUPERMAN 640-641, 644-647. Copyright ©
2005, 2006 DC Comics. All Rights Reserved. All characters, their distinctive likenesses and related elements featured in this publication
are trademarks of DC Comics. The stories, characters and incidents featured in this publication are entirely fictional. DC Comics does
not read or accept unsolicited submissions of ideas, stories or artwork.   DC Comics, 1700 Broadway, New York, NY 10019.
A Warner Bros. Entertainment Company.   Printed in Canada.   First Printing.   ISBN: 1-4012-0920-3.   ISBN 13: 978-1-4012-0920-9.
Cover illustration by **Karl Kerschl**.   Publication design by **John J. Hill**.

OUR STORY SO FAR...

Faster than a speeding bullet, more powerful than a locomotive, able to leap the tallest buildings with a single bound...**Superman** is known to all as the world's greatest super-hero. While he has faced many challenges that have tested his heroic abilities — including his own death and resurrection — the Man of Steel now finds his life in a downward spiral due to his most recent adventures...

Clark Kent and his *Daily Planet* editor Perry White faked Clark's firing, allowing him to go undercover to look for proof that then-President Lex Luthor was engaged in criminal activities. Meantime, White seemingly hired Clark's newspaper-office rival Jack Ryder to fill his investigative reporting slot. When Clark was finally ready to return to work, he was forced to settle for something lower on the food chain, the police beat.

Clark's wife, Lois Lane, had known about the demotion for weeks, but was sworn to secrecy by White. Once Clark found out, he was naturally upset. And before he had a chance to react to the news, he was needed again as Superman.

In Smallville, he had to deal with the wrathful Gog, seeking to kill Superman to prevent a particular future from coming to pass. He had to call upon other heroes — including Steel, Wonder Woman and the Teen Titans — to help him defeat his foe.

The Man of Steel again had to put his marital woes on hold when a new threat named Ruin arrived in Metropolis. For unknown reasons, Ruin made his attacks personal, and he was aided by twins with parasitic powers. During all of this, Lois was embedded with the U.S. armed forces to cover a Middle East conflict in Umec. Her assignment was interrupted when a sniper shot her, nearly killing her. It took all of Dr. Mid-Nite's skills and resources to save her life.

Soon thereafter, Superman created what he believed to be paradise, a better world beyond ours in the Phantom Zone. Paradise was, instead, lost to the essence of the Kryptonian villain Zod, and it quickly became a living hell for the one million people — including Superman's recovering wife — who had been whisked there during the "vanishing."

Back in the real world, as others conspired against him, the Man of Steel found himself at odds with several of his fellow heroes, coming to blows with his dearest friends.

After Superman and Wonder Woman destroyed his Arctic home, the Fortress of Solitude, Superman searched for a new location for his personal refuge. He continued to watch for Ruin, who remained a threat, and for another, more ominous danger the Fifth Dimensional imp Mr. Mxyzptlk had warned him about not once, but twice.

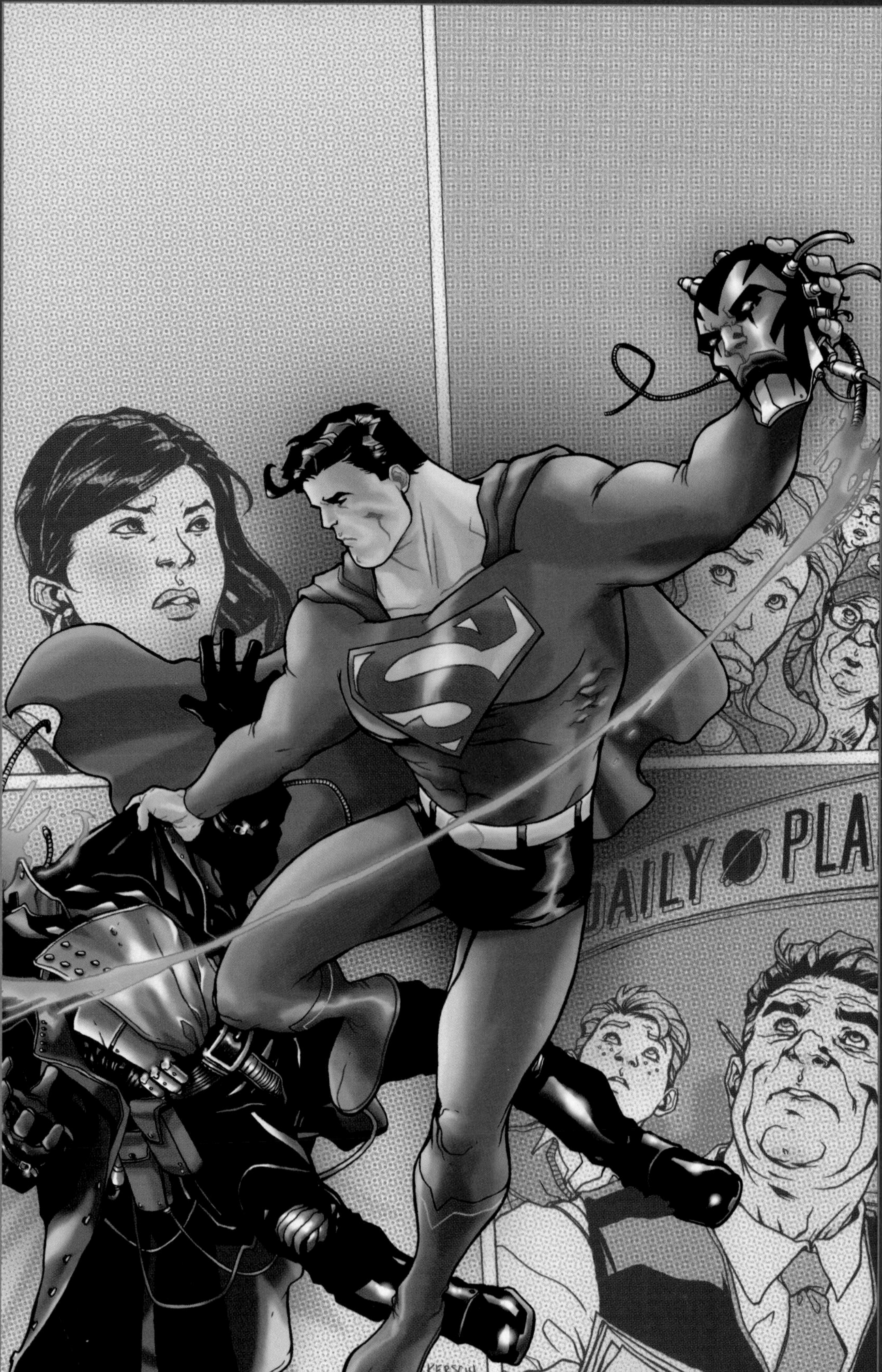
DAILY PLA
KERSCHL
'05

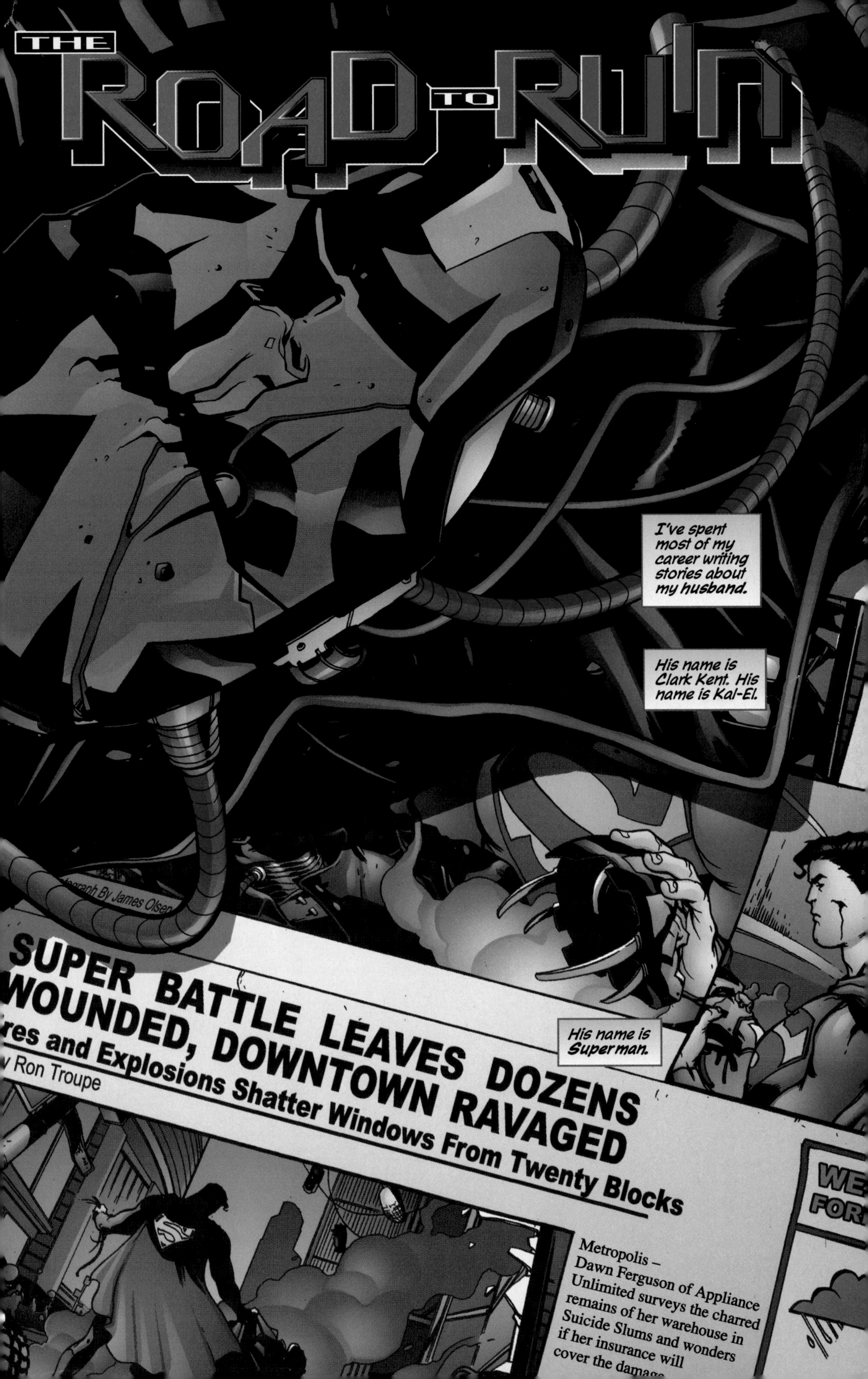
THE ROAD TO RUIN
I've spent most of my career writing stories about my husband.
His name is Clark Kent. His name is Kal-El.
His name is Superman.
By James Olsen
SUPER BATTLE LEAVES DOZENS WOUNDED, DOWNTOWN RAVAGED
res and Explosions Shatter Windows From Twenty Blocks
y Ron Troupe
Metropolis – Dawn Ferguson of Appliance Unlimited surveys the charred remains of her warehouse in Suicide Slums and wonders if her insurance will cover the damag

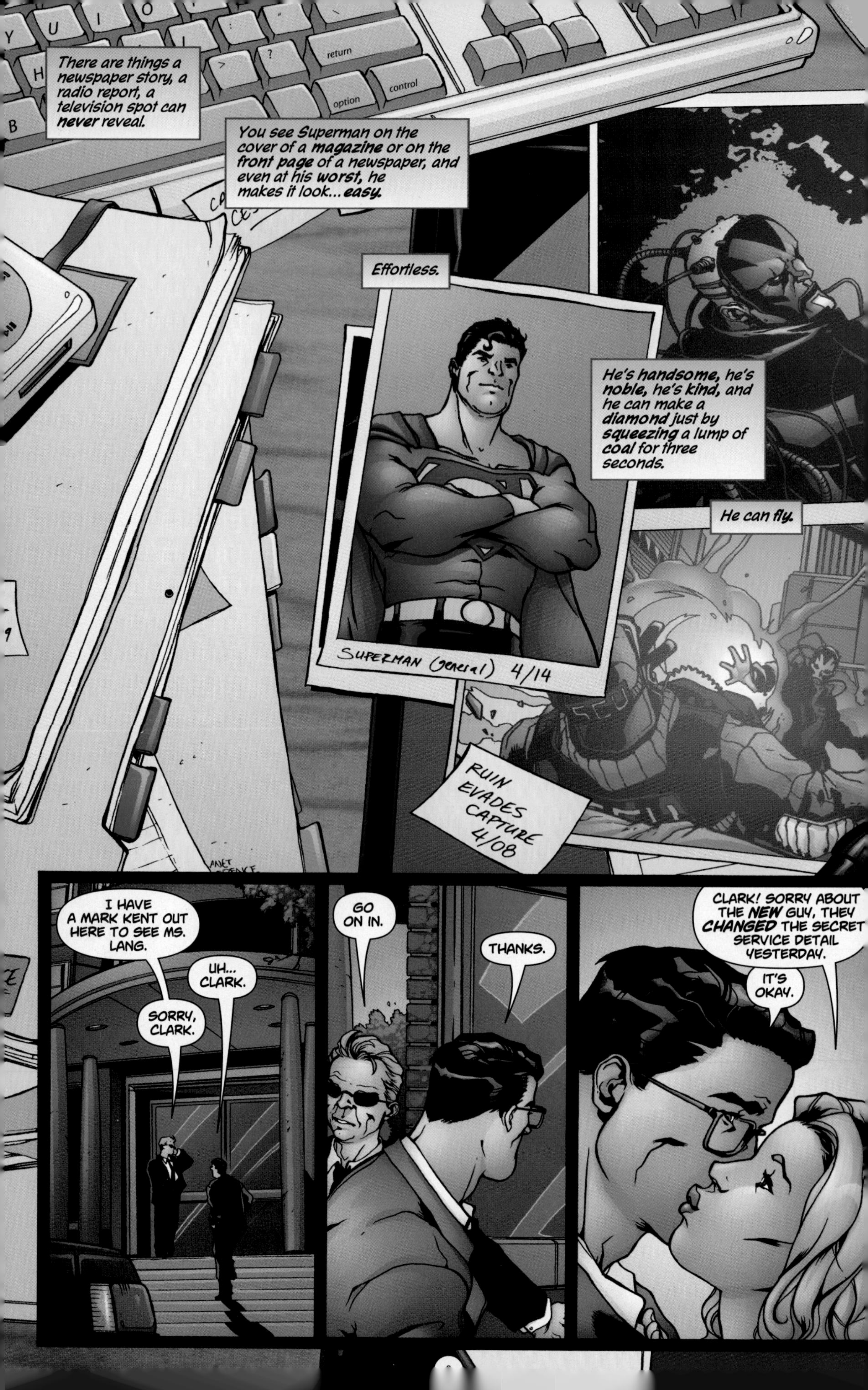

There are things a newspaper story, a radio report, a television spot can never reveal.
You see Superman on the cover of a magazine or on the front page of a newspaper, and even at his worst, he makes it look... easy.
Effortless.
SUPERMAN (general) 4/14
He's handsome, he's noble, he's kind, and he can make a diamond just by squeezing a lump of coal for three seconds.
He can fly.
RUIN EVADES CAPTURE 4/08
I HAVE A MARK KENT OUT HERE TO SEE MS. LANG.
UH... CLARK.
SORRY, CLARK.
GO ON IN.
THANKS.
CLARK! SORRY ABOUT THE NEW GUY, THEY CHANGED THE SECRET SERVICE DETAIL YESTERDAY.
IT'S OKAY.

You look at Superman, and you wonder, what can he possibly have to worry about? What could possibly ever hurt him?

But just because his skin is invulnerable, that doesn't mean his *heart* is.

STEEL WORKS METROPOLIS — IRONS, JOHN HENRY & NIECE, NATASHA (FILE)

STEEL IV - HANSON FIRE 3/29

And that's how you hurt Superman.

You break his *heart*.

YOUR *UNCLE'S* HERE, HONEY! SAY HI!

YOU SOUNDED *SERIOUS* ON THE *PHONE*, CLARK.

AM I IN *TROUBLE* OR *SOMETHING*?

PETE CAME TO SEE ME, LANA.

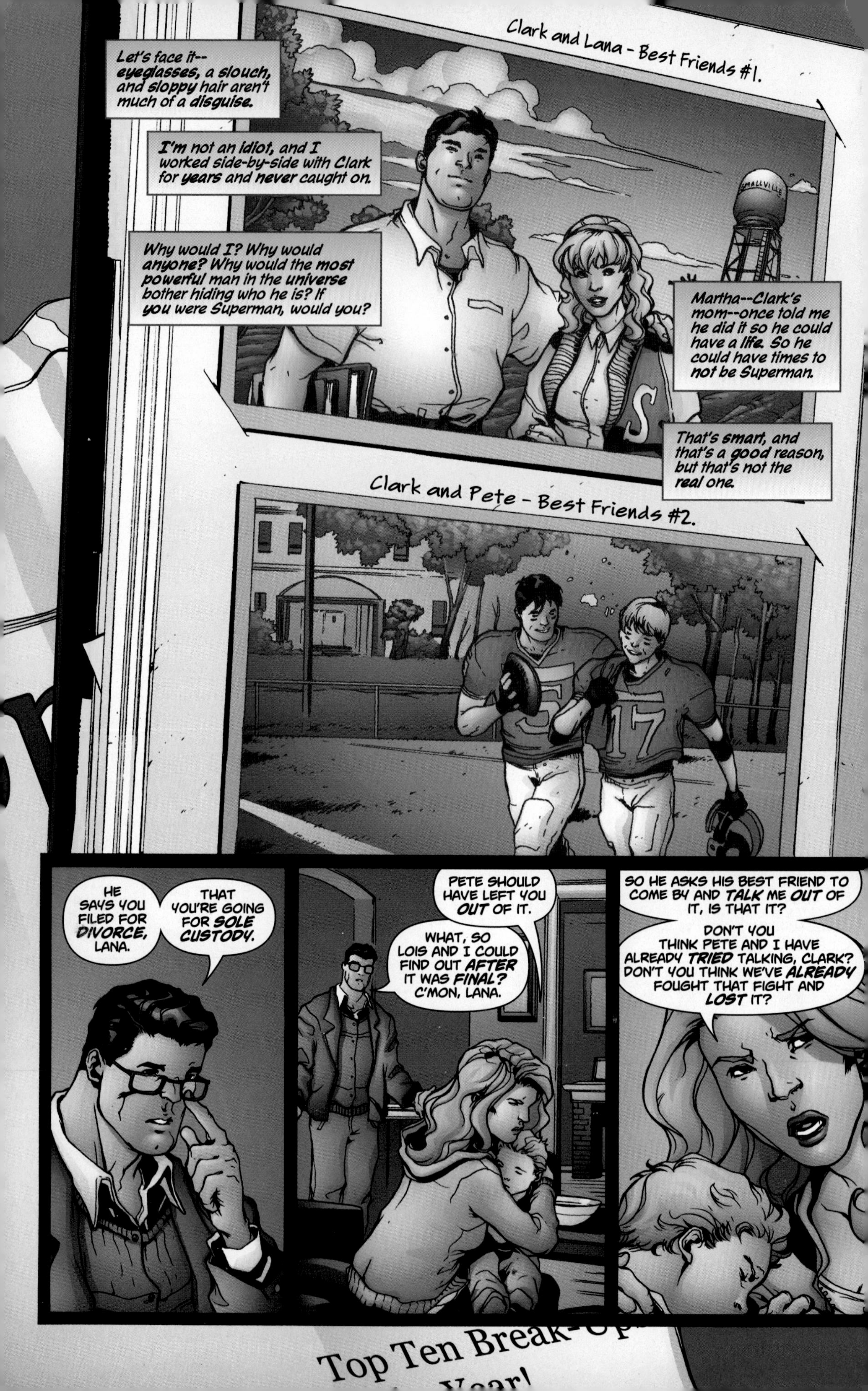
Clark and Lana - Best Friends #1.
Let's face it-- eyeglasses, a slouch, and sloppy hair aren't much of a disguise.
I'm not an idiot, and I worked side-by-side with Clark for years and never caught on.
Why would I? Why would anyone? Why would the most powerful man in the universe bother hiding who he is? If you were Superman, would you?
SMALLVILLE
Martha--Clark's mom--once told me he did it so he could have a life. So he could have times to not be Superman.
That's smart, and that's a good reason, but that's not the real one.
Clark and Pete - Best Friends #2.
HE SAYS YOU FILED FOR DIVORCE, LANA.
THAT YOU'RE GOING FOR SOLE CUSTODY.
PETE SHOULD HAVE LEFT YOU OUT OF IT.
WHAT, SO LOIS AND I COULD FIND OUT AFTER IT WAS FINAL? C'MON, LANA.
SO HE ASKS HIS BEST FRIEND TO COME BY AND TALK ME OUT OF IT, IS THAT IT?
DON'T YOU THINK PETE AND I HAVE ALREADY TRIED TALKING, CLARK? DON'T YOU THINK WE'VE ALREADY FOUGHT THAT FIGHT AND LOST IT?
Top Ten Break-Up

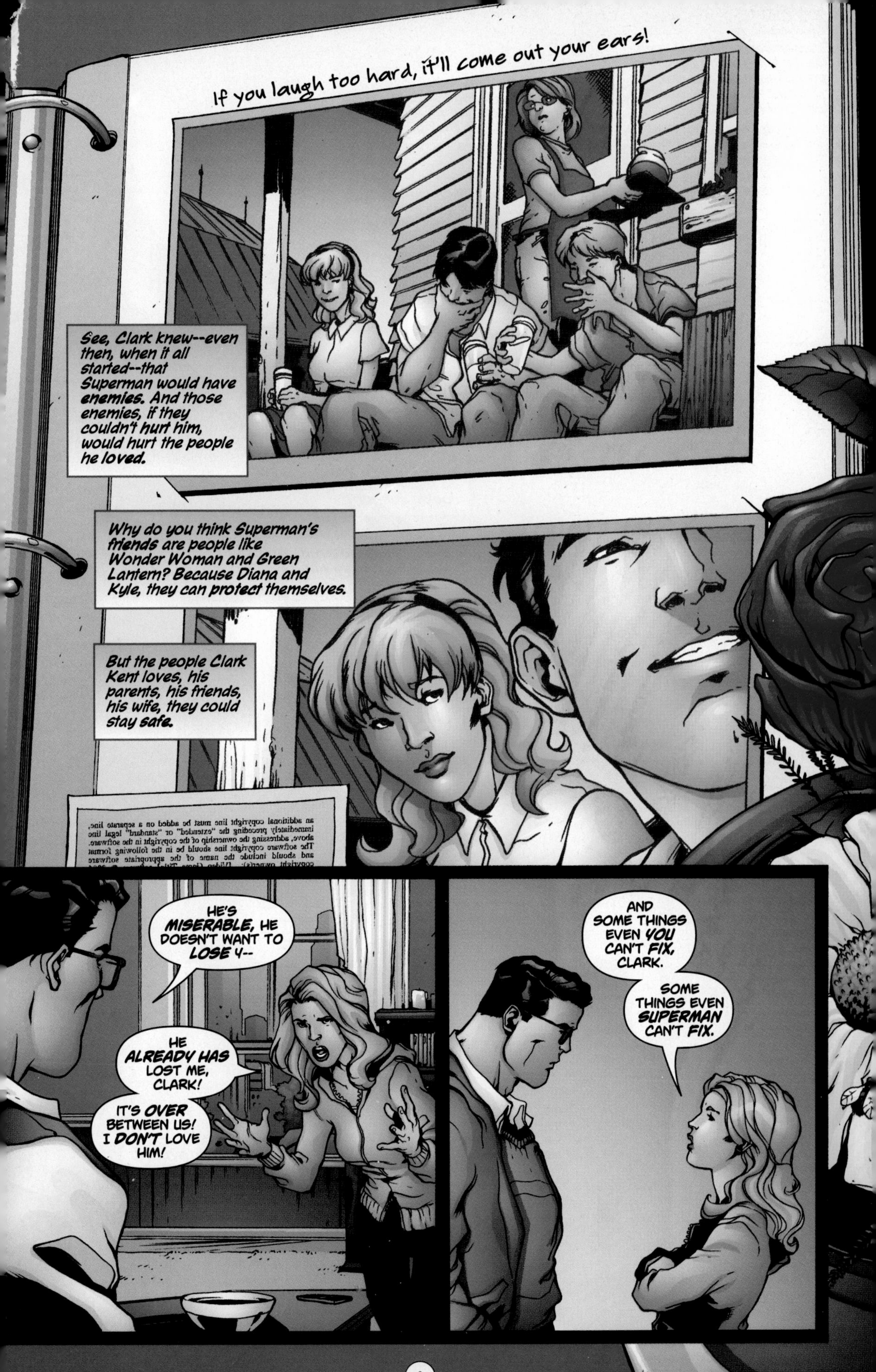
If you laugh too hard, it'll come out your ears!
See, Clark knew--even then, when it all started--that Superman would have enemies. And those enemies, if they couldn't hurt him, would hurt the people he loved.
Why do you think Superman's friends are people like Wonder Woman and Green Lantern? Because Diana and Kyle, they can protect themselves.
But the people Clark Kent loves, his parents, his friends, his wife, they could stay safe.
HE'S MISERABLE, HE DOESN'T WANT TO LOSE Y--
HE ALREADY HAS LOST ME, CLARK!
IT'S OVER BETWEEN US! I DON'T LOVE HIM!
AND SOME THINGS EVEN YOU CAN'T FIX, CLARK.
SOME THINGS EVEN SUPERMAN CAN'T FIX.

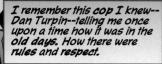

I remember this **cop** I knew--Dan Turpin--telling me once upon a time how it was in the old days. How there were rules and **respect**.

How the robbers knew they were robbers and the **cops** knew they were cops, and everyone played their part.

This one time, he chased this **crook** he knew, and the guy was going over a **fence**.

Dan drew and fired a warning shot.

Crook drops off the fence, stares at Dan, and he's seriously upset.

Says, "What'd you do that for, Dan? I coulda got **hurt!**"

And Dan apologized, because the guy was right.

That's how it used to be.

DIDN'T GO WELL, DID IT?

I'M SORRY, PETE.

I TRIED, I REALLY DID...

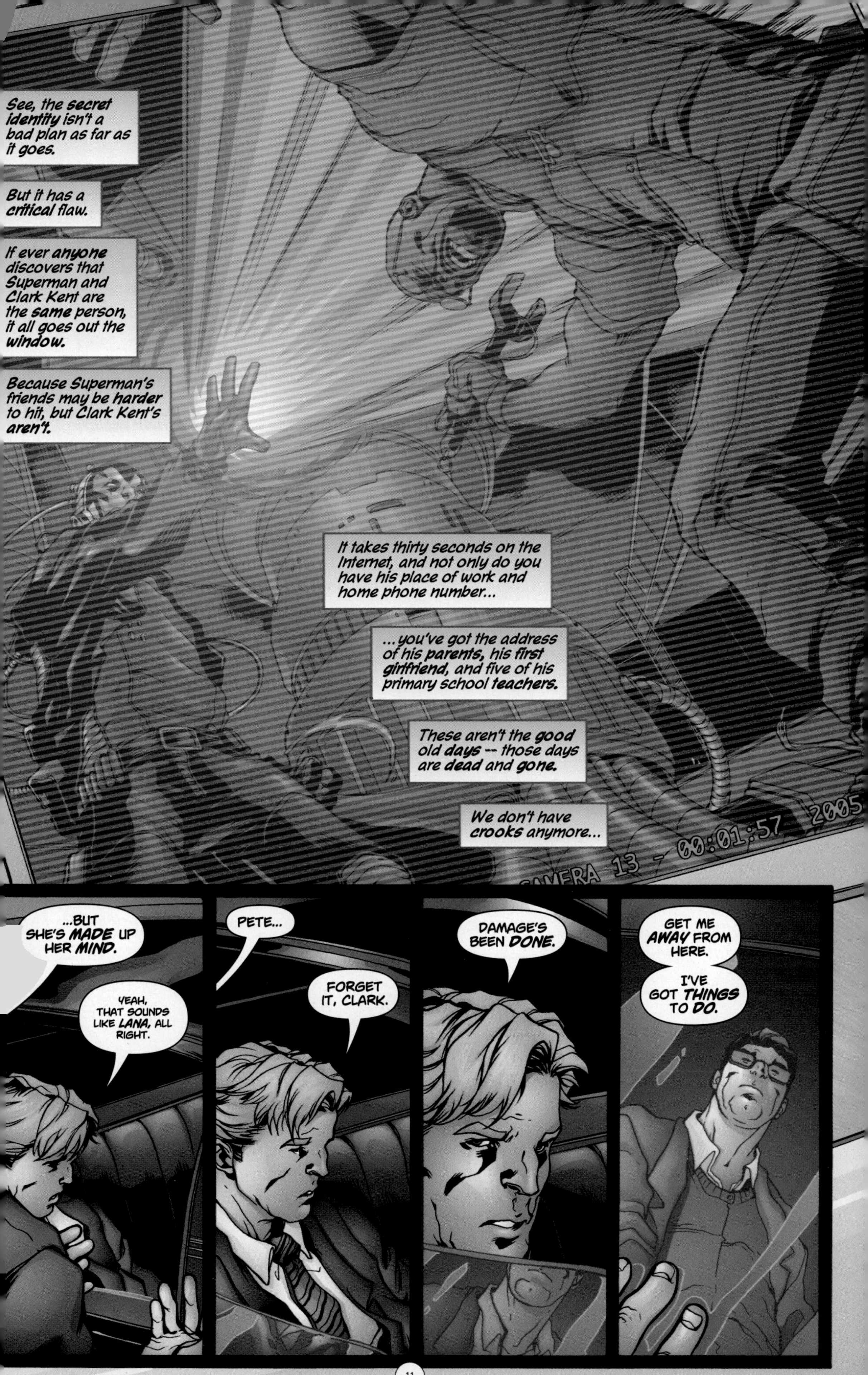
See, the secret identity isn't a bad plan as far as it goes.
But it has a critical flaw.
If ever anyone discovers that Superman and Clark Kent are the same person, it all goes out the window.
Because Superman's friends may be harder to hit, but Clark Kent's aren't.
It takes thirty seconds on the Internet, and not only do you have his place of work and home phone number...
...you've got the address of his parents, his first girlfriend, and five of his primary school teachers.
These aren't the good old days -- those days are dead and gone.
We don't have crooks anymore...
CAMERA 13 - 00:01:57 2005
...BUT SHE'S MADE UP HER MIND.
YEAH, THAT SOUNDS LIKE LANA, ALL RIGHT.
PETE...
FORGET IT, CLARK.
DAMAGE'S BEEN DONE.
GET ME AWAY FROM HERE.
I'VE GOT THINGS TO DO.

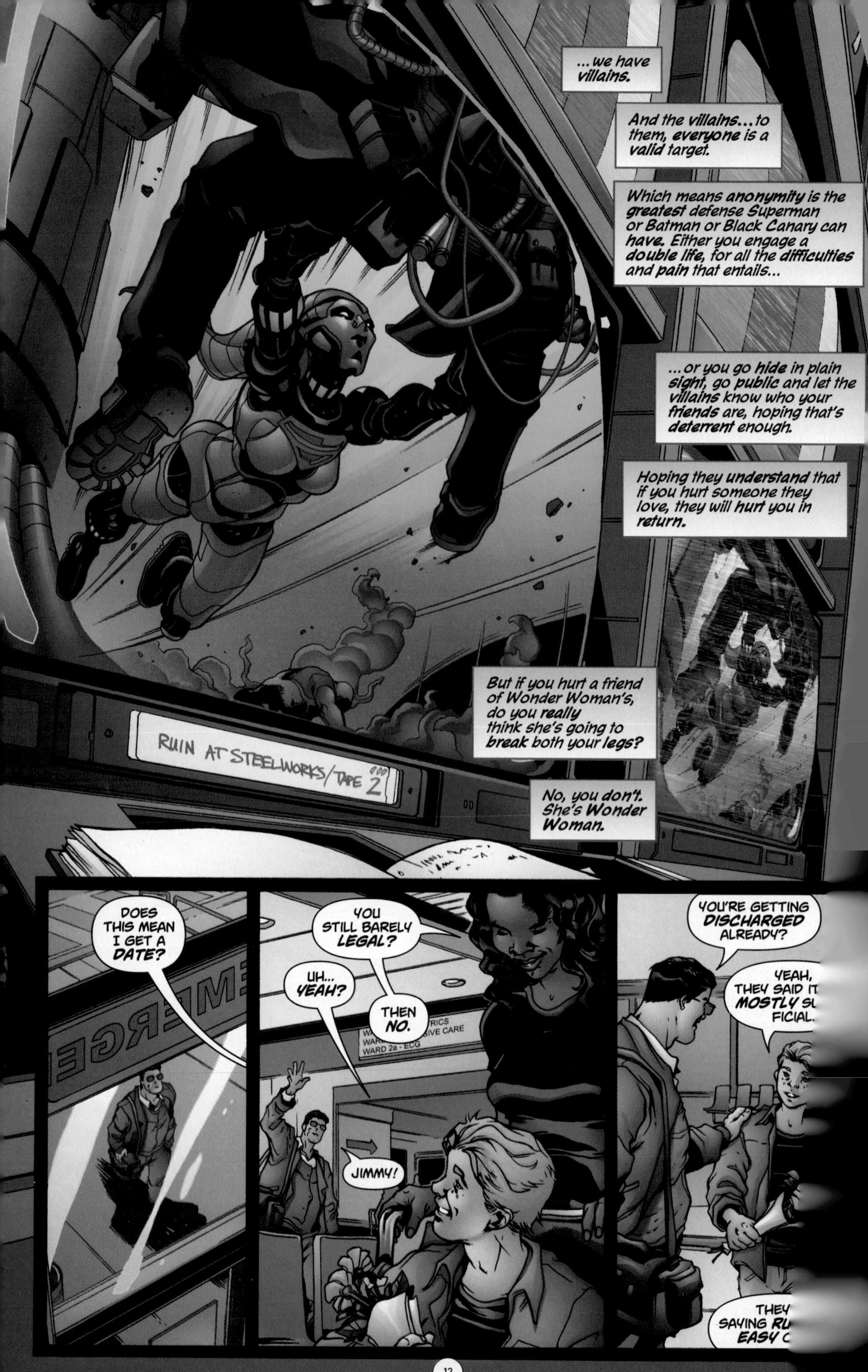
...we have villains.
And the villains...to them, everyone is a valid target.
Which means anonymity is the greatest defense Superman or Batman or Black Canary can have. Either you engage a double life, for all the difficulties and pain that entails...
...or you go hide in plain sight, go public and let the villains know who your friends are, hoping that's deterrent enough.
Hoping they understand that if you hurt someone they love, they will hurt you in return.
But if you hurt a friend of Wonder Woman's, do you really think she's going to break both your legs?
RUIN AT STEELWORKS/TAPE 2
No, you don't. She's Wonder Woman.
DOES THIS MEAN I GET A DATE?
YOU STILL BARELY LEGAL?
UH... YEAH?
THEN NO.
WARD 2a - ECG
JIMMY!
YOU'RE GETTING DISCHARGED ALREADY?
YEAH, THEY SAID IT MOSTLY SU FICIAL.
THEY SAYING RU EASY

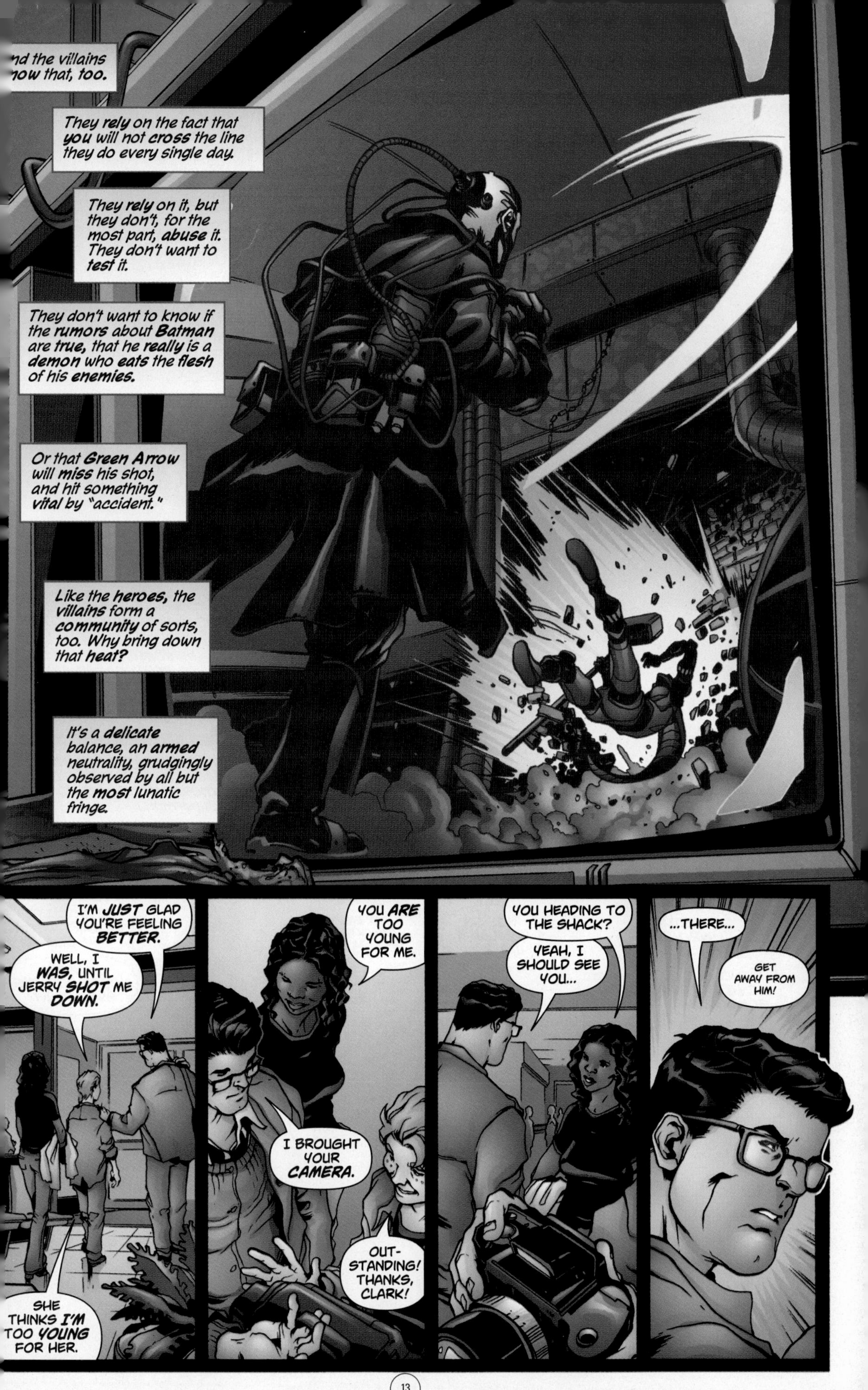
nd the villains now that, too.
They rely on the fact that you will not cross the line they do every single day.
They rely on it, but they don't, for the most part, abuse it. They don't want to test it.
They don't want to know if the rumors about Batman are true, that he really is a demon who eats the flesh of his enemies.
Or that Green Arrow will miss his shot, and hit something vital by "accident."
Like the heroes, the villains form a community of sorts, too. Why bring down that heat?
It's a delicate balance, an armed neutrality, grudgingly observed by all but the most lunatic fringe.
I'M JUST GLAD YOU'RE FEELING BETTER.
WELL, I WAS, UNTIL JERRY SHOT ME DOWN.
SHE THINKS I'M TOO YOUNG FOR HER.
YOU ARE TOO YOUNG FOR ME.
I BROUGHT YOUR CAMERA.
OUT-STANDING! THANKS, CLARK!
YOU HEADING TO THE SHACK?
YEAH, I SHOULD SEE YOU...
...THERE...
GET AWAY FROM HIM!

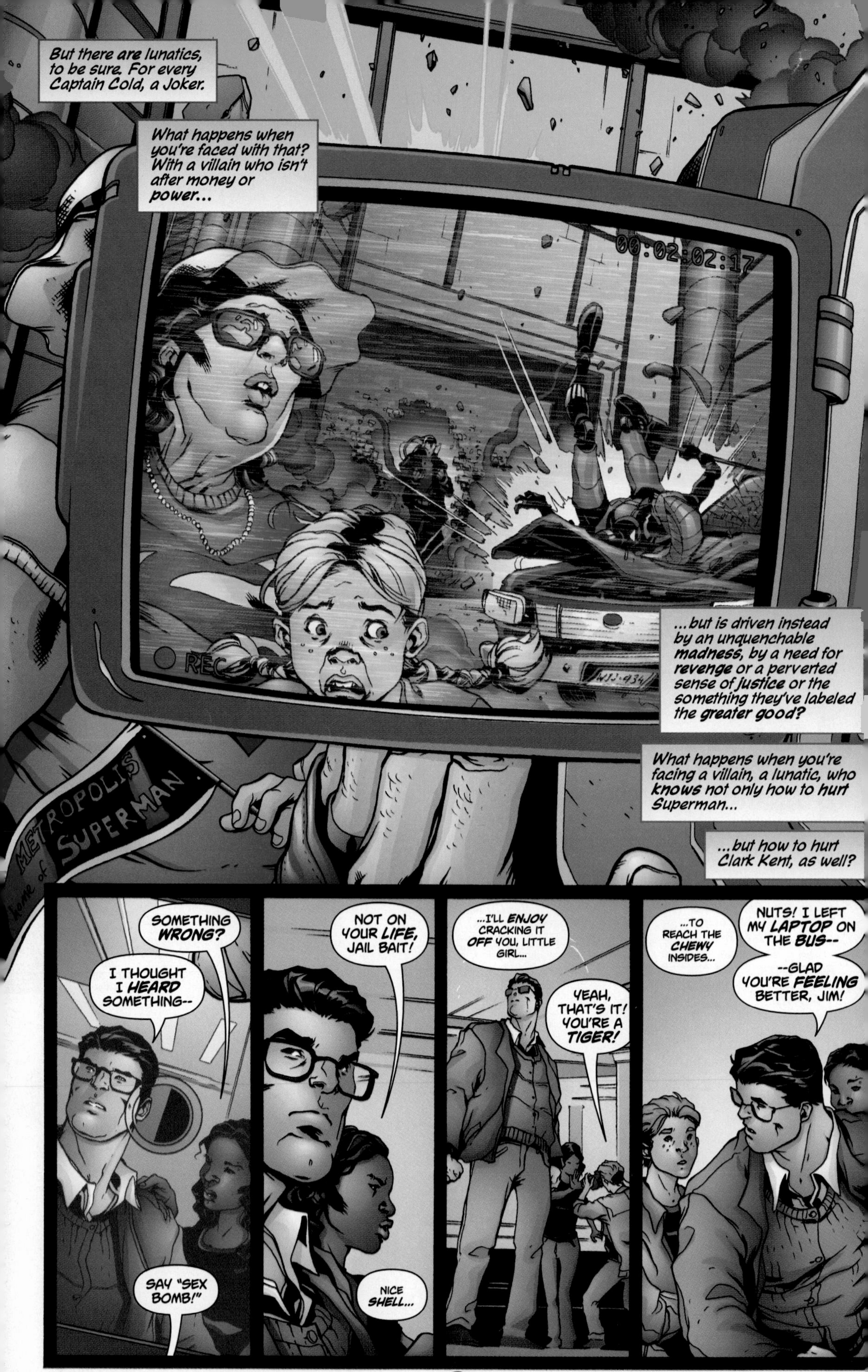

But there are lunatics, to be sure. For every Captain Cold, a Joker.
What happens when you're faced with that? With a villain who isn't after money or power...
00:02:02:17
REC
...but is driven instead by an unquenchable madness, by a need for revenge or a perverted sense of justice or the something they've labeled the greater good?
What happens when you're facing a villain, a lunatic, who knows not only how to hurt Superman...
...but how to hurt Clark Kent, as well?
home of METROPOLIS SUPERMAN
SOMETHING WRONG?
I THOUGHT I HEARD SOMETHING--
SAY "SEX BOMB!"
NOT ON YOUR LIFE, JAIL BAIT!
NICE SHELL...
...I'LL ENJOY CRACKING IT OFF YOU, LITTLE GIRL...
YEAH, THAT'S IT! YOU'RE A TIGER!
...TO REACH THE CHEWY INSIDES...
NUTS! I LEFT MY LAPTOP ON THE BUS--
--GLAD YOU'RE FEELING BETTER, JIM!

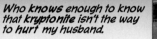

Enter Ruin, a lunatic who, for one reason or another, has fixated on Superman.

Who knows enough to know that kryptonite isn't the way to *hurt* my husband.

Kill him, sure. But hurt him? Really hurt him so the wound will never heal?

Ruin knows you go for the heart, and that's what he's doing.

He's targeting Clark's friends. He already went after Jimmy.

Clark's scared, because he knows Jimmy's just the start.

I do, too.

DID HE ACTUALLY SAY "NUTS"?

HE GREW UP IN KANSAS.

OH.

HNNNN

THERE'S A LITTLE GIRL IN THAT BIG SUIT, ISN'T THERE?

A SOON TO BE DEAD LITTLE GIRL...

...AND SUPERMAN WILL WEEP AT YOUR PASSING--

15

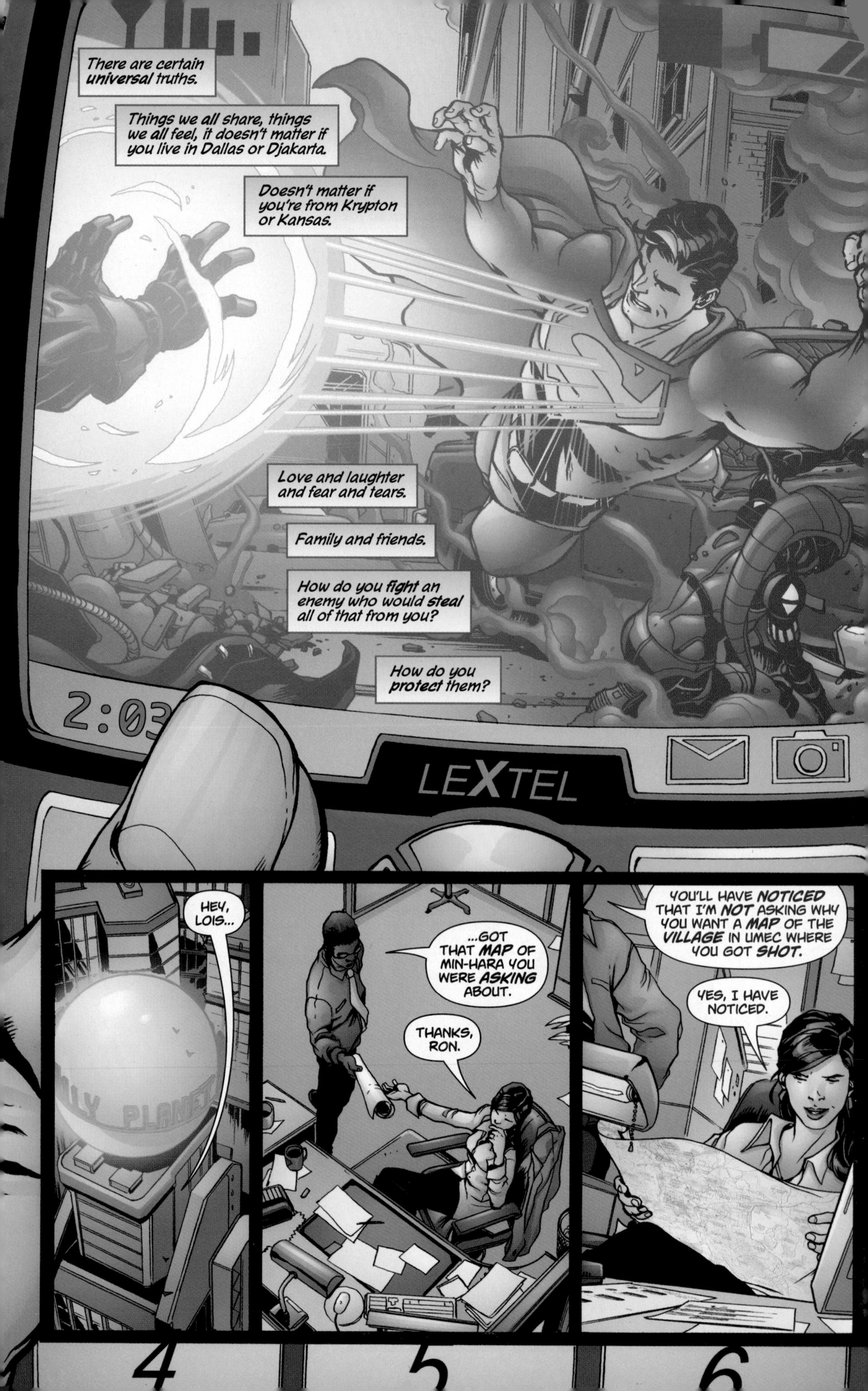
There are certain universal truths.
Things we all share, things we all feel, it doesn't matter if you live in Dallas or Djakarta.
Doesn't matter if you're from Krypton or Kansas.
Love and laughter and fear and tears.
Family and friends.
How do you fight an enemy who would steal all of that from you?
How do you protect them?
2:03
LEXTEL
HEY, LOIS...
...GOT THAT MAP OF MIN-HARA YOU WERE ASKING ABOUT.
THANKS, RON.
YOU'LL HAVE NOTICED THAT I'M NOT ASKING WHY YOU WANT A MAP OF THE VILLAGE IN UMEC WHERE YOU GOT SHOT.
YES, I HAVE NOTICED.
4
5
6

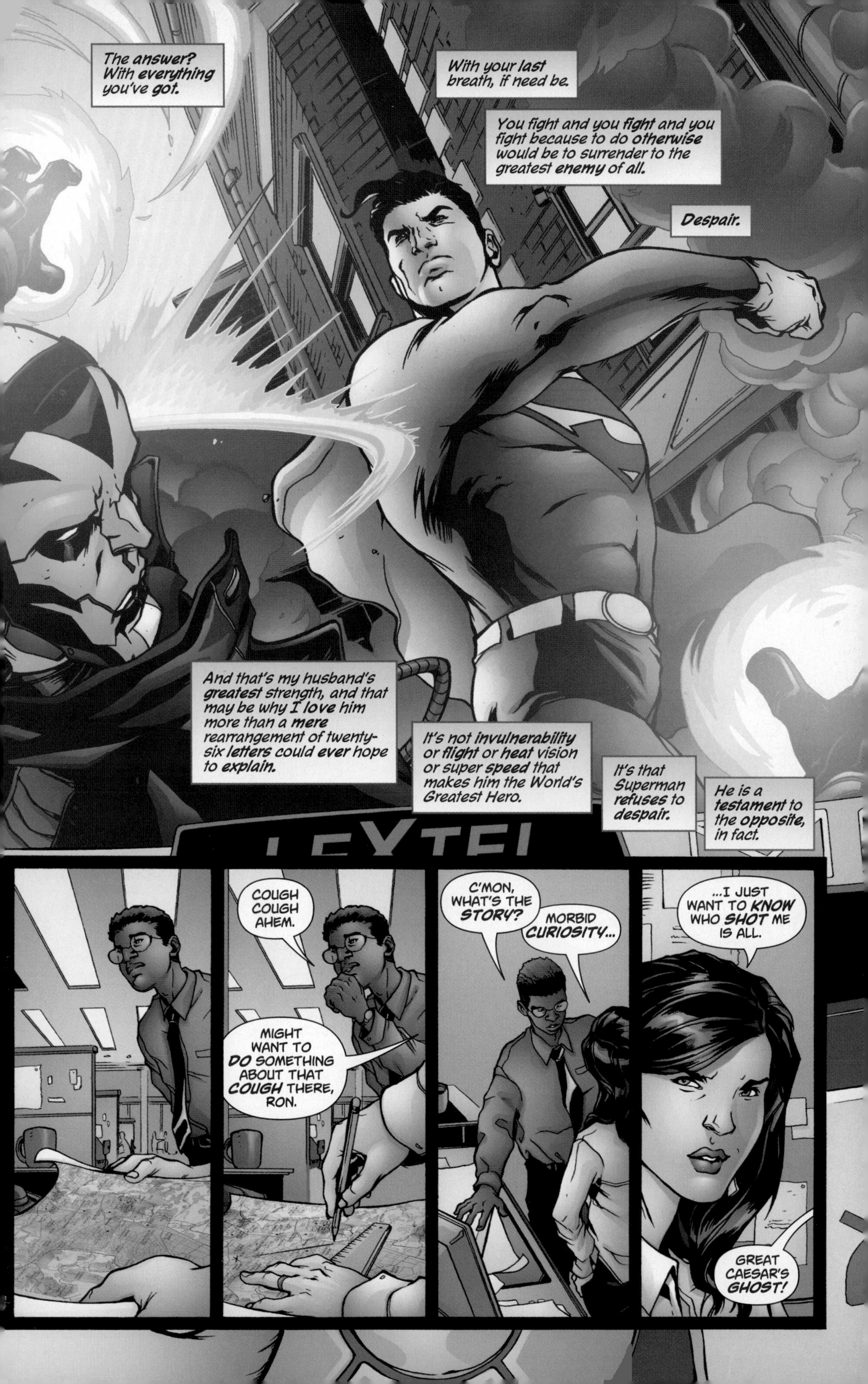
The answer? With everything you've got.
With your last breath, if need be.
You fight and you fight and you fight because to do otherwise would be to surrender to the greatest enemy of all.
Despair.
And that's my husband's greatest strength, and that may be why I love him more than a mere rearrangement of twenty-six letters could ever hope to explain.
It's not invulnerability or flight or heat vision or super speed that makes him the World's Greatest Hero.
It's that Superman refuses to despair.
He is a testament to the opposite, in fact.
COUGH COUGH AHEM.
MIGHT WANT TO DO SOMETHING ABOUT THAT COUGH THERE, RON.
C'MON, WHAT'S THE STORY?
MORBID CURIOSITY...
...I JUST WANT TO KNOW WHO SHOT ME IS ALL.
GREAT CAESAR'S GHOST!

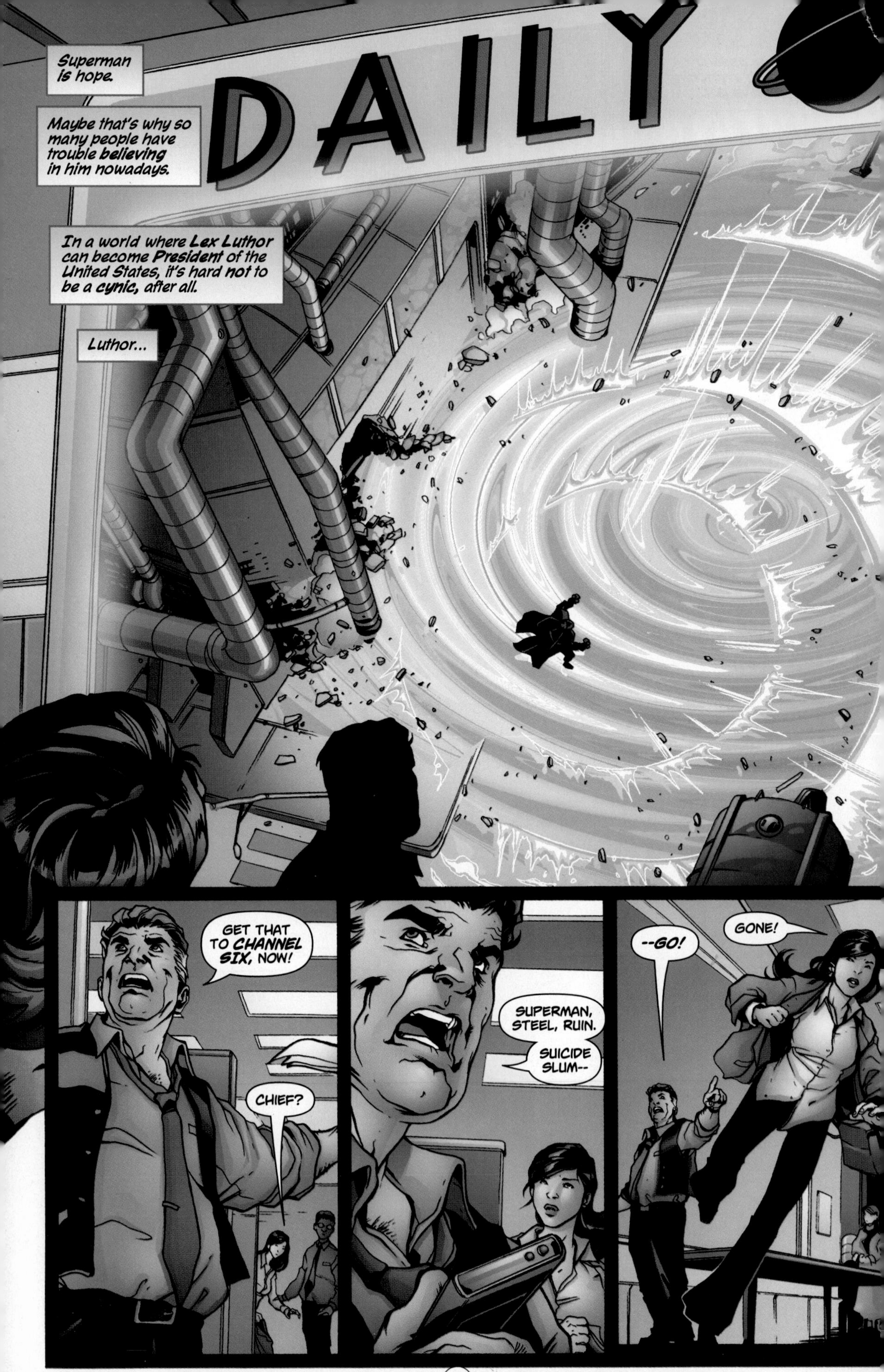
DAILY
Superman is hope.
Maybe that's why so many people have trouble believing in him nowadays.
In a world where Lex Luthor can become President of the United States, it's hard not to be a cynic, after all.
Luthor...
GET THAT TO CHANNEL SIX, NOW!
CHIEF?
SUPERMAN, STEEL, RUIN.
SUICIDE SLUM--
--GO!
GONE!

...is it *Lex* under Ruin's mask?

Is this where his *madness* has led him?

I mentioned the idea to Clark, and he said that *Batman* had suggested the *same* thing.

But he didn't sound *convinced.*

If not *Lex,* then *who?*

Who is Ruin?

FOR LEASE
office/business l...
inc: 1-800-555-4832

FORGET THE ELEVATOR, RON!

THAT WAS THE STEELWORKS, IT LOOKS LIKE THE *PLACE* GOT *LEVELED*--

I KNOW, I *SAW.*

JIMMY? YOU *OUT* OF THE *HOSPITAL?*

GREAT, NOW *SHUT UP.*

GET DOWN TO SUICIDE SLUM *PRONTO*--

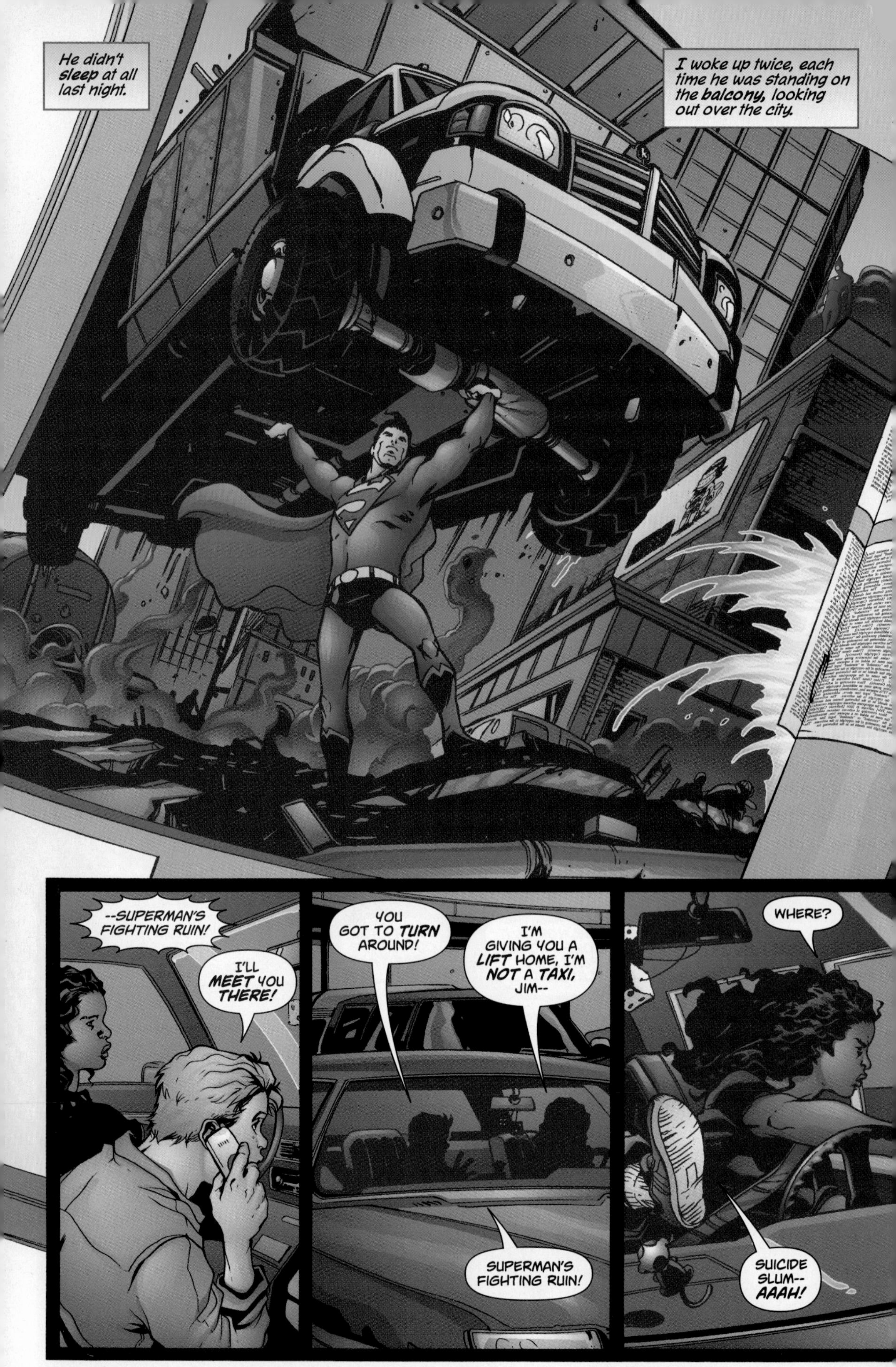
He didn't sleep at all last night.
I woke up twice, each time he was standing on the balcony, looking out over the city.
--SUPERMAN'S FIGHTING RUIN!
I'LL MEET YOU THERE!
YOU GOT TO TURN AROUND!
I'M GIVING YOU A LIFT HOME, I'M NOT A TAXI, JIM--
SUPERMAN'S FIGHTING RUIN!
WHERE?
SUICIDE SLUM-- AAAH!

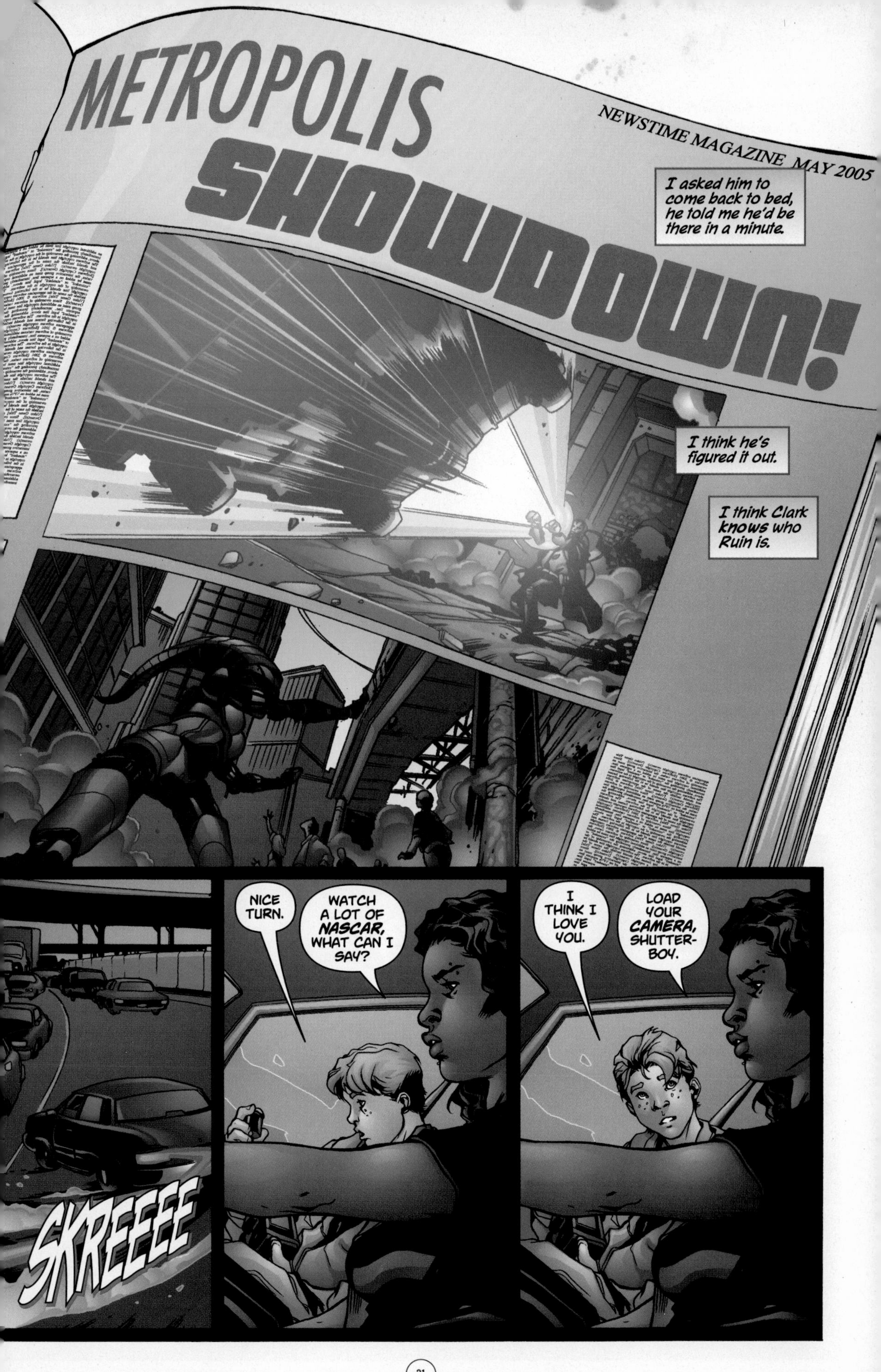
METROPOLIS
SHOWDOWN!
NEWSTIME MAGAZINE MAY 2005
I asked him to come back to bed, he told me he'd be there in a minute.
I think he's figured it out.
I think Clark knows who Ruin is.
SKREEEE
NICE TURN.
WATCH A LOT OF NASCAR, WHAT CAN I SAY?
I THINK I LOVE YOU.
LOAD YOUR CAMERA, SHUTTER-BOY.

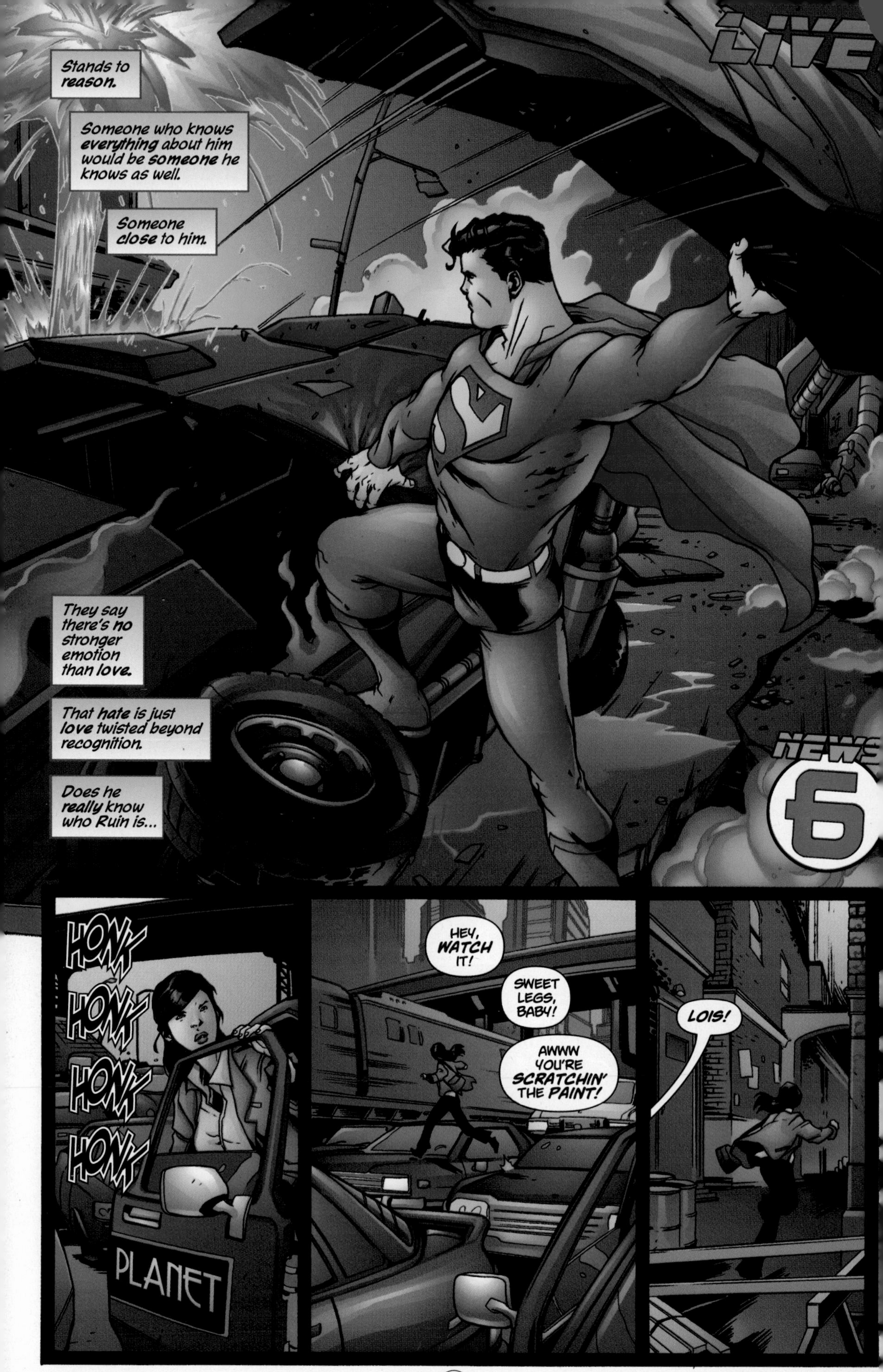
LIVE
Stands to reason.
Someone who knows everything about him would be someone he knows as well.
Someone close to him.
They say there's no stronger emotion than love.
That hate is just love twisted beyond recognition.
Does he really know who Ruin is...
NEWS 6
HONK HONK HONK HONK
PLANET
HEY, WATCH IT!
SWEET LEGS, BABY!
AWWW YOU'RE SCRATCHIN' THE PAINT!
LOIS!

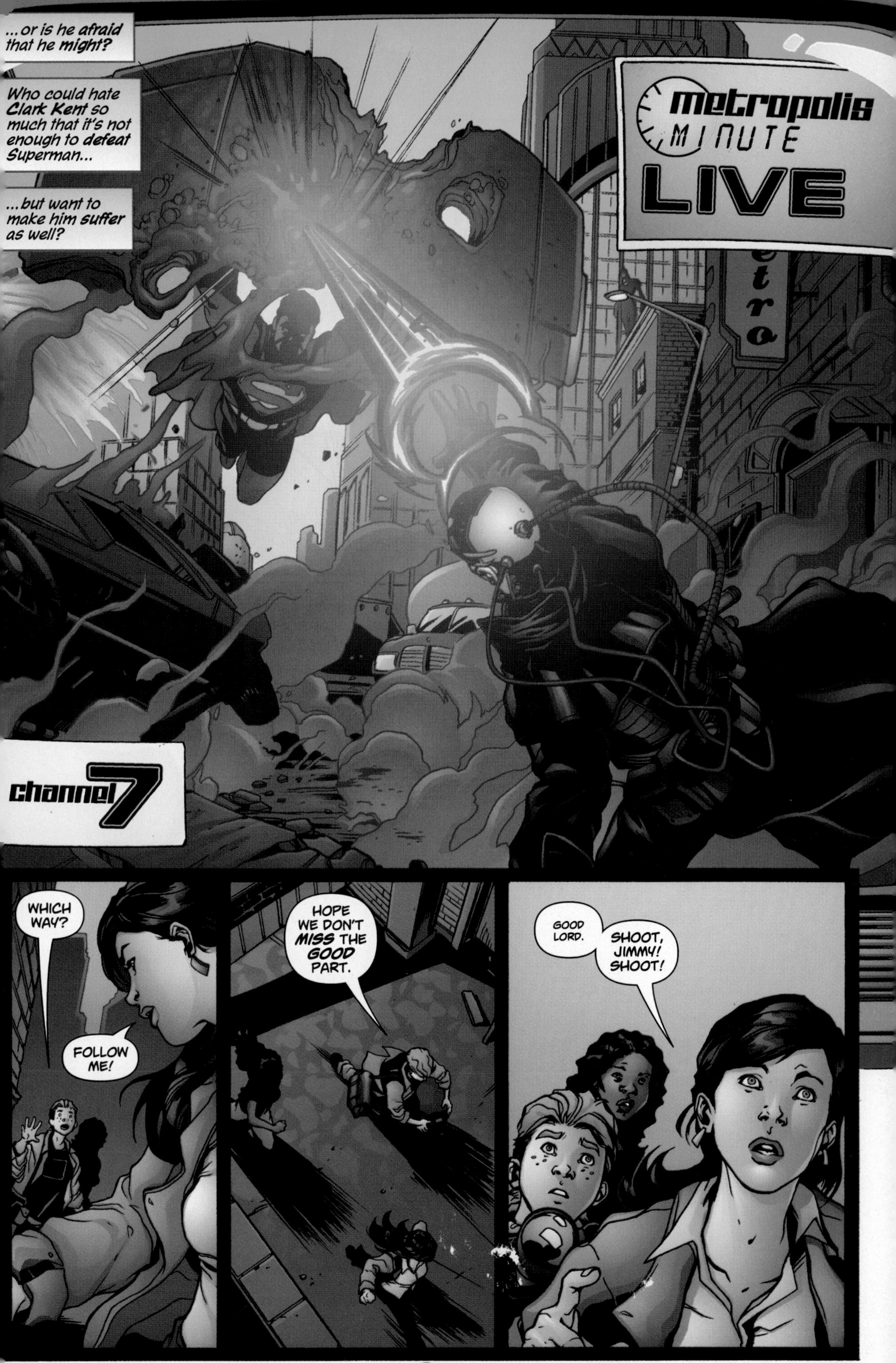
...or is he afraid that he might?
Who could hate Clark Kent so much that it's not enough to defeat Superman...
...but want to make him suffer as well?
metropolis MINUTE LIVE
channel 7
WHICH WAY?
FOLLOW ME!
HOPE WE DON'T MISS THE GOOD PART.
GOOD LORD.
SHOOT, JIMMY! SHOOT!

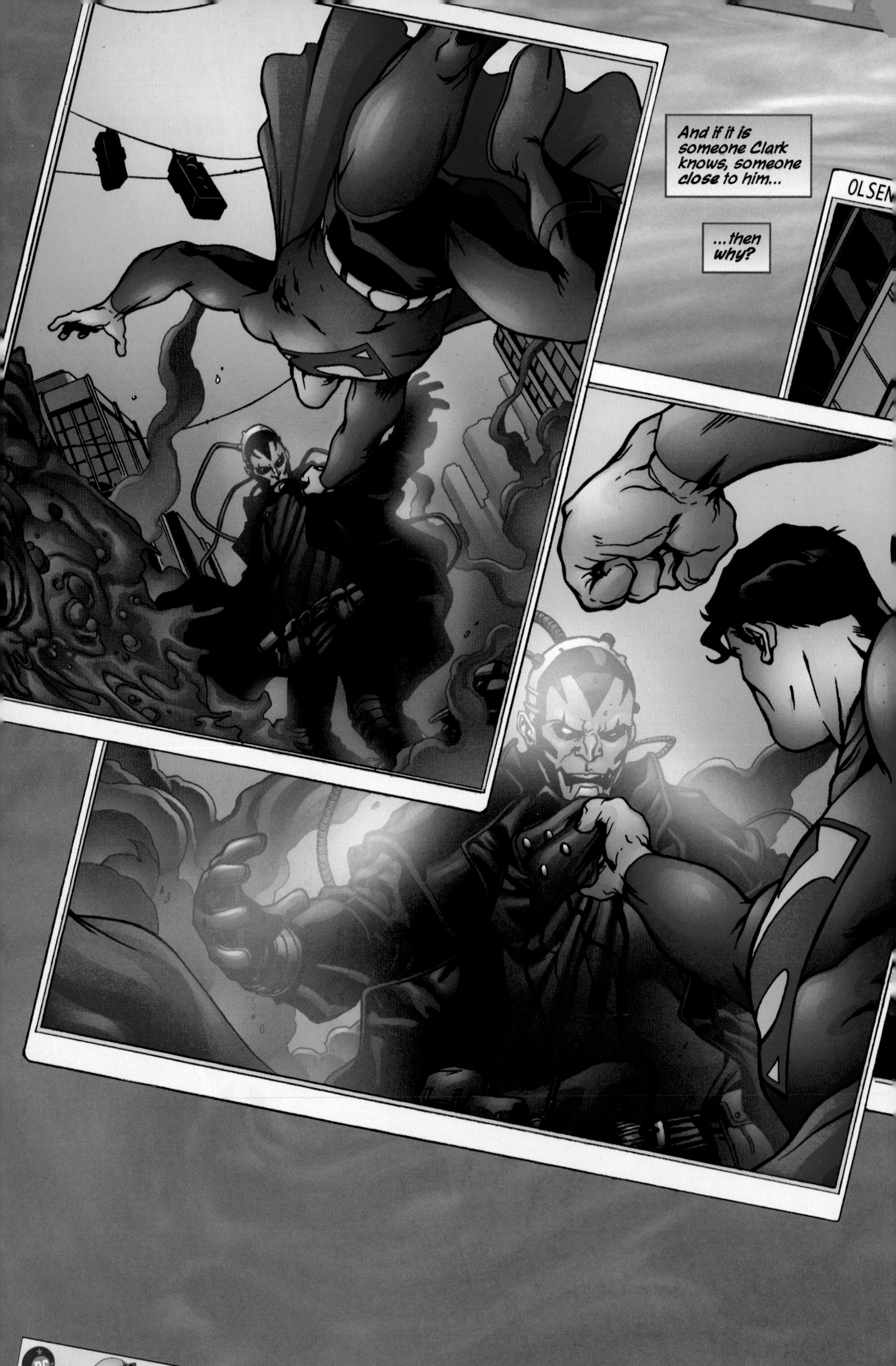
And if it is someone Clark knows, someone close to him...
...then why?
OLSEN

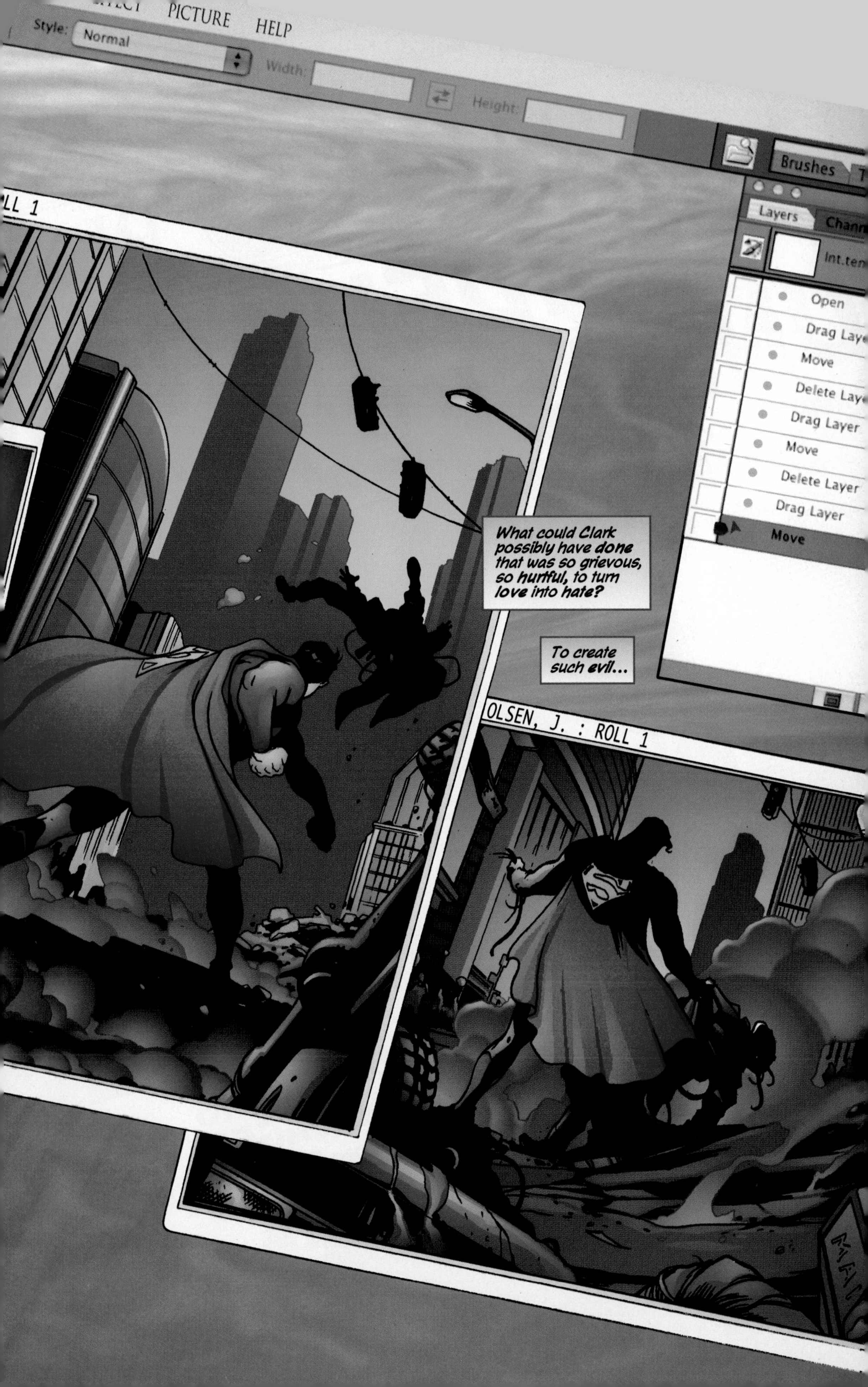

PICTURE
HELP
Style:
Normal
Width:
Height:
Brushes
Layers
Open
Drag Layer
Move
Delete Layer
Drag Layer
Move
Delete Layer
Drag Layer
Move
LL 1
What could Clark possibly have done that was so grievous, so hurtful, to turn love into hate?
To create such evil...
OLSEN, J. : ROLL 1

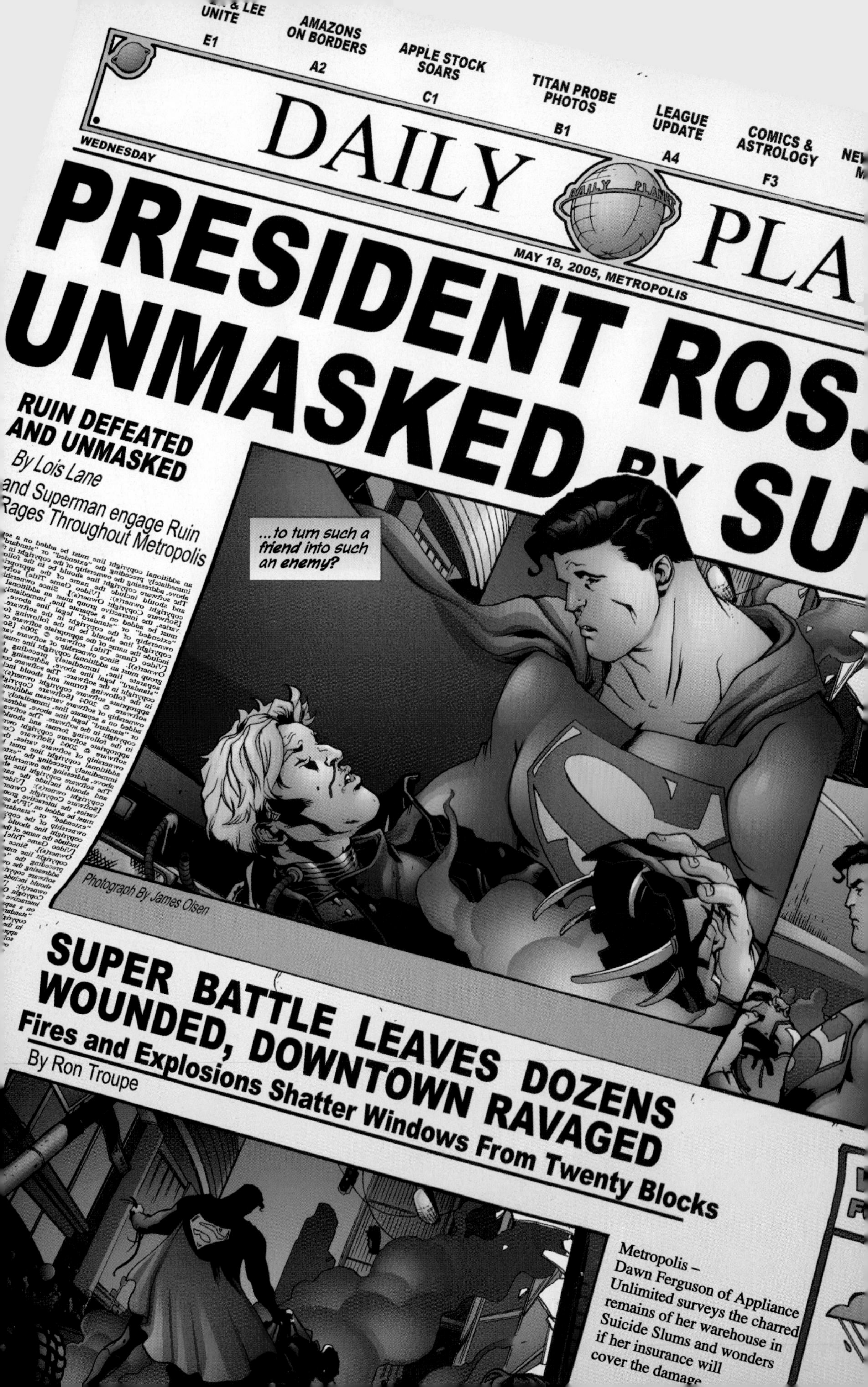
& LEE UNITE E1
AMAZONS ON BORDERS A2
APPLE STOCK SOARS C1
TITAN PROBE PHOTOS B1
LEAGUE UPDATE A4
COMICS & ASTROLOGY F3
WEDNESDAY
DAILY PLA
MAY 18, 2005, METROPOLIS
PRESIDENT ROS
UNMASKED BY SU
RUIN DEFEATED AND UNMASKED
By Lois Lane
and Superman engage Ruin
Rages Throughout Metropolis
...to turn such a friend into such an enemy?
Photograph By James Olsen
SUPER BATTLE LEAVES DOZENS WOUNDED, DOWNTOWN RAVAGED
Fires and Explosions Shatter Windows From Twenty Blocks
By Ron Troupe
Metropolis – Dawn Ferguson of Appliance Unlimited surveys the charred remains of her warehouse in Suicide Slums and wonders if her insurance will cover the damage

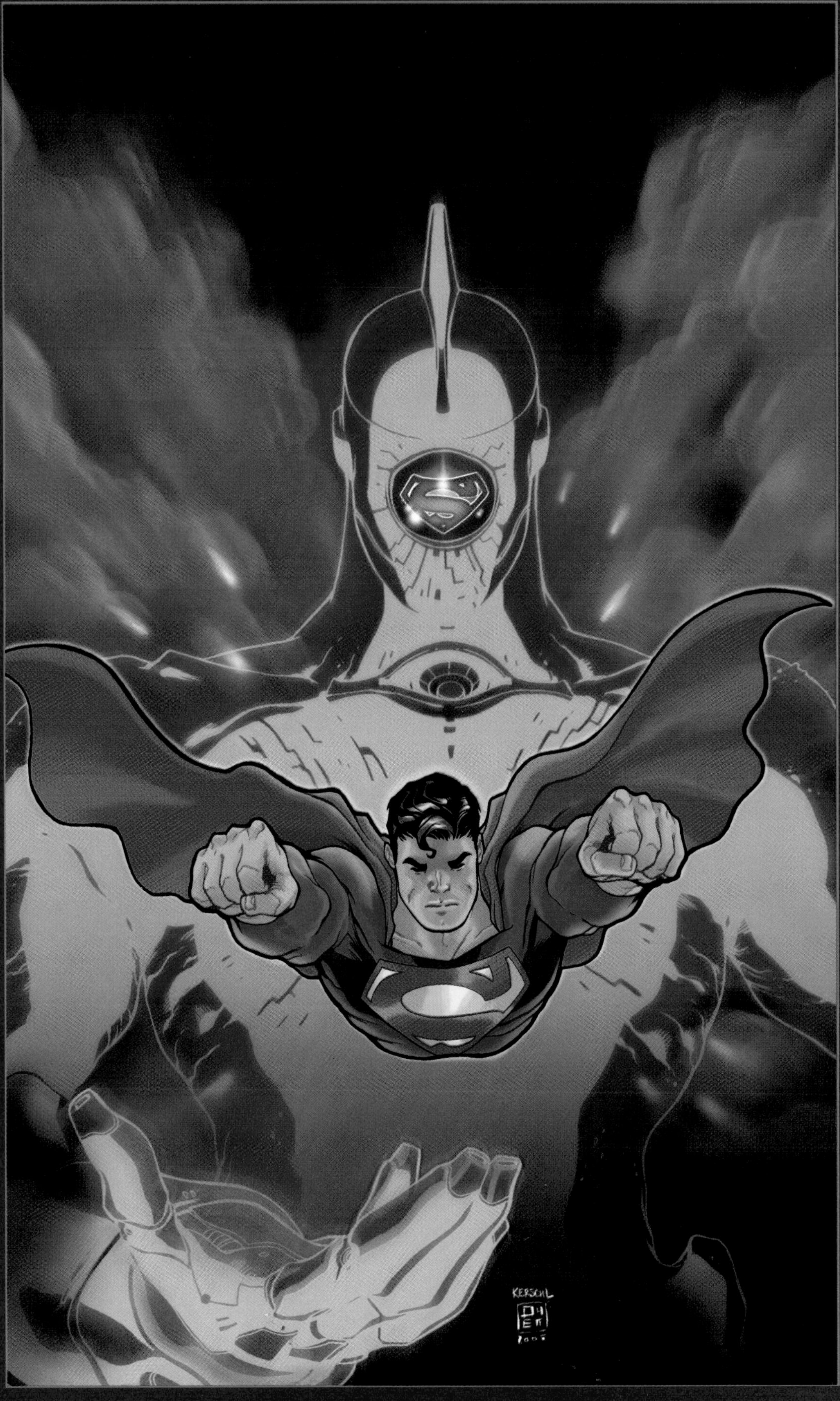
KERSCHL

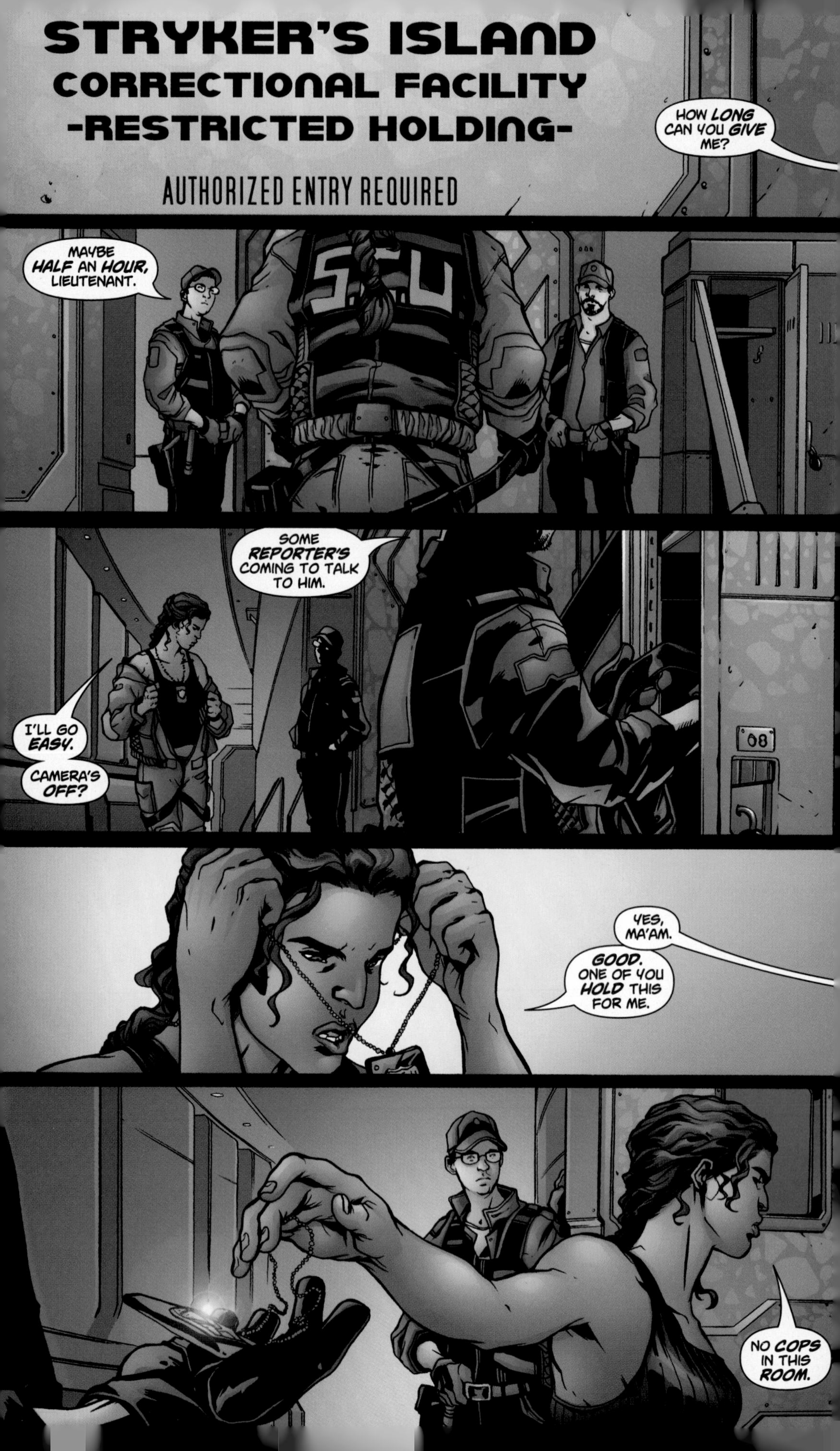

STRYKER'S ISLAND
CORRECTIONAL FACILITY
-RESTRICTED HOLDING-
AUTHORIZED ENTRY REQUIRED
HOW LONG CAN YOU GIVE ME?
MAYBE HALF AN HOUR, LIEUTENANT.
S.C.U
SOME REPORTER'S COMING TO TALK TO HIM.
I'LL GO EASY.
CAMERA'S OFF?
08
YES, MA'AM.
GOOD. ONE OF YOU HOLD THIS FOR ME.
NO COPS IN THIS ROOM.

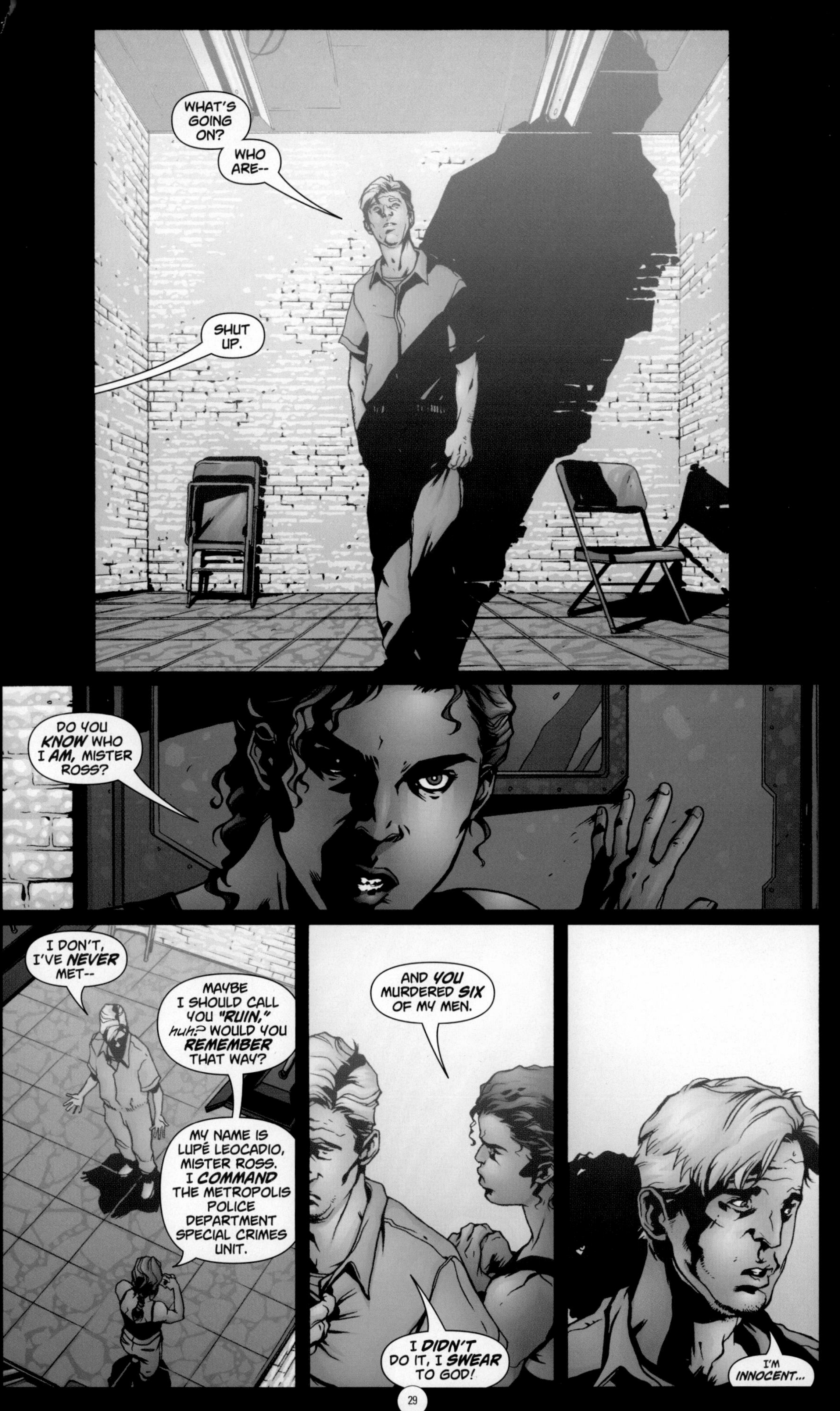
WHAT'S GOING ON?
WHO ARE--
SHUT UP.
DO YOU KNOW WHO I AM, MISTER ROSS?
I DON'T, I'VE NEVER MET--
MAYBE I SHOULD CALL YOU "RUIN," huh? WOULD YOU REMEMBER THAT WAY?
MY NAME IS LUPÉ LEOCADIO, MISTER ROSS. I COMMAND THE METROPOLIS POLICE DEPARTMENT SPECIAL CRIMES UNIT.
AND YOU MURDERED SIX OF MY MEN.
I DIDN'T DO IT, I SWEAR TO GOD!
I'M INNOCENT...

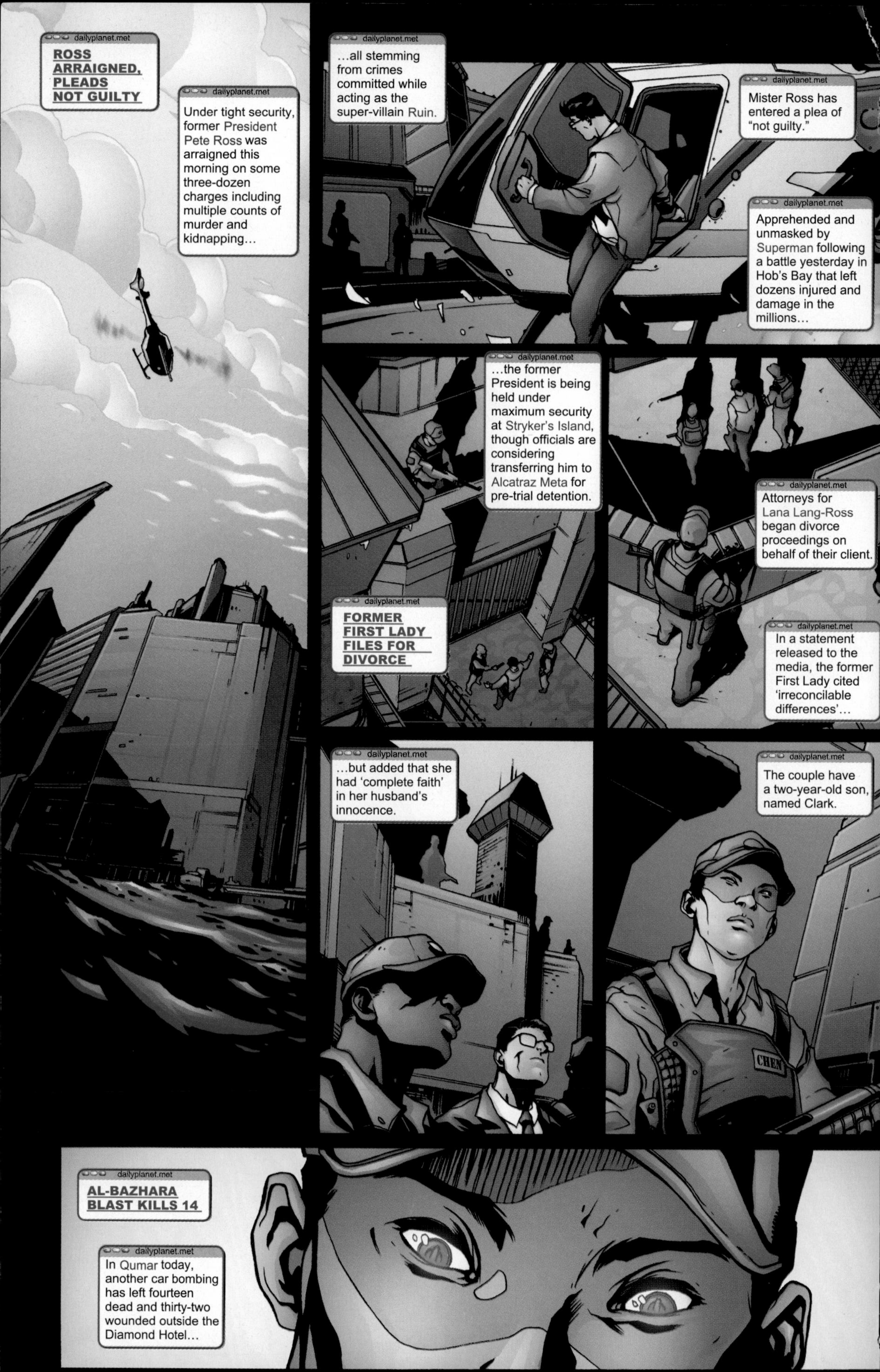
dailyplanet.met
ROSS ARRAIGNED, PLEADS NOT GUILTY
dailyplanet.met
Under tight security, former President Pete Ross was arraigned this morning on some three-dozen charges including multiple counts of murder and kidnapping…
dailyplanet.met
…all stemming from crimes committed while acting as the super-villain Ruin.
dailyplanet.met
Mister Ross has entered a plea of "not guilty."
dailyplanet.met
Apprehended and unmasked by Superman following a battle yesterday in Hob's Bay that left dozens injured and damage in the millions…
dailyplanet.met
…the former President is being held under maximum security at Stryker's Island, though officials are considering transferring him to Alcatraz Meta for pre-trial detention.
dailyplanet.met
FORMER FIRST LADY FILES FOR DIVORCE
dailyplanet.met
Attorneys for Lana Lang-Ross began divorce proceedings on behalf of their client.
dailyplanet.met
In a statement released to the media, the former First Lady cited 'irreconcilable differences'…
dailyplanet.met
…but added that she had 'complete faith' in her husband's innocence.
dailyplanet.met
The couple have a two-year-old son, named Clark.
CHEN
dailyplanet.met
AL-BAZHARA BLAST KILLS 14
dailyplanet.met
In Qumar today, another car bombing has left fourteen dead and thirty-two wounded outside the Diamond Hotel…

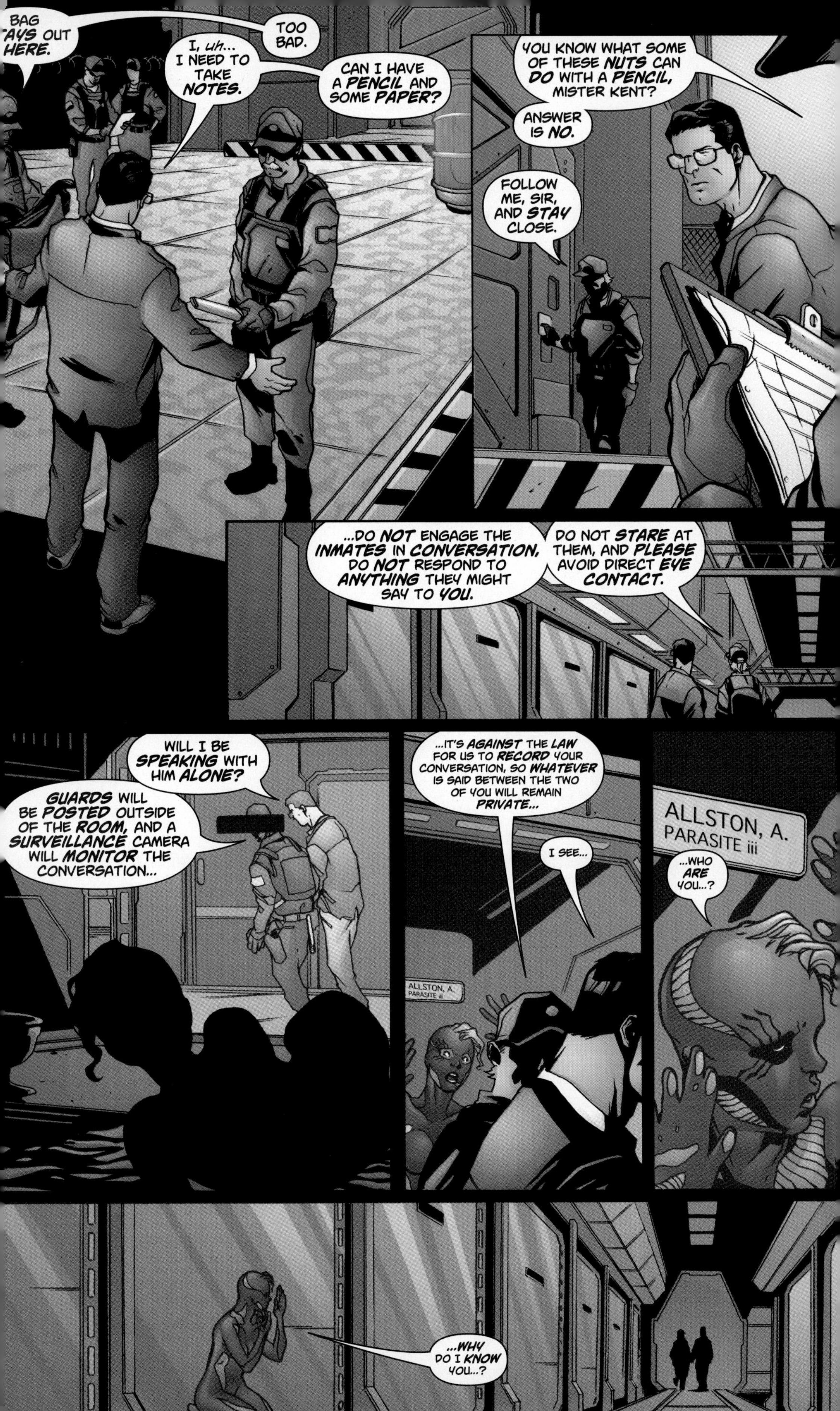

BAG TAYS OUT HERE.
I, *uh*... I NEED TO TAKE **NOTES.**
TOO BAD.
CAN I HAVE A **PENCIL** AND SOME **PAPER?**
YOU KNOW WHAT SOME OF THESE **NUTS** CAN **DO** WITH A **PENCIL,** MISTER KENT?
ANSWER IS **NO.**
FOLLOW ME, SIR, AND **STAY** CLOSE.
...DO **NOT** ENGAGE THE **INMATES** IN **CONVERSATION,** DO **NOT** RESPOND TO **ANYTHING** THEY MIGHT SAY TO **YOU.**
DO NOT **STARE** AT THEM, AND **PLEASE** AVOID DIRECT **EYE CONTACT.**
WILL I BE **SPEAKING** WITH HIM **ALONE?**
GUARDS WILL BE **POSTED** OUTSIDE OF THE **ROOM,** AND A **SURVEILLANCE** CAMERA WILL **MONITOR** THE CONVERSATION...
...IT'S **AGAINST** THE **LAW** FOR US TO **RECORD** YOUR CONVERSATION, SO **WHATEVER** IS SAID BETWEEN THE TWO OF YOU WILL REMAIN **PRIVATE...**
I SEE...
ALLSTON, A.
PARASITE iii
ALLSTON, A.
PARASITE iii
...WHO **ARE** YOU...?
...**WHY** DO I **KNOW** YOU...?

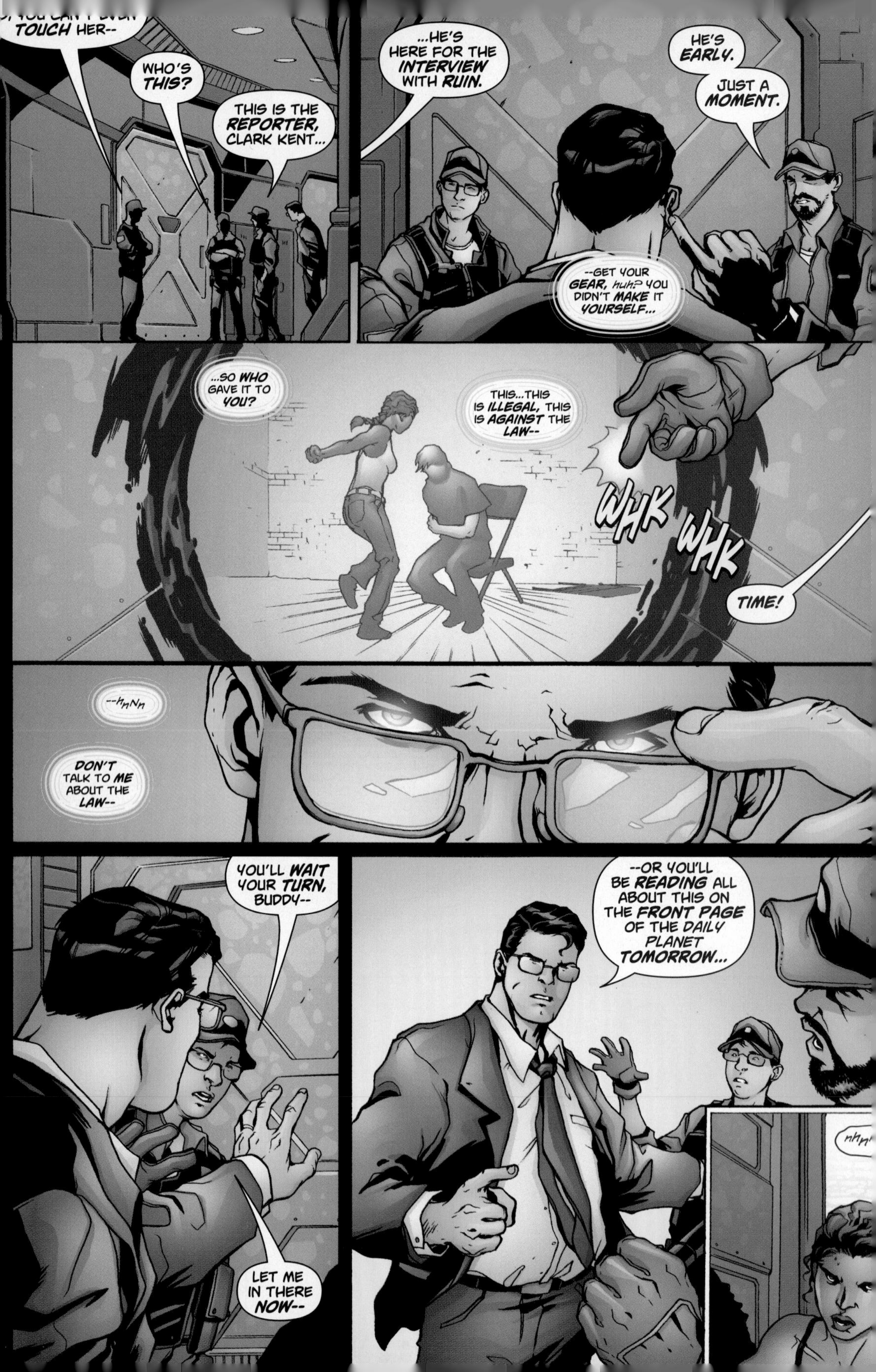
TOUCH HER--
WHO'S THIS?
THIS IS THE REPORTER, CLARK KENT...
...HE'S HERE FOR THE INTERVIEW WITH RUIN.
HE'S EARLY.
JUST A MOMENT.
--GET YOUR GEAR, huh? YOU DIDN'T MAKE IT YOURSELF...
...SO WHO GAVE IT TO YOU?
THIS...THIS IS ILLEGAL, THIS IS AGAINST THE LAW--
WHK
WHK
TIME!
--hnnn
DON'T TALK TO ME ABOUT THE LAW--
YOU'LL WAIT YOUR TURN, BUDDY--
LET ME IN THERE NOW--
--OR YOU'LL BE READING ALL ABOUT THIS ON THE FRONT PAGE OF THE DAILY PLANET TOMORROW...

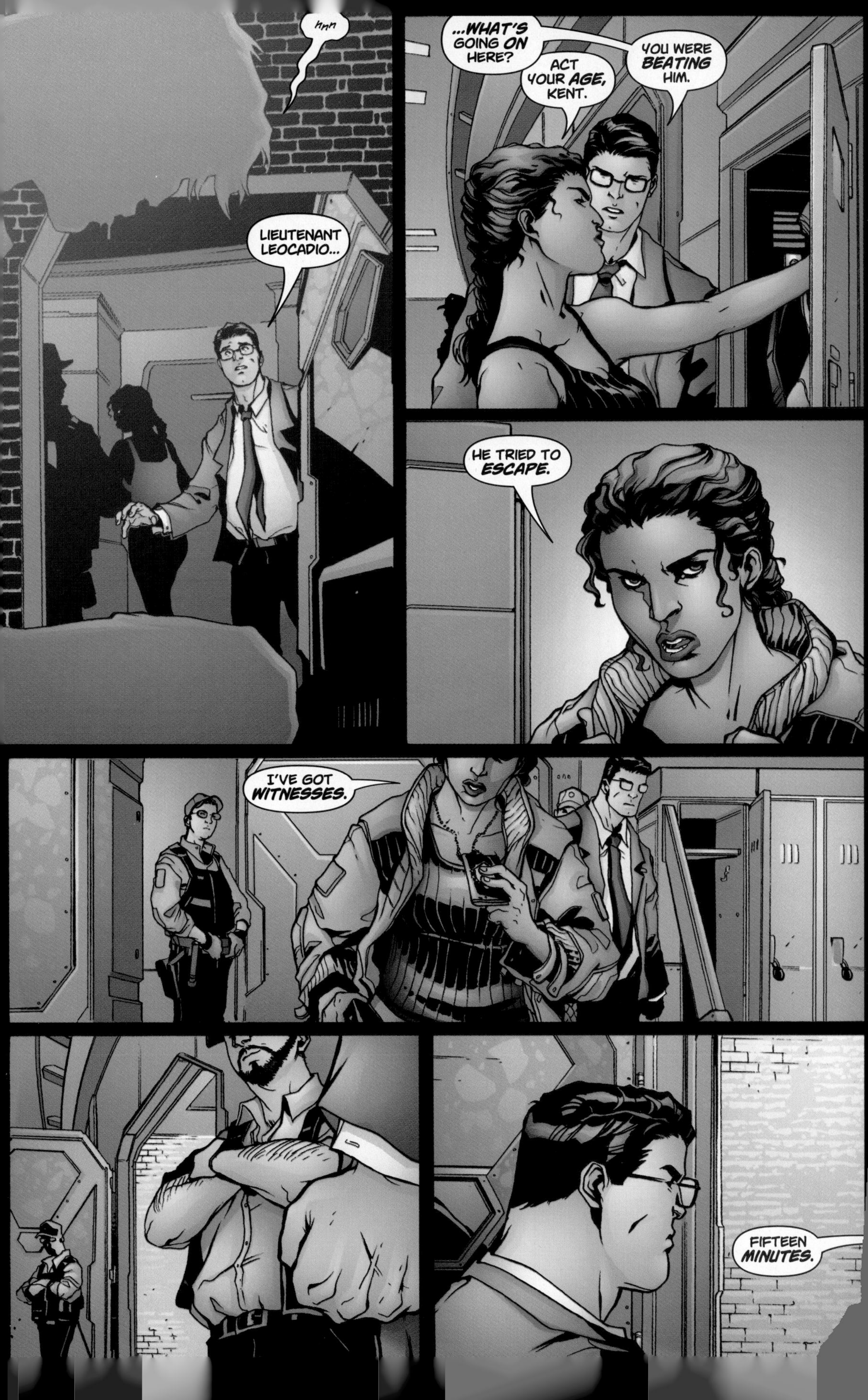
hnn
LIEUTENANT LEOCADIO...
...WHAT'S GOING ON HERE?
ACT YOUR AGE, KENT.
YOU WERE BEATING HIM.
HE TRIED TO ESCAPE.
I'VE GOT WITNESSES.
FIFTEEN MINUTES.

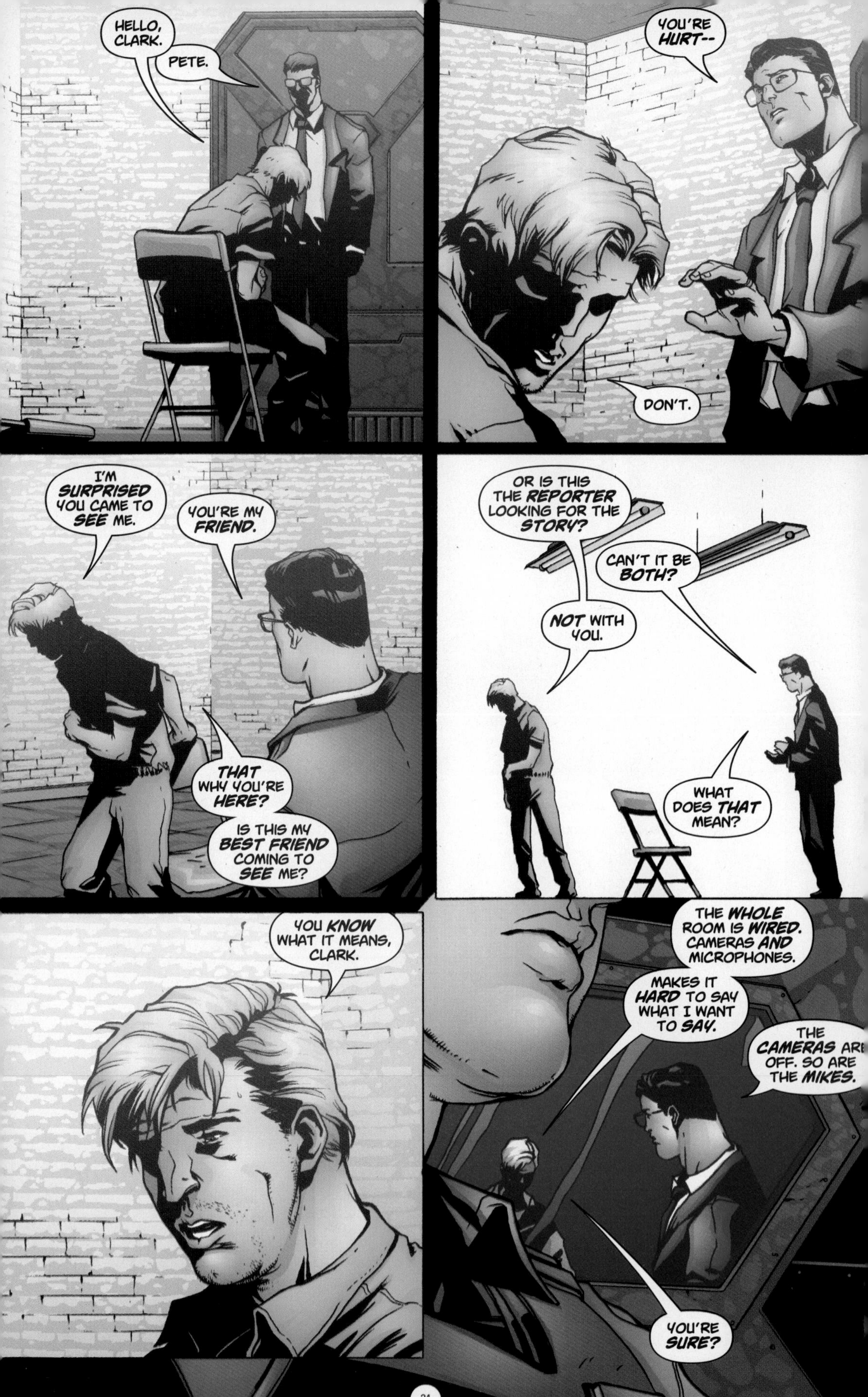
HELLO, CLARK.
PETE.
YOU'RE HURT--
DON'T.
I'M SURPRISED YOU CAME TO SEE ME.
YOU'RE MY FRIEND.
THAT WHY YOU'RE HERE?
IS THIS MY BEST FRIEND COMING TO SEE ME?
OR IS THIS THE REPORTER LOOKING FOR THE STORY?
CAN'T IT BE BOTH?
NOT WITH YOU.
WHAT DOES THAT MEAN?
YOU KNOW WHAT IT MEANS, CLARK.
THE WHOLE ROOM IS WIRED. CAMERAS AND MICROPHONES.
MAKES IT HARD TO SAY WHAT I WANT TO SAY.
THE CAMERAS ARE OFF. SO ARE THE MIKES.
YOU'RE SURE?

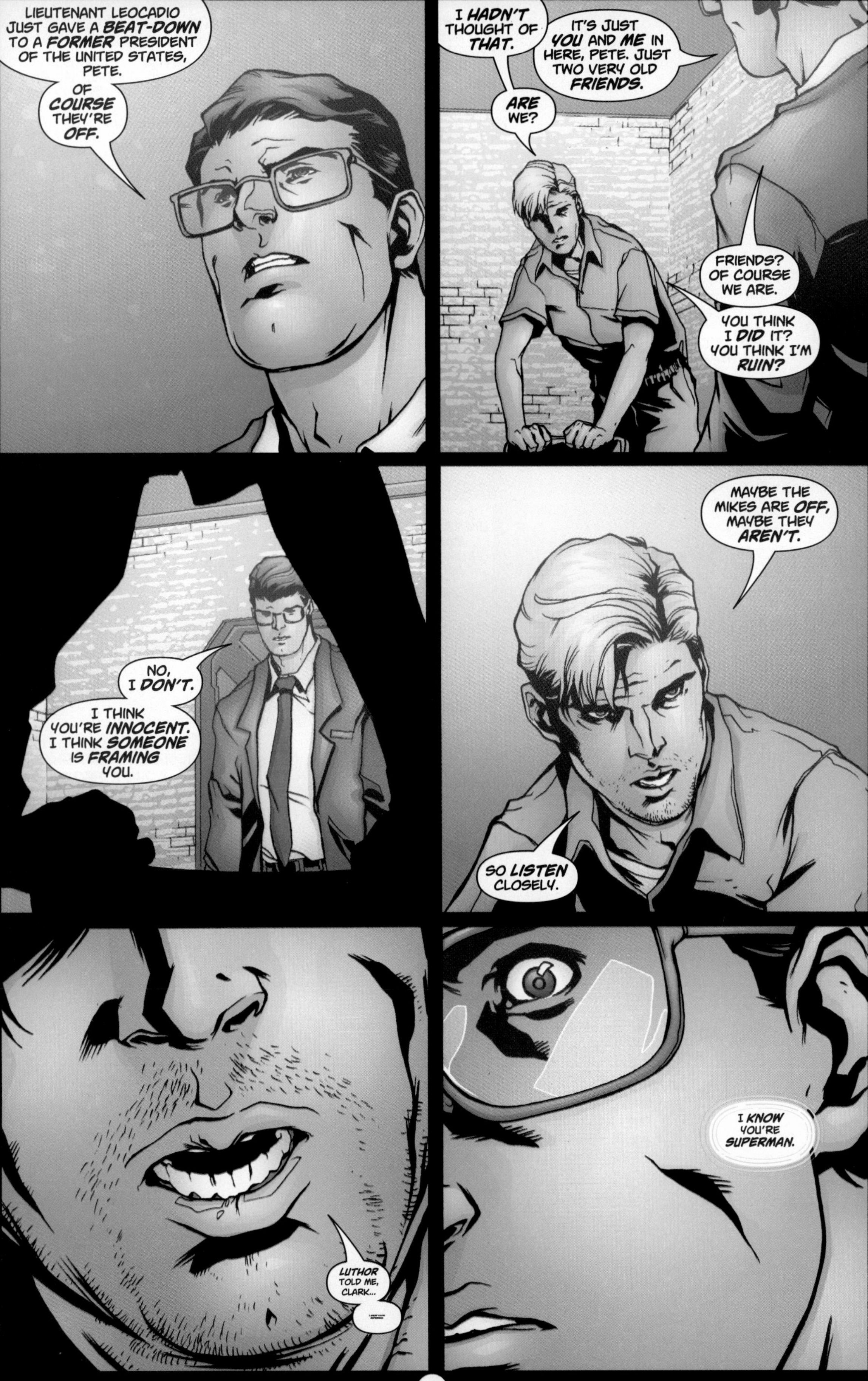
LIEUTENANT LEOCADIO JUST GAVE A BEAT-DOWN TO A FORMER PRESIDENT OF THE UNITED STATES, PETE.
OF COURSE THEY'RE OFF.
I HADN'T THOUGHT OF THAT.
IT'S JUST YOU AND ME IN HERE, PETE. JUST TWO VERY OLD FRIENDS.
ARE WE?
FRIENDS? OF COURSE WE ARE.
YOU THINK I DID IT? YOU THINK I'M RUIN?
NO, I DON'T.
I THINK YOU'RE INNOCENT. I THINK SOMEONE IS FRAMING YOU.
MAYBE THE MIKES ARE OFF, MAYBE THEY AREN'T.
SO LISTEN CLOSELY.
LUTHOR TOLD ME, CLARK...
I KNOW YOU'RE SUPERMAN.

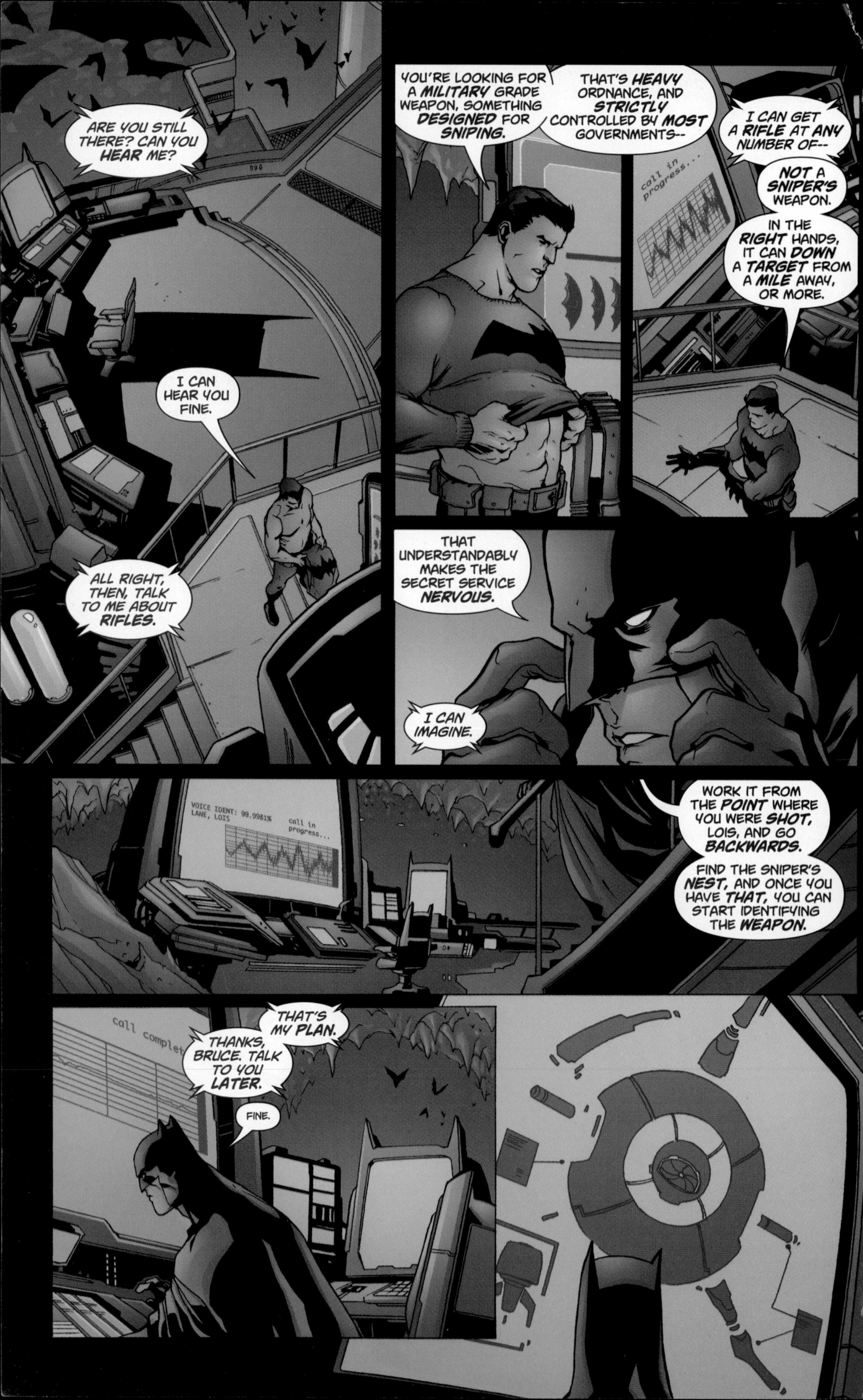
ARE YOU STILL THERE? CAN YOU HEAR ME?
I CAN HEAR YOU FINE.
ALL RIGHT, THEN, TALK TO ME ABOUT RIFLES.
YOU'RE LOOKING FOR A MILITARY GRADE WEAPON, SOMETHING DESIGNED FOR SNIPING.
THAT'S HEAVY ORDNANCE, AND STRICTLY CONTROLLED BY MOST GOVERNMENTS--
call in progress...
I CAN GET A RIFLE AT ANY NUMBER OF--
NOT A SNIPER'S WEAPON.
IN THE RIGHT HANDS, IT CAN DOWN A TARGET FROM A MILE AWAY, OR MORE.
THAT UNDERSTANDABLY MAKES THE SECRET SERVICE NERVOUS.
I CAN IMAGINE.
VOICE IDENT: 99.9981%
LANE, LOIS
call in progress...
WORK IT FROM THE POINT WHERE YOU WERE SHOT, LOIS, AND GO BACKWARDS.
FIND THE SNIPER'S NEST, AND ONCE YOU HAVE THAT, YOU CAN START IDENTIFYING THE WEAPON.
THAT'S MY PLAN.
THANKS, BRUCE. TALK TO YOU LATER.
FINE.

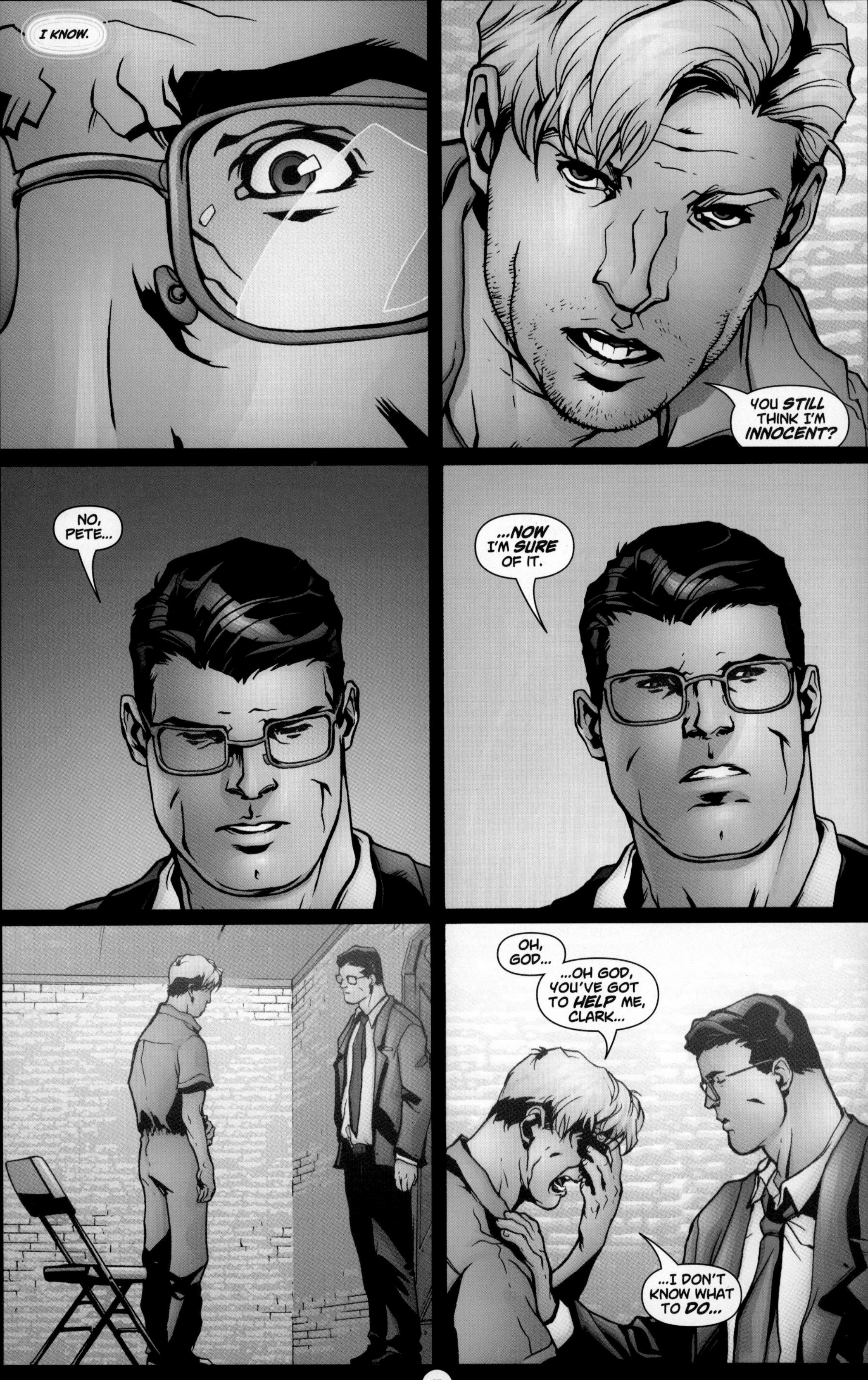
I KNOW.
YOU STILL THINK I'M INNOCENT?
NO, PETE...
...NOW I'M SURE OF IT.
OH, GOD...
...OH GOD, YOU'VE GOT TO HELP ME, CLARK...
...I DON'T KNOW WHAT TO DO...

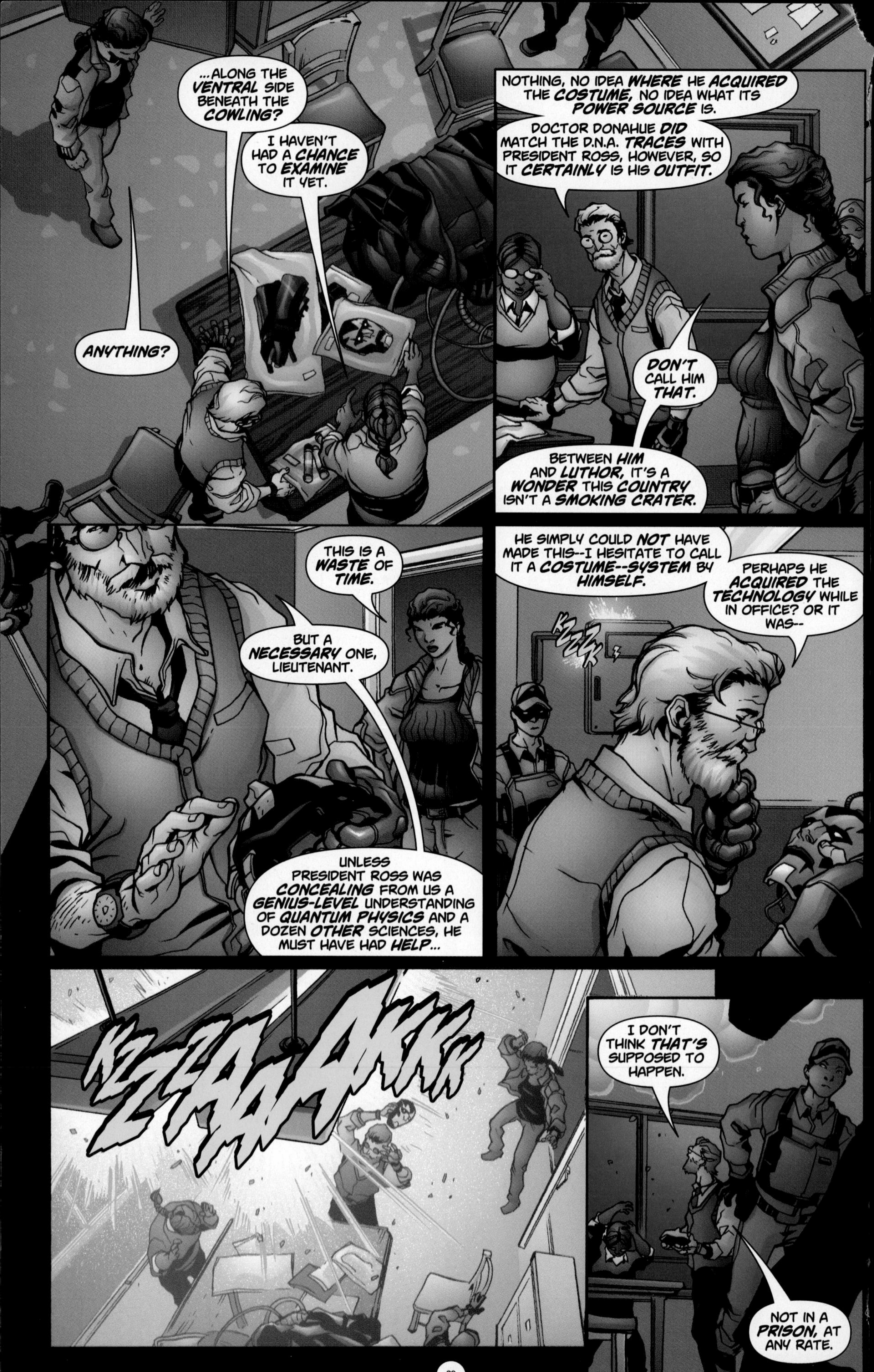
...ALONG THE VENTRAL SIDE BENEATH THE COWLING?
I HAVEN'T HAD A CHANCE TO EXAMINE IT YET.
ANYTHING?
NOTHING, NO IDEA WHERE HE ACQUIRED THE COSTUME, NO IDEA WHAT ITS POWER SOURCE IS.
DOCTOR DONAHUE DID MATCH THE D.N.A. TRACES WITH PRESIDENT ROSS, HOWEVER, SO IT CERTAINLY IS HIS OUTFIT.
DON'T CALL HIM THAT.
BETWEEN HIM AND LUTHOR, IT'S A WONDER THIS COUNTRY ISN'T A SMOKING CRATER.
THIS IS A WASTE OF TIME.
BUT A NECESSARY ONE, LIEUTENANT.
UNLESS PRESIDENT ROSS WAS CONCEALING FROM US A GENIUS-LEVEL UNDERSTANDING OF QUANTUM PHYSICS AND A DOZEN OTHER SCIENCES, HE MUST HAVE HAD HELP...
HE SIMPLY COULD NOT HAVE MADE THIS--I HESITATE TO CALL IT A COSTUME--SYSTEM BY HIMSELF.
PERHAPS HE ACQUIRED THE TECHNOLOGY WHILE IN OFFICE? OR IT WAS--
KZZZK
KZZAAAAKKKK
I DON'T THINK THAT'S SUPPOSED TO HAPPEN.
NOT IN A PRISON, AT ANY RATE.

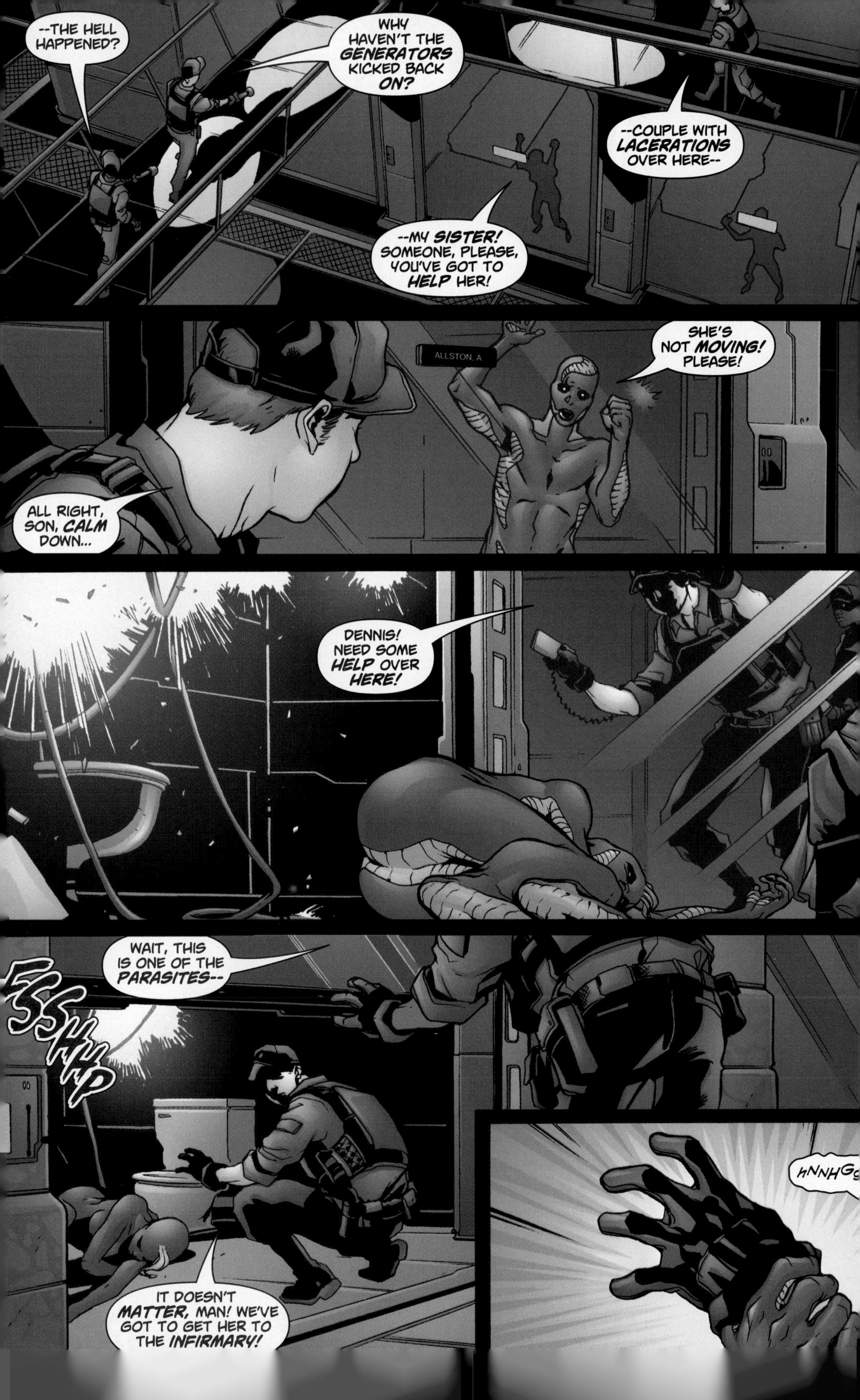
--THE HELL HAPPENED?
WHY HAVEN'T THE GENERATORS KICKED BACK ON?
--COUPLE WITH LACERATIONS OVER HERE--
--MY SISTER! SOMEONE, PLEASE, YOU'VE GOT TO HELP HER!
ALLSTON, A
SHE'S NOT MOVING! PLEASE!
ALL RIGHT, SON, CALM DOWN...
DENNIS! NEED SOME HELP OVER HERE!
FSSHHP
WAIT, THIS IS ONE OF THE PARASITES--
IT DOESN'T MATTER, MAN! WE'VE GOT TO GET HER TO THE INFIRMARY!
hNNHG

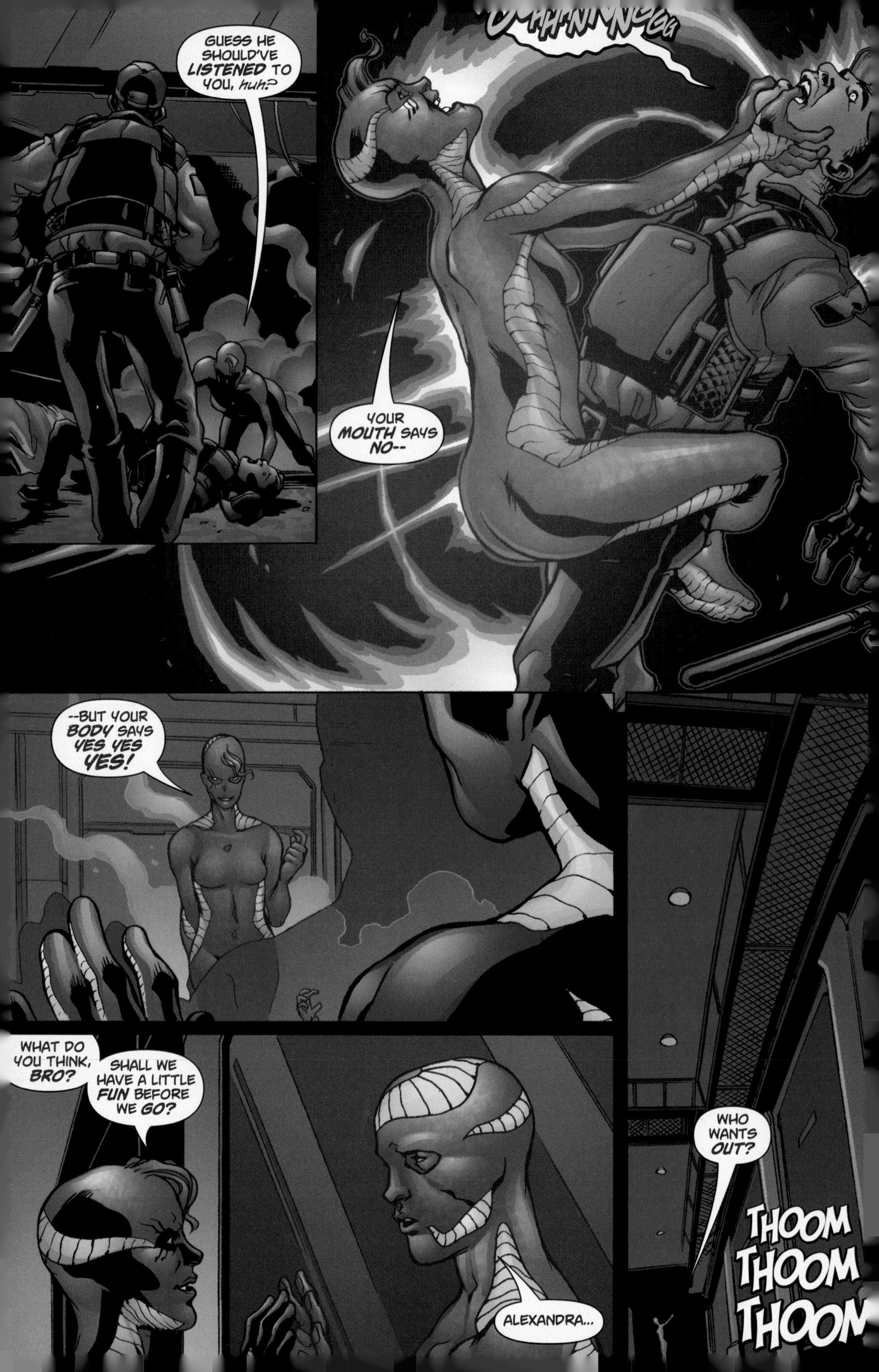
GUESS HE SHOULD'VE LISTENED TO YOU, huh?
YOUR MOUTH SAYS NO--
--BUT YOUR BODY SAYS YES YES YES!
WHAT DO YOU THINK, BRO?
SHALL WE HAVE A LITTLE FUN BEFORE WE GO?
ALEXANDRA...
WHO WANTS OUT?
THOOM
THOOM

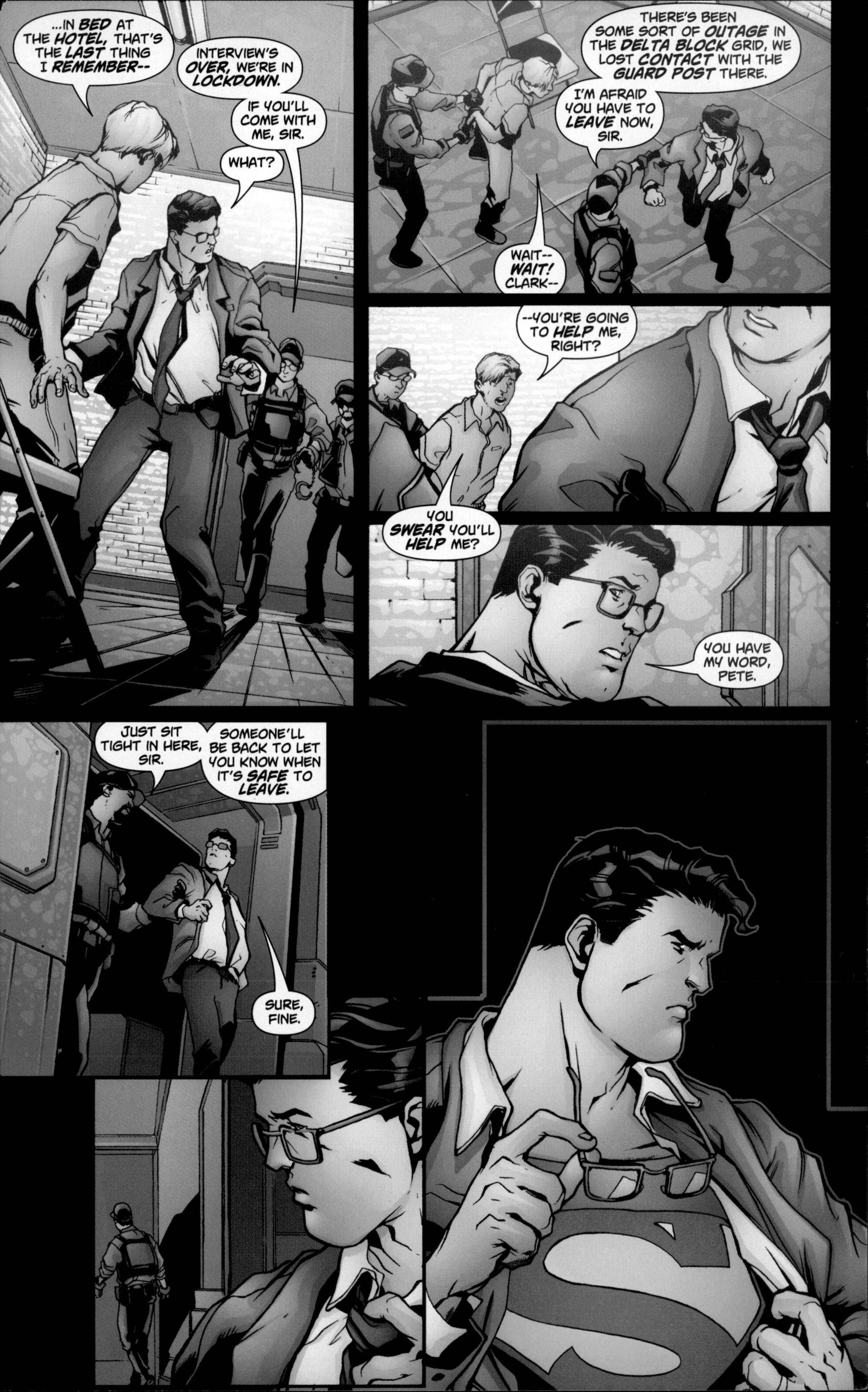
...IN BED AT THE HOTEL, THAT'S THE LAST THING I REMEMBER--
INTERVIEW'S OVER, WE'RE IN LOCKDOWN.
IF YOU'LL COME WITH ME, SIR.
WHAT?
THERE'S BEEN SOME SORT OF OUTAGE IN THE DELTA BLOCK GRID, WE LOST CONTACT WITH THE GUARD POST THERE.
I'M AFRAID YOU HAVE TO LEAVE NOW, SIR.
WAIT-- WAIT! CLARK--
--YOU'RE GOING TO HELP ME, RIGHT?
YOU SWEAR YOU'LL HELP ME?
YOU HAVE MY WORD, PETE.
JUST SIT TIGHT IN HERE, SIR.
SOMEONE'LL BE BACK TO LET YOU KNOW WHEN IT'S SAFE TO LEAVE.
SURE, FINE.

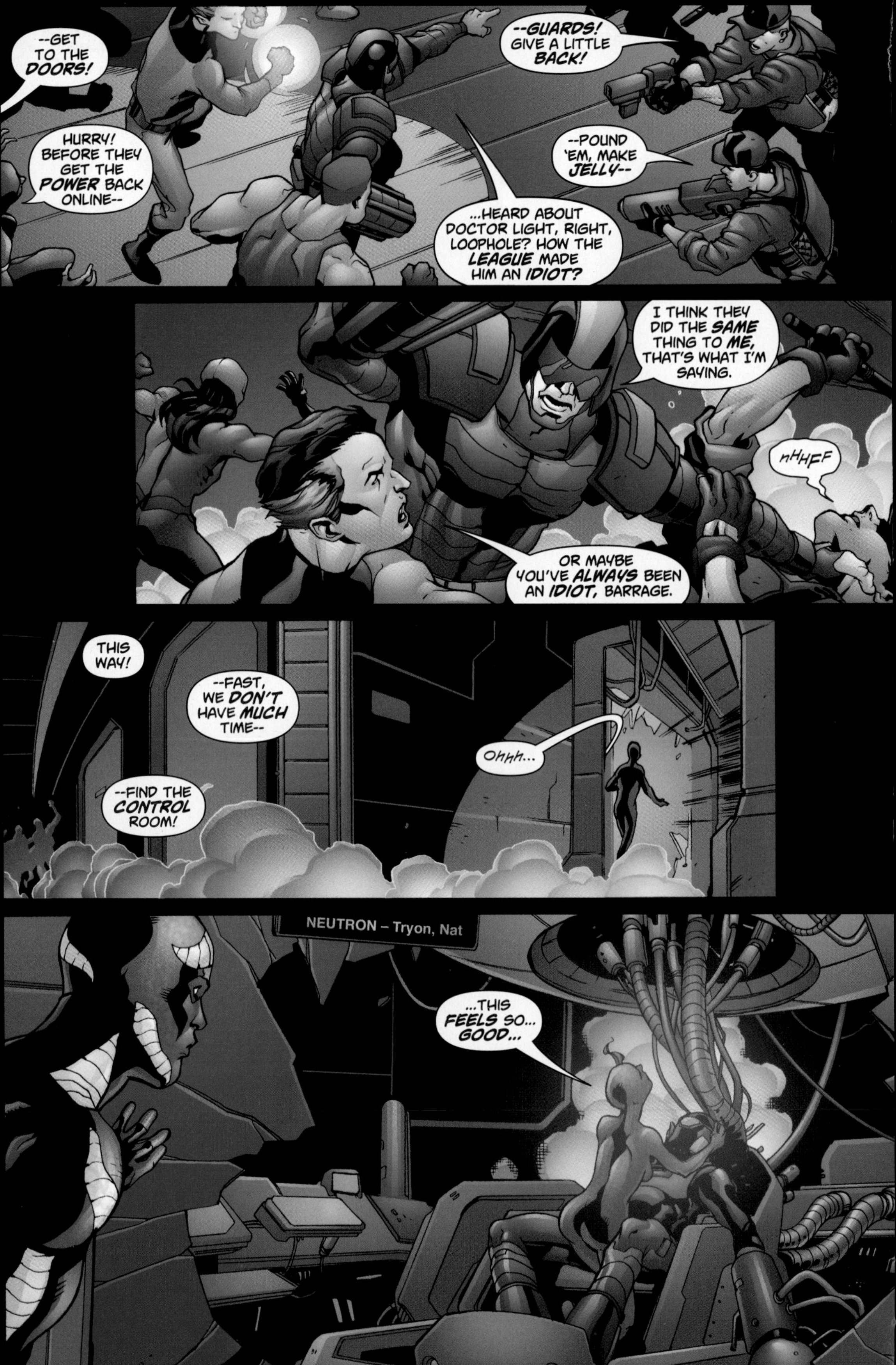
--GET TO THE DOORS!
HURRY! BEFORE THEY GET THE POWER BACK ONLINE--
--GUARDS! GIVE A LITTLE BACK!
--POUND 'EM, MAKE JELLY--
...HEARD ABOUT DOCTOR LIGHT, RIGHT, LOOPHOLE? HOW THE LEAGUE MADE HIM AN IDIOT?
I THINK THEY DID THE SAME THING TO ME, THAT'S WHAT I'M SAYING.
nHHFF
OR MAYBE YOU'VE ALWAYS BEEN AN IDIOT, BARRAGE.
THIS WAY!
--FAST, WE DON'T HAVE MUCH TIME--
Ohhh...
--FIND THE CONTROL ROOM!
NEUTRON – Tryon, Nat
...THIS FEELS SO... GOOD...

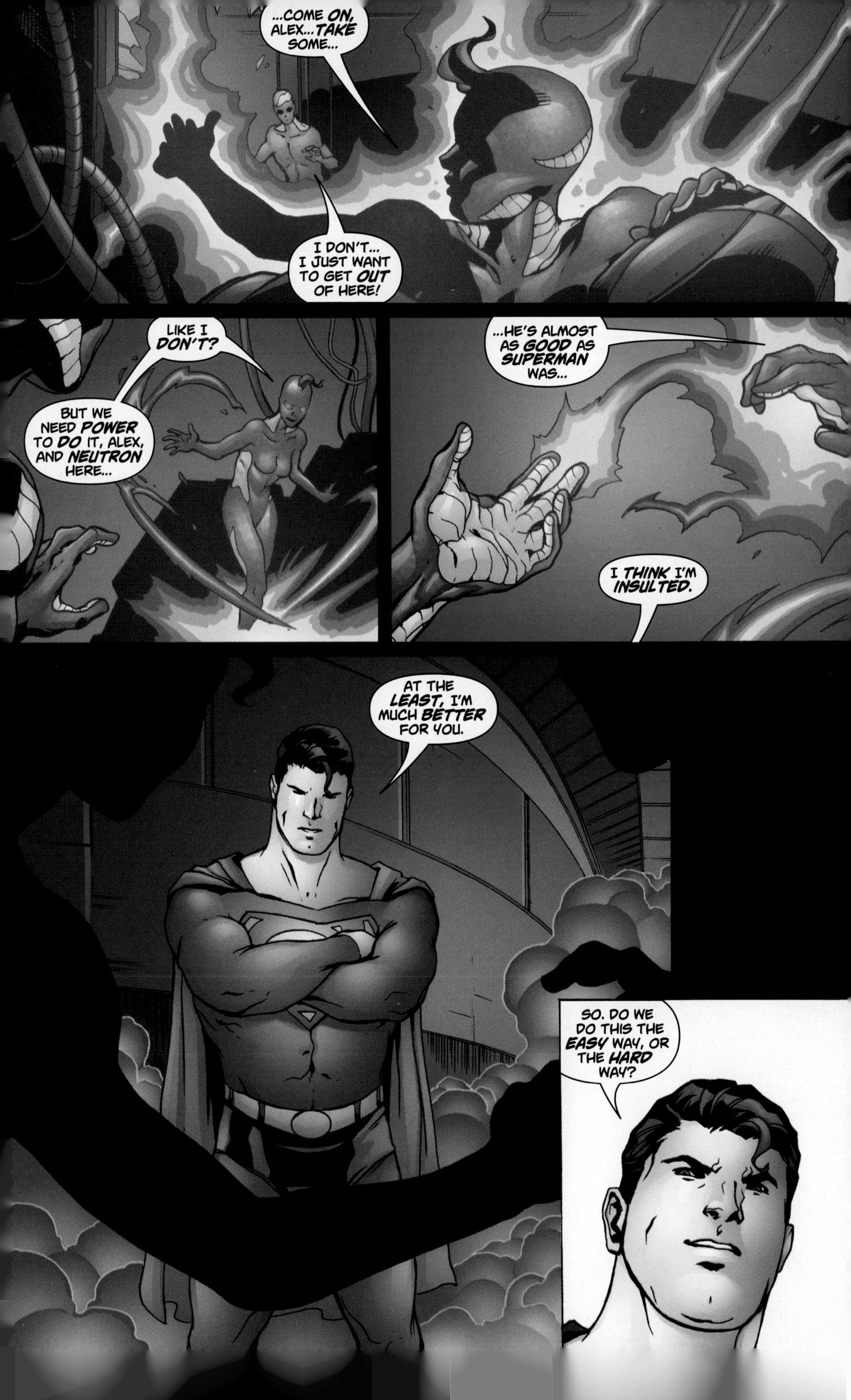
...COME ON, ALEX...TAKE SOME...
I DON'T... I JUST WANT TO GET OUT OF HERE!
LIKE I DON'T?
BUT WE NEED POWER TO DO IT, ALEX, AND NEUTRON HERE...
...HE'S ALMOST AS GOOD AS SUPERMAN WAS...
I THINK I'M INSULTED.
AT THE LEAST, I'M MUCH BETTER FOR YOU.
SO. DO WE DO THIS THE EASY WAY, OR THE HARD WAY?

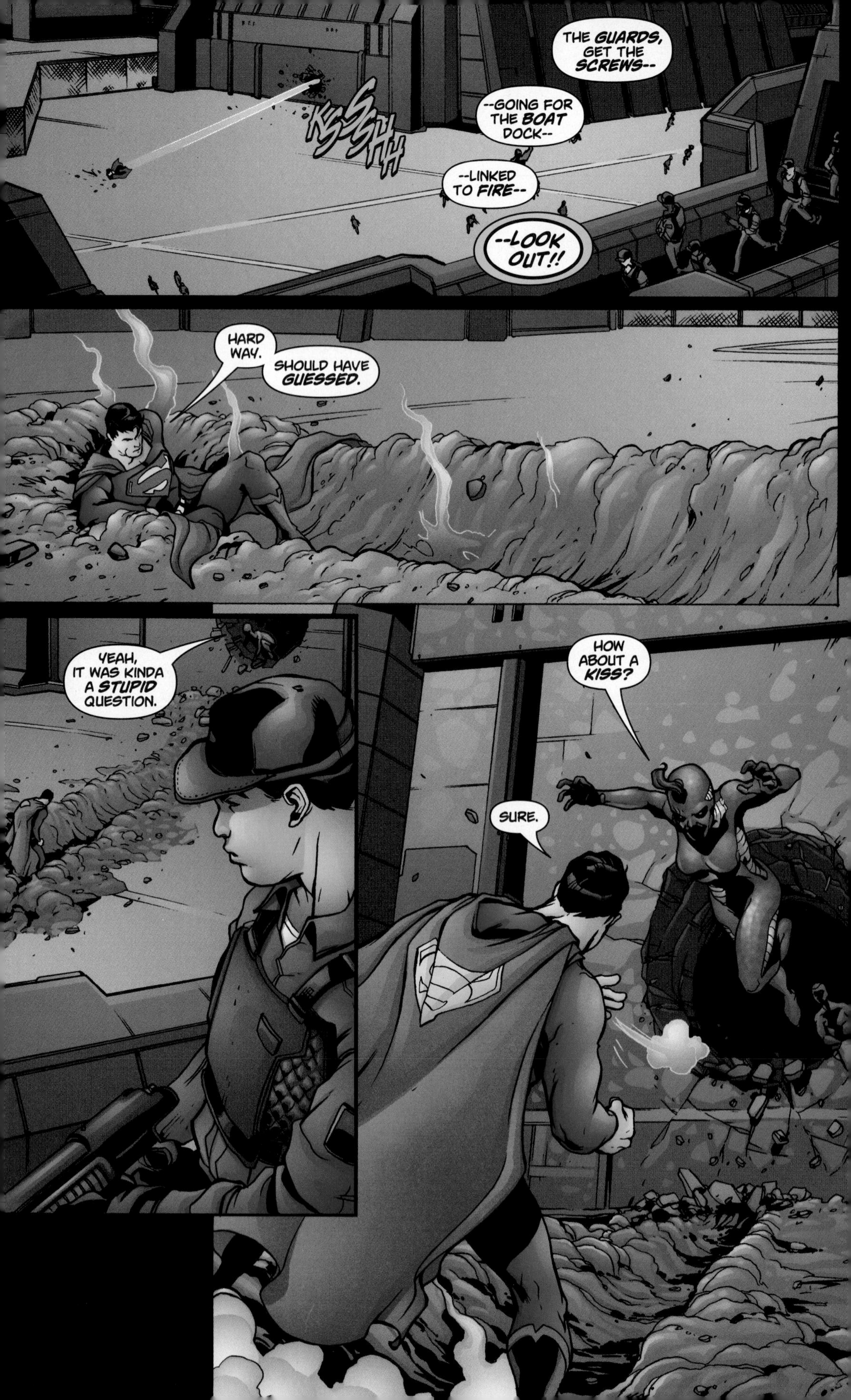
THE GUARDS, GET THE SCREWS--
--GOING FOR THE BOAT DOCK--
--LINKED TO FIRE--
KSSSHH
--LOOK OUT!!
HARD WAY.
SHOULD HAVE GUESSED.
YEAH, IT WAS KINDA A STUPID QUESTION.
HOW ABOUT A KISS?
SURE.

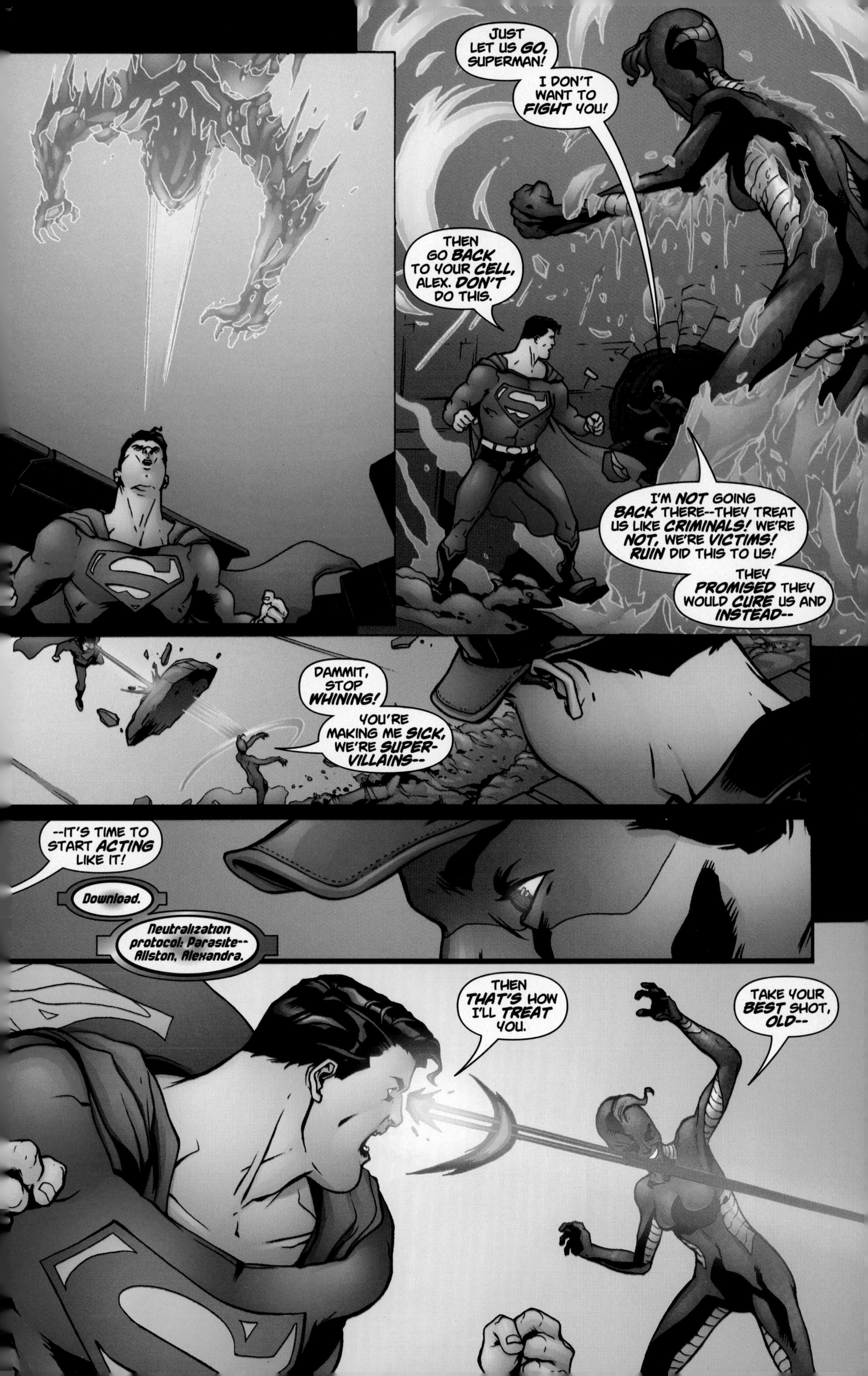
JUST LET US GO, SUPERMAN!
I DON'T WANT TO FIGHT YOU!
THEN GO BACK TO YOUR CELL, ALEX. DON'T DO THIS.
I'M NOT GOING BACK THERE--THEY TREAT US LIKE CRIMINALS! WE'RE NOT, WE'RE VICTIMS! RUIN DID THIS TO US!
THEY PROMISED THEY WOULD CURE US AND INSTEAD--
DAMMIT, STOP WHINING!
YOU'RE MAKING ME SICK, WE'RE SUPER-VILLAINS--
--IT'S TIME TO START ACTING LIKE IT!
Download.
Neutralization protocol: Parasite--Allston, Alexandra.
THEN THAT'S HOW I'LL TREAT YOU.
TAKE YOUR BEST SHOT, OLD--

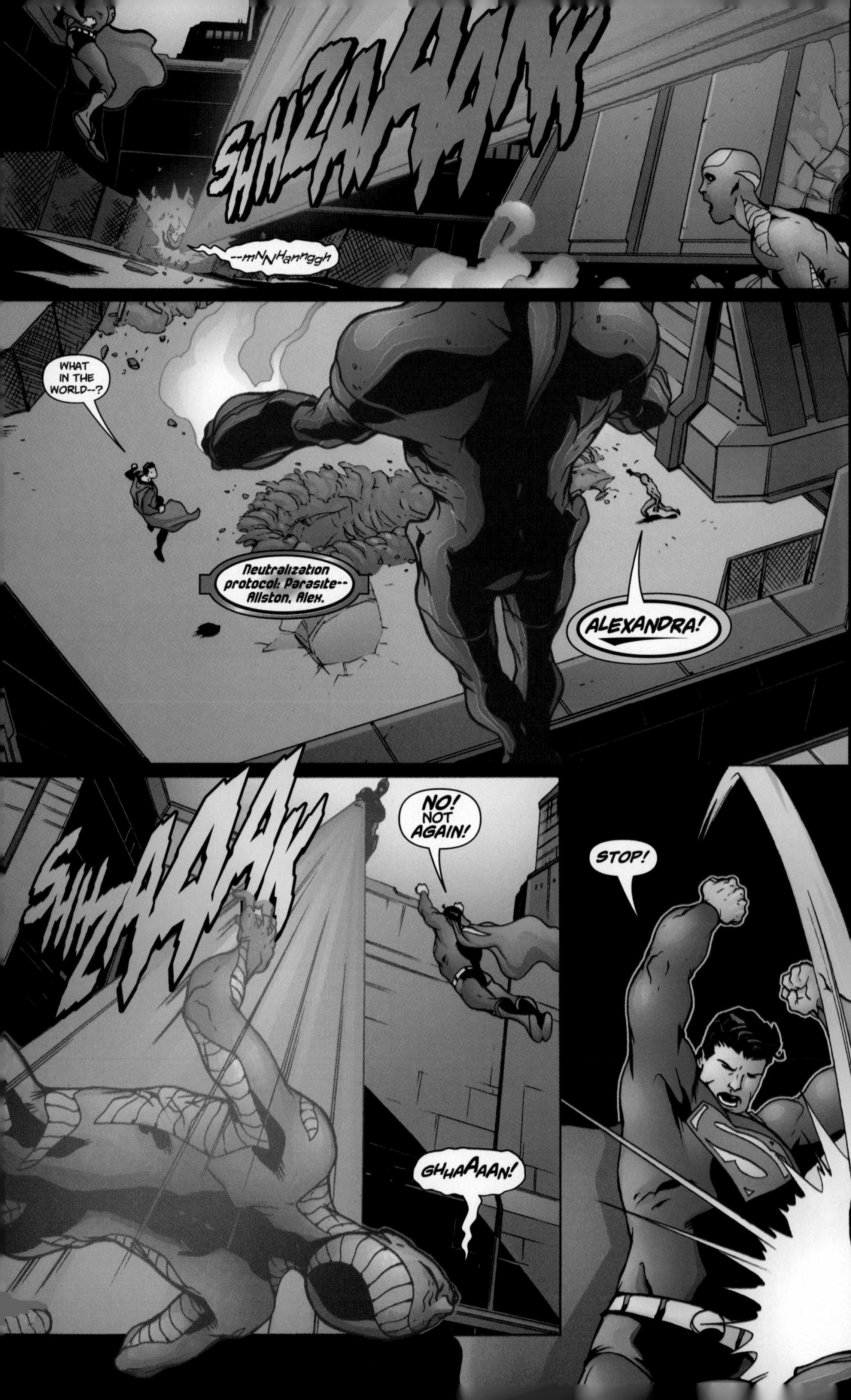
SHHZAHAHAK
--mNNHannggh
WHAT IN THE WORLD--?
Neutralization protocol: Parasite-- Allston, Alex.
ALEXANDRA!
SHHZAAAK
NO! NOT AGAIN!
GHHAAAAN!
STOP!

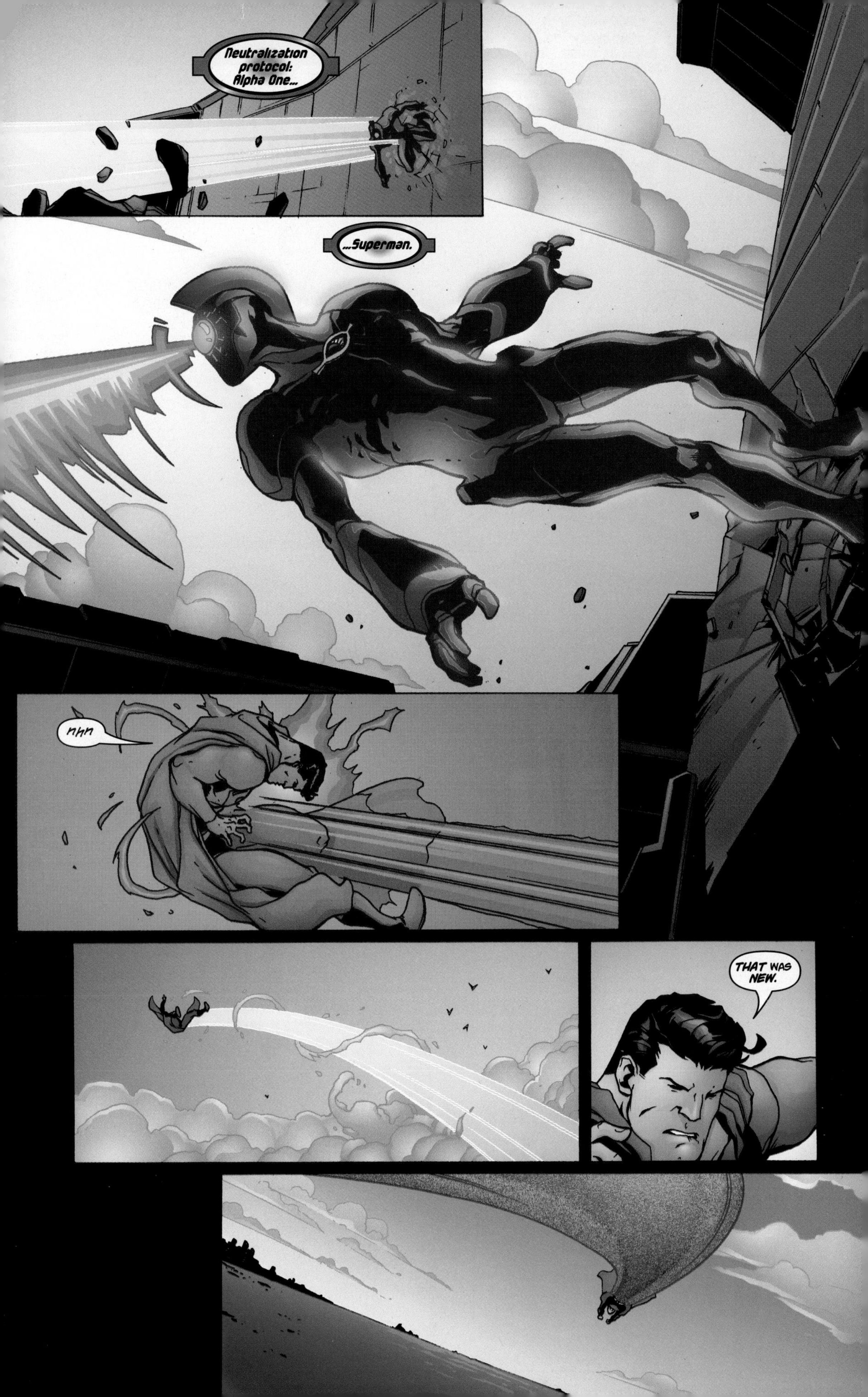
Neutralization protocol: Alpha One...
...Superman.
nhn
THAT WAS NEW.

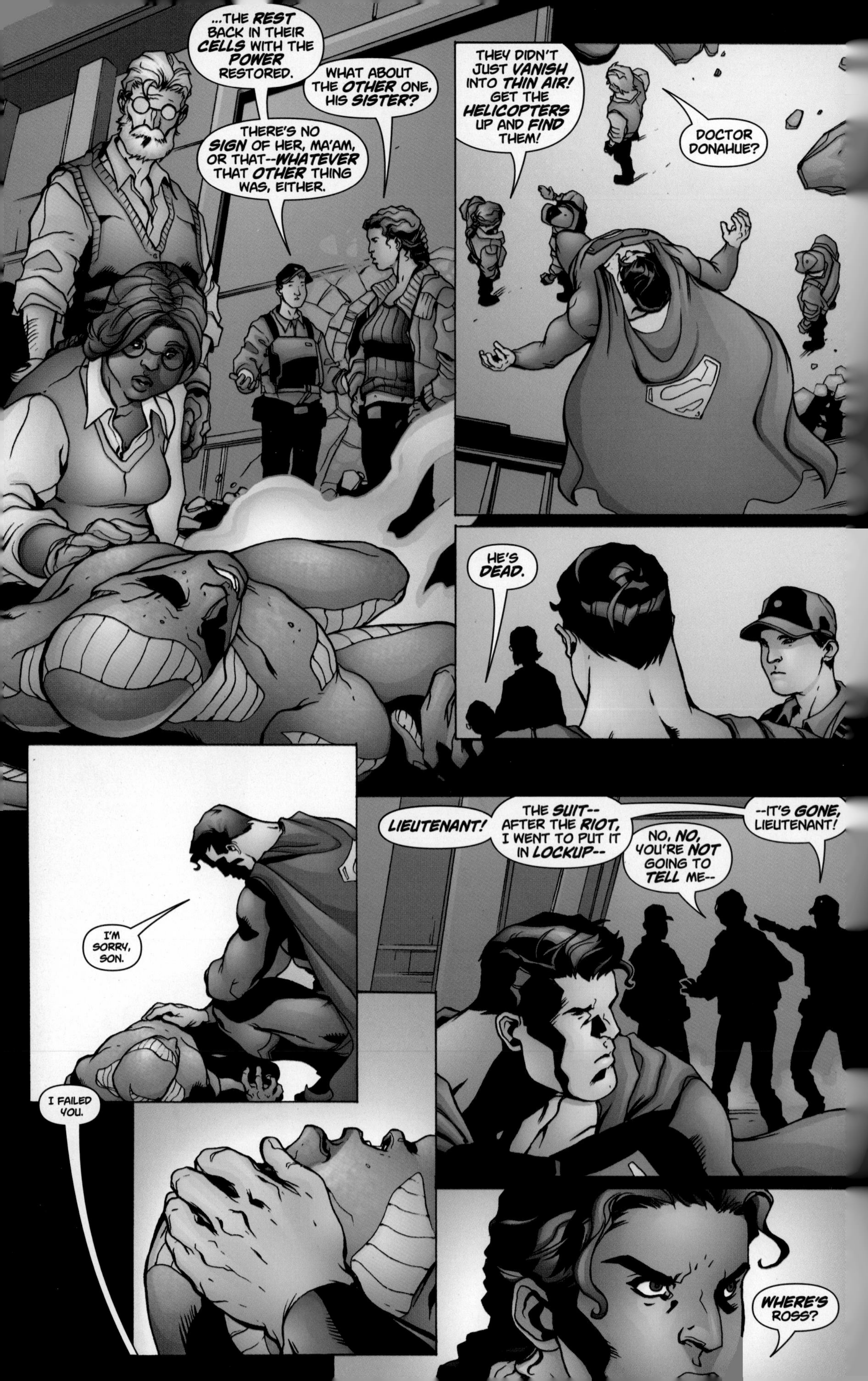
...THE REST BACK IN THEIR CELLS WITH THE POWER RESTORED.
WHAT ABOUT THE OTHER ONE, HIS SISTER?
THERE'S NO SIGN OF HER, MA'AM, OR THAT--WHATEVER THAT OTHER THING WAS, EITHER.
THEY DIDN'T JUST VANISH INTO THIN AIR! GET THE HELICOPTERS UP AND FIND THEM!
DOCTOR DONAHUE?
HE'S DEAD.
I'M SORRY, SON.
I FAILED YOU.
LIEUTENANT!
THE SUIT-- AFTER THE RIOT, I WENT TO PUT IT IN LOCKUP--
--IT'S GONE, LIEUTENANT!
NO, NO, YOU'RE NOT GOING TO TELL ME--
WHERE'S ROSS?

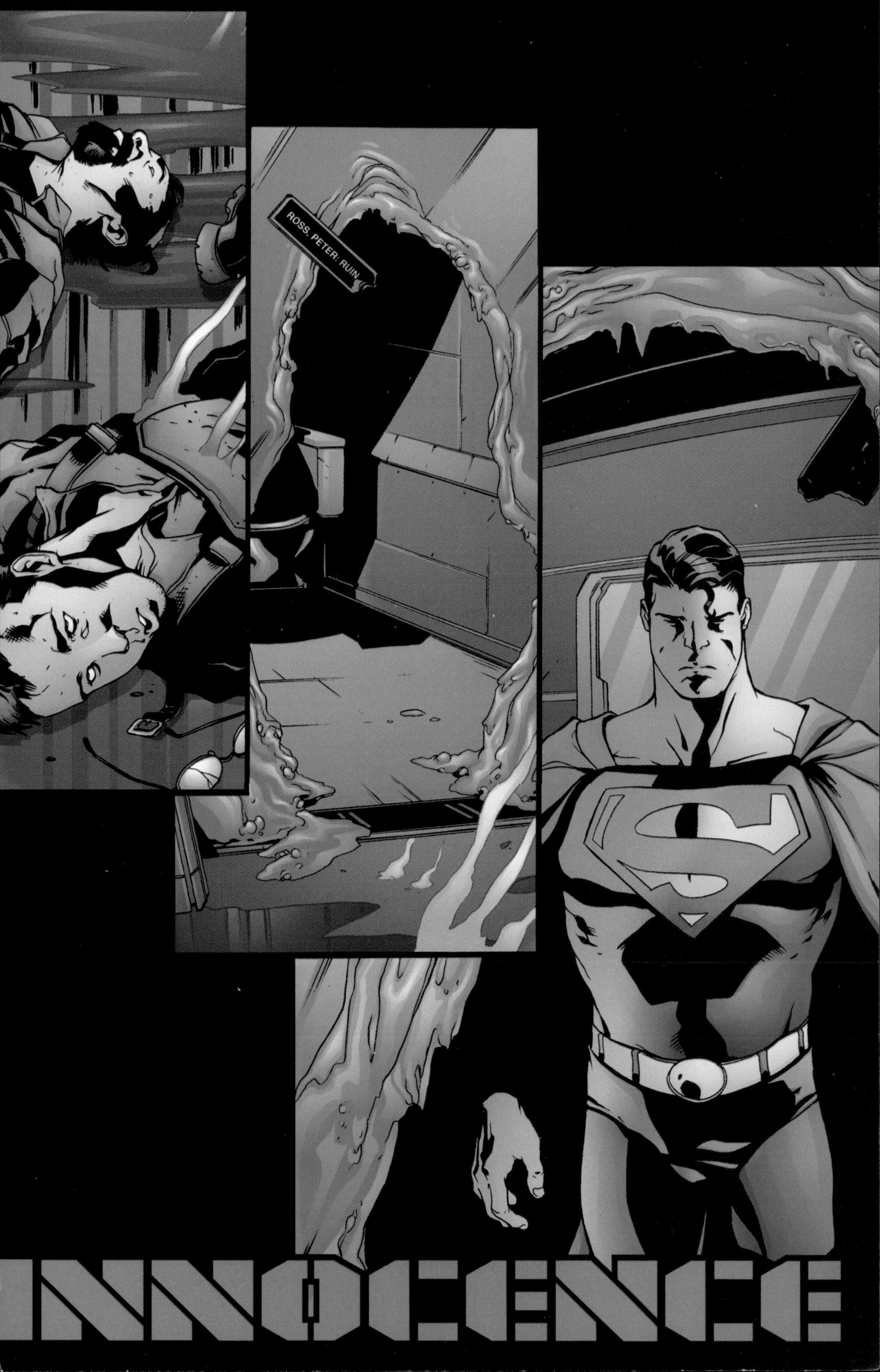
ROSS, PETER: RUIN
INNOCENCE

The cybernetic attack by the OMACs was just a hint of the terror to come, one that would grip every man, woman and child living on Earth.

Superman's peers have had to cope with the violent death of several comrades, including the Blue Beetle and Sue Dibny, wife of the Elongated Man. This burden was compounded by a grim revelation: that various heroes had conspired to allow Zatanna to alter the memories and even the personalities of their criminal opponents. Word of this has spread among the costumed champions and their deadliest opponents. The resulting rift among the members of the JLA has led to physical conflict, and that gap is growing.

As a result of this disclosure, the villains have been working together to see to it that such affronts never occur again. Several of Superman's foes have joined an organization called the Society, but not all. Those who have declined include the reincarnation of an old minor villain named Blackrock, who has appeared more powerful than ever.

The telepathic Maxwell Lord began to slowly usurp Superman's mind at this time. Lord, having taken over the clandestine organization Checkmate, also stole access to Brother Eye, the artificial intelligence satellite that controls the OMACs. After nearly killing Batman, Superman was opposed by Wonder Woman and their confrontation, the second in a short span of time, was bloody. When Lord refused to release his control, the Amazon Princess saw no other choice but to snap Lord's neck, killing him, an act recorded and subsequently broadcast worldwide by Brother Eye.

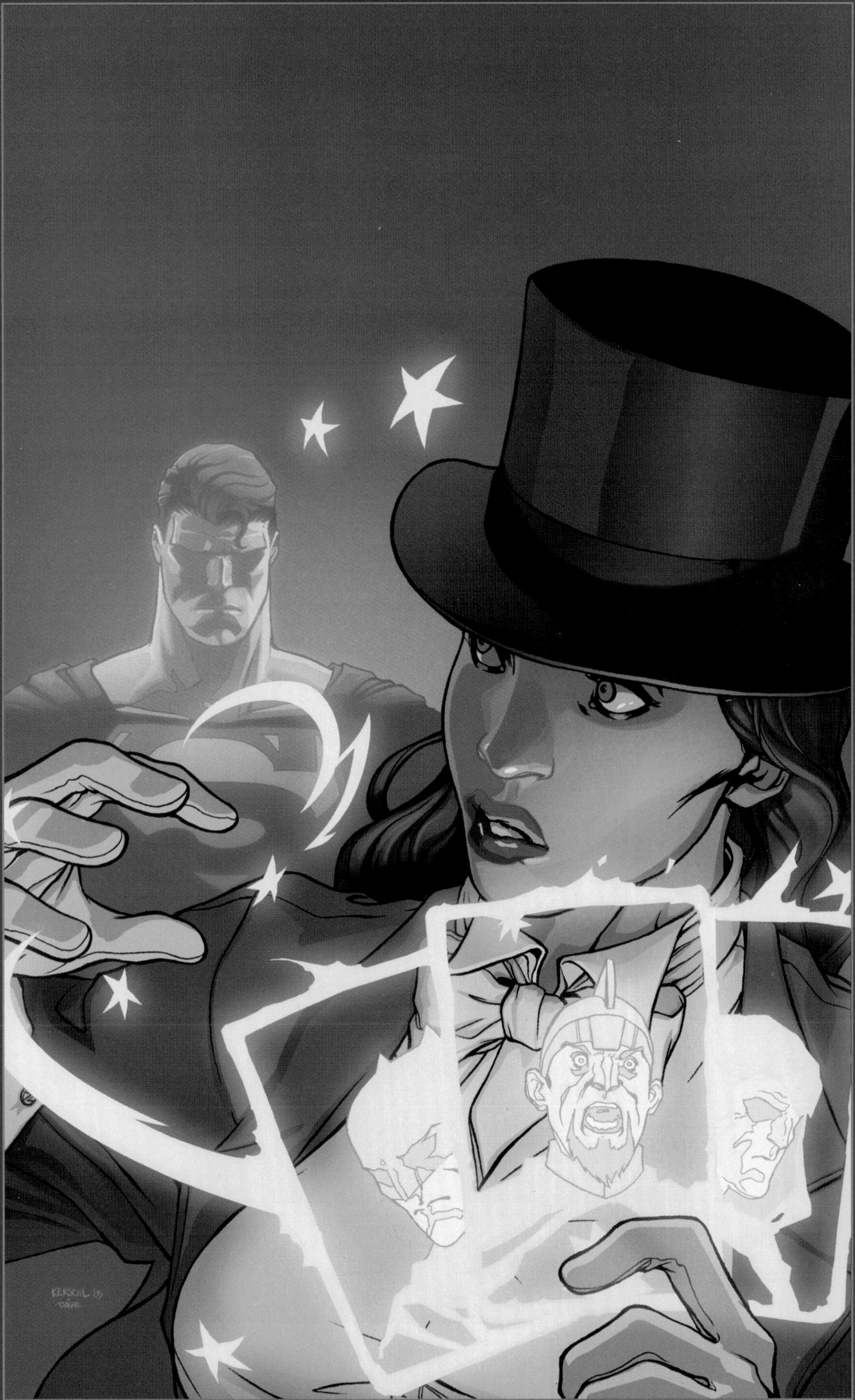

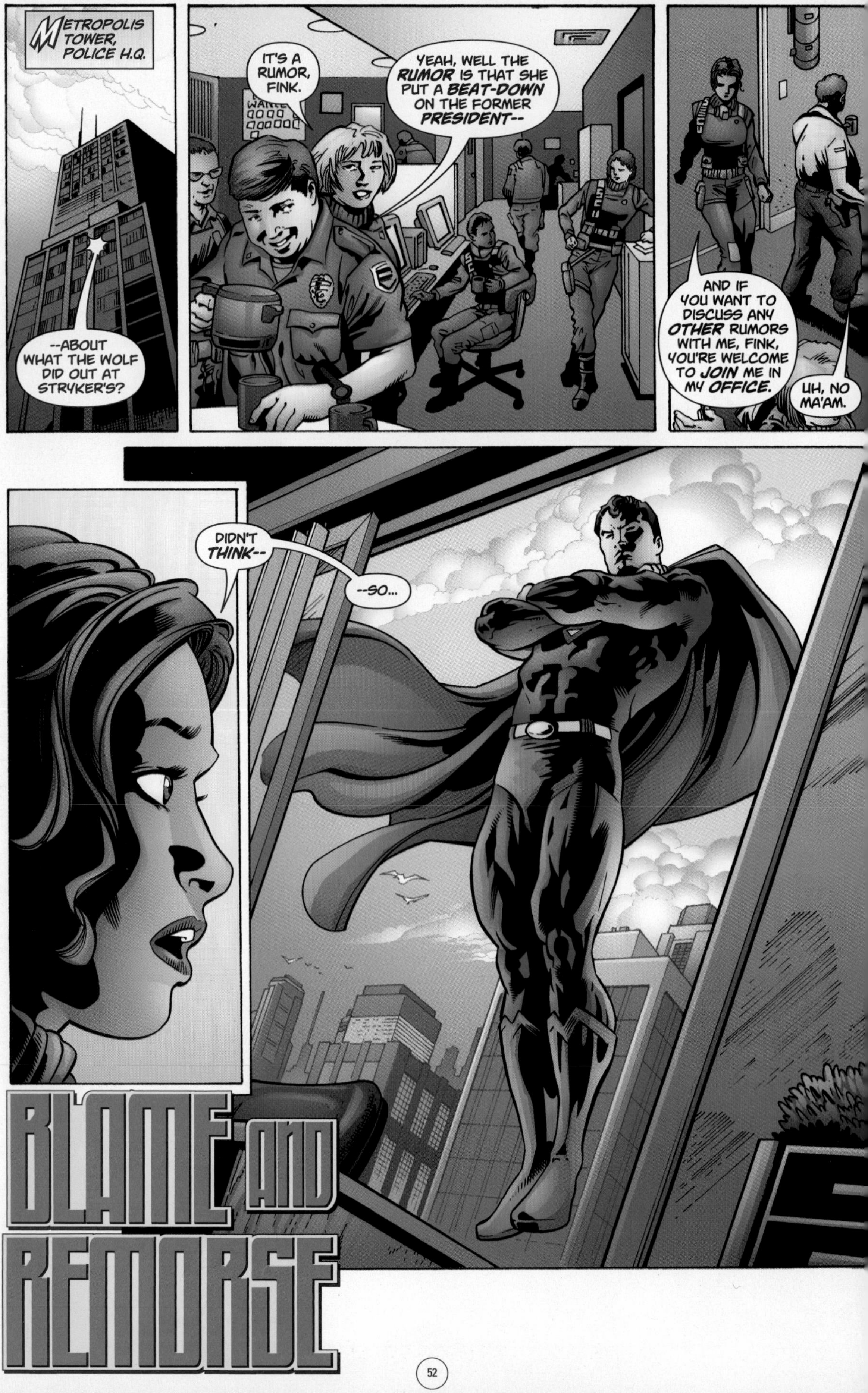
METROPOLIS TOWER, POLICE H.Q.
--ABOUT WHAT THE WOLF DID OUT AT STRYKER'S?
IT'S A RUMOR, FINK.
YEAH, WELL THE RUMOR IS THAT SHE PUT A BEAT-DOWN ON THE FORMER PRESIDENT--
AND IF YOU WANT TO DISCUSS ANY OTHER RUMORS WITH ME, FINK, YOU'RE WELCOME TO JOIN ME IN MY OFFICE.
UH, NO MA'AM.
DIDN'T THINK--
--SO...
BLAME AND REMORSE

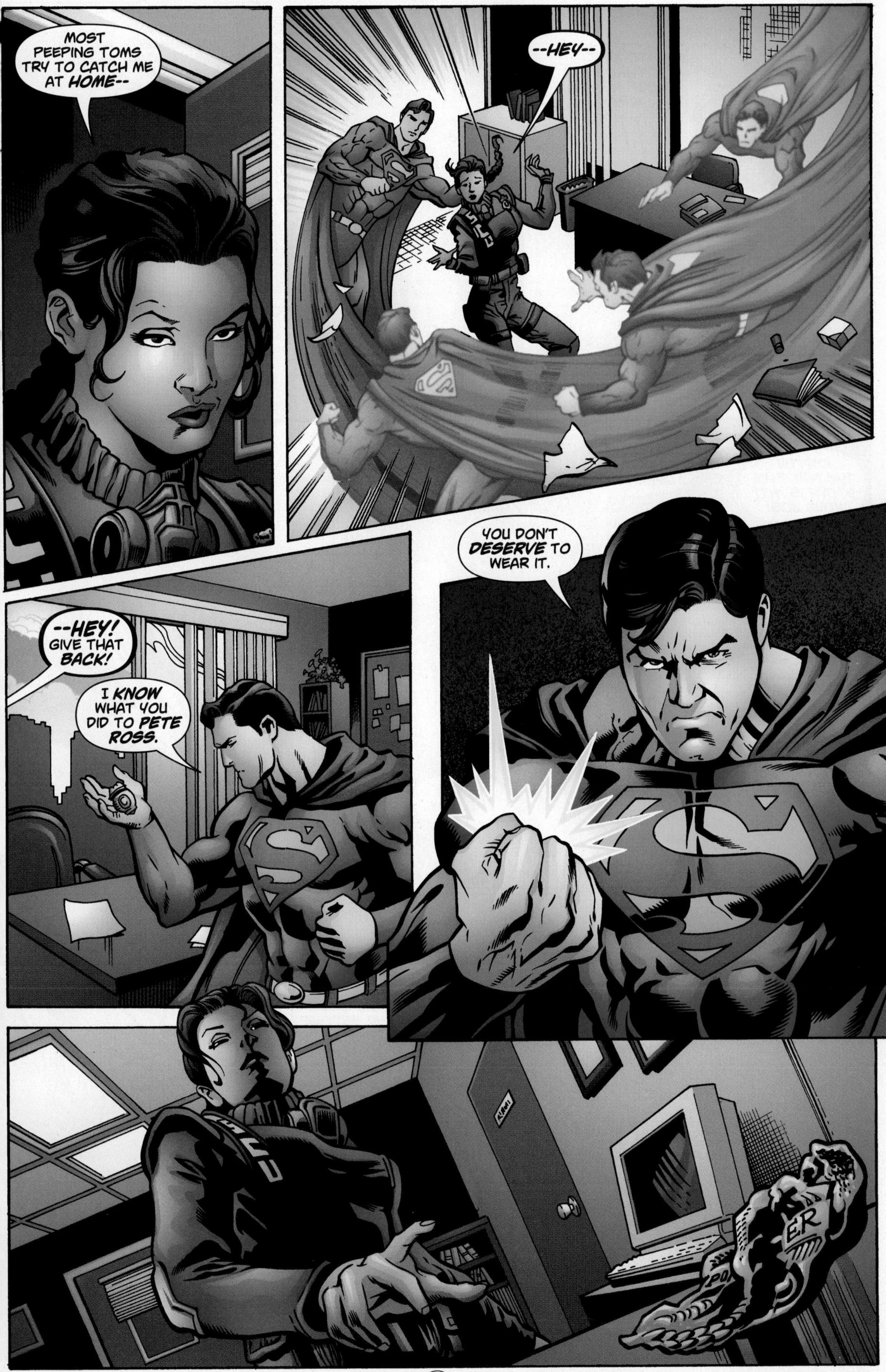
MOST PEEPING TOMS TRY TO CATCH ME AT HOME--
--HEY--
--HEY! GIVE THAT BACK!
I KNOW WHAT YOU DID TO PETE ROSS.
YOU DON'T DESERVE TO WEAR IT.

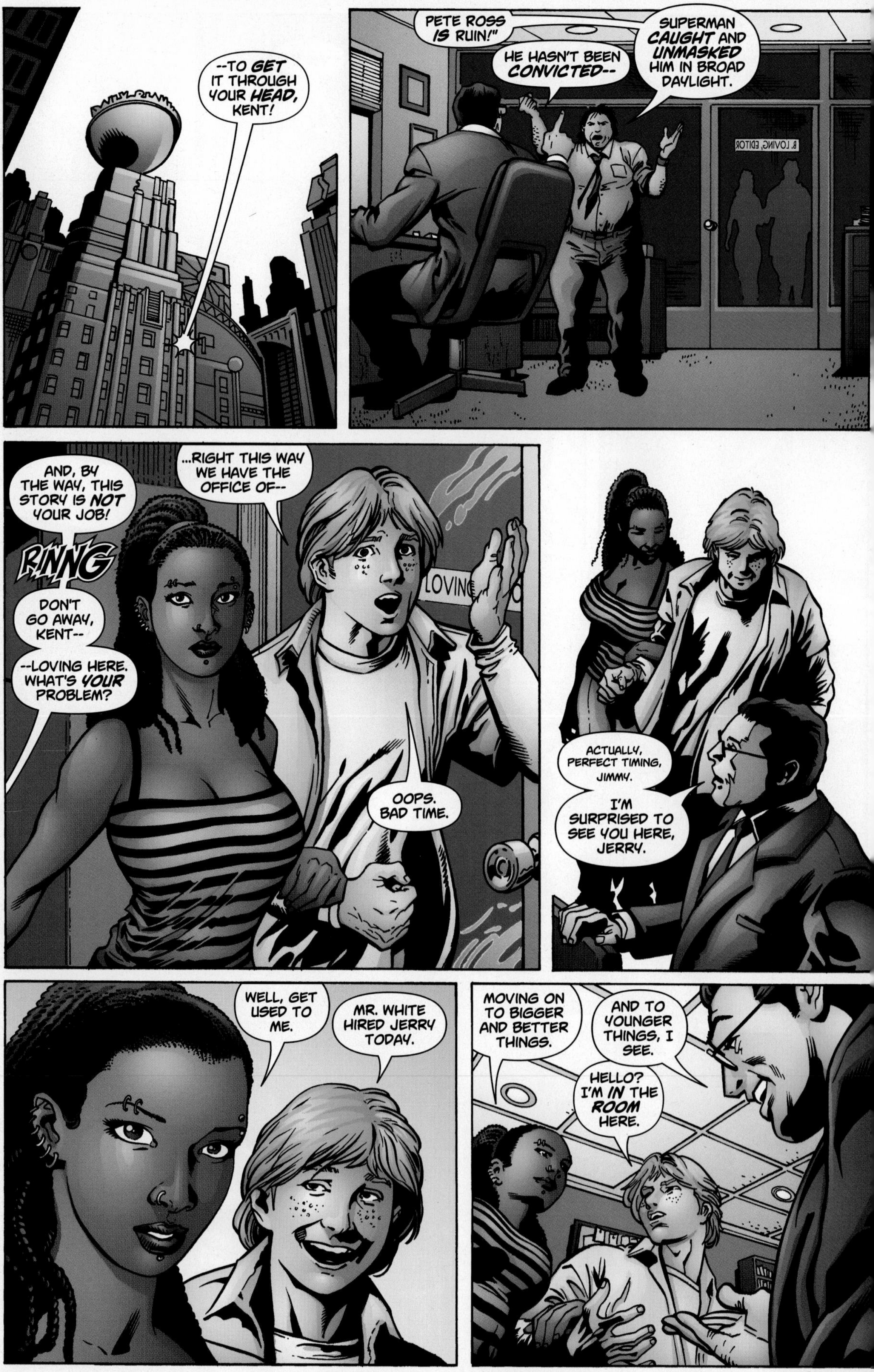
--TO GET IT THROUGH YOUR HEAD, KENT!
PETE ROSS IS RUIN!"
HE HASN'T BEEN CONVICTED--
SUPERMAN CAUGHT AND UNMASKED HIM IN BROAD DAYLIGHT.
AND, BY THE WAY, THIS STORY IS NOT YOUR JOB!
RINNG
DON'T GO AWAY, KENT--
--LOVING HERE. WHAT'S YOUR PROBLEM?
...RIGHT THIS WAY WE HAVE THE OFFICE OF--
LOVING
OOPS. BAD TIME.
ACTUALLY, PERFECT TIMING, JIMMY.
I'M SURPRISED TO SEE YOU HERE, JERRY.
WELL, GET USED TO ME.
MR. WHITE HIRED JERRY TODAY.
MOVING ON TO BIGGER AND BETTER THINGS.
AND TO YOUNGER THINGS, I SEE.
HELLO? I'M IN THE ROOM HERE.

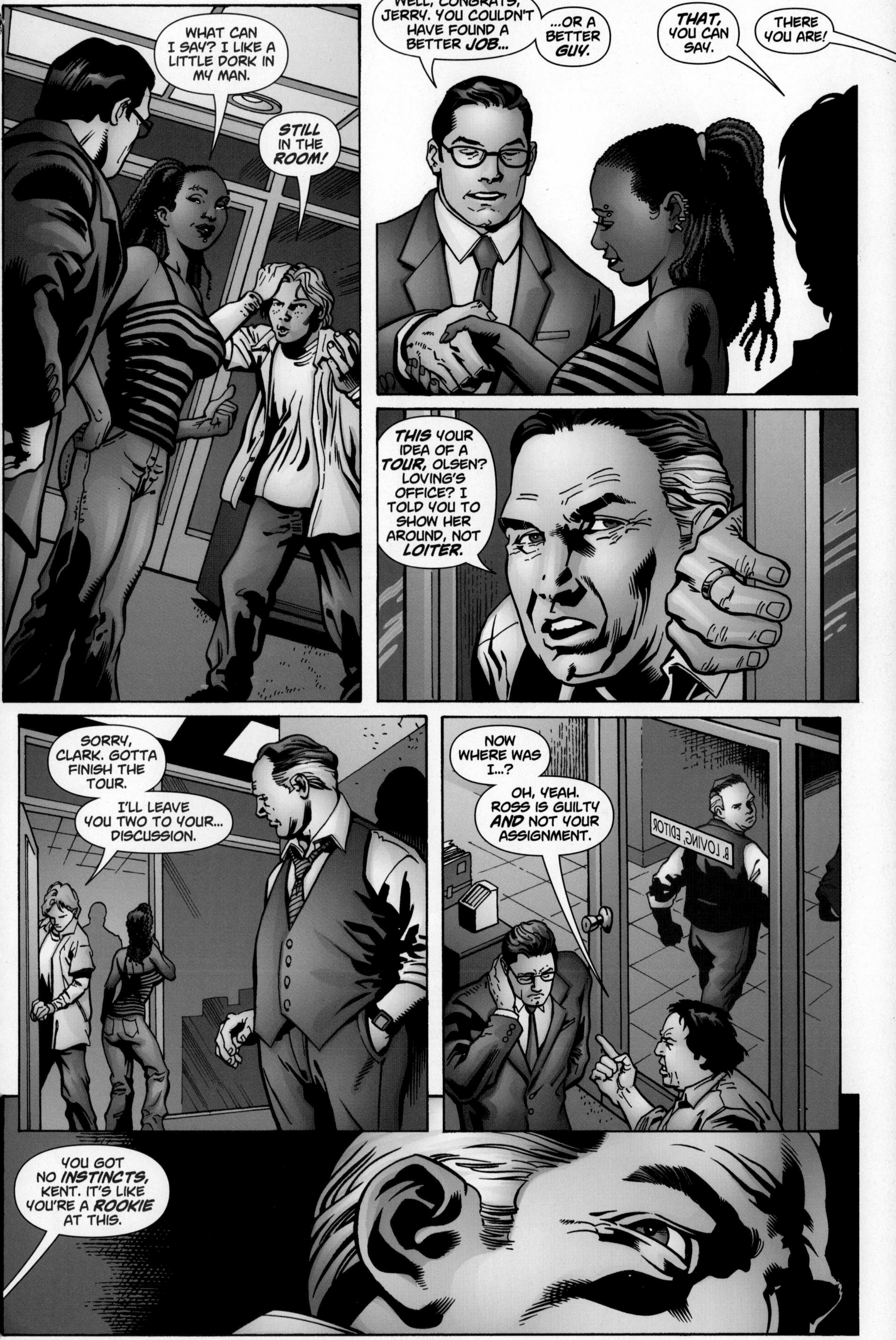
WHAT CAN I SAY? I LIKE A LITTLE DORK IN MY MAN.
STILL IN THE ROOM!
WELL, CONGRATS, JERRY. YOU COULDN'T HAVE FOUND A BETTER JOB...
...OR A BETTER GUY.
THAT, YOU CAN SAY.
THERE YOU ARE!
THIS YOUR IDEA OF A TOUR, OLSEN? LOVING'S OFFICE? I TOLD YOU TO SHOW HER AROUND, NOT LOITER.
SORRY, CLARK. GOTTA FINISH THE TOUR.
I'LL LEAVE YOU TWO TO YOUR... DISCUSSION.
NOW WHERE WAS I...?
OH, YEAH. ROSS IS GUILTY AND NOT YOUR ASSIGNMENT.
B. LOVING, EDITOR
YOU GOT NO INSTINCTS, KENT. IT'S LIKE YOU'RE A ROOKIE AT THIS.

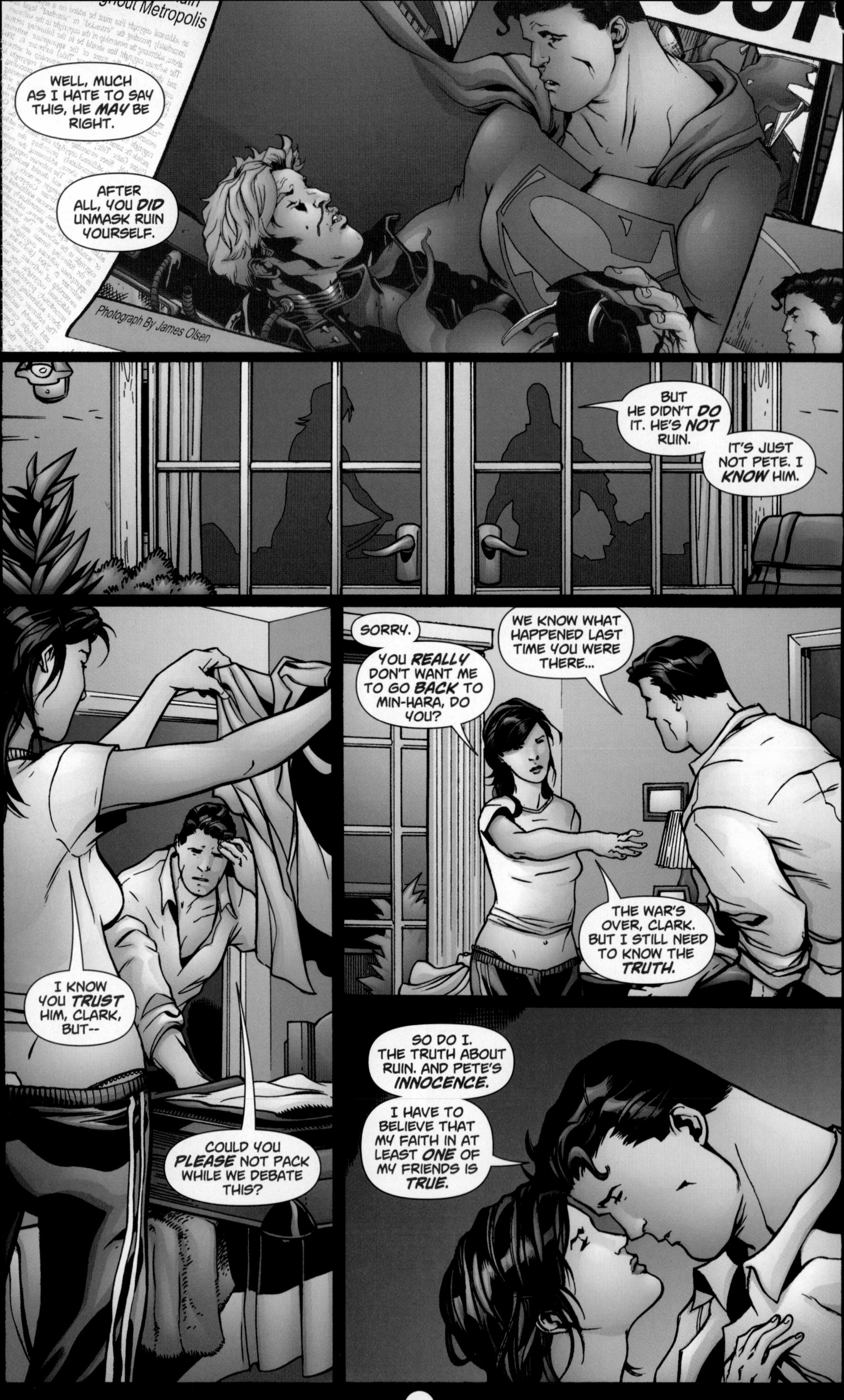

Metropolis
WELL, MUCH AS I HATE TO SAY THIS, HE MAY BE RIGHT.
AFTER ALL, YOU DID UNMASK RUIN YOURSELF.
Photograph By James Olsen
BUT HE DIDN'T DO IT. HE'S NOT RUIN.
IT'S JUST NOT PETE. I KNOW HIM.
I KNOW YOU TRUST HIM, CLARK, BUT--
COULD YOU PLEASE NOT PACK WHILE WE DEBATE THIS?
SORRY.
YOU REALLY DON'T WANT ME TO GO BACK TO MIN-HARA, DO YOU?
WE KNOW WHAT HAPPENED LAST TIME YOU WERE THERE...
THE WAR'S OVER, CLARK. BUT I STILL NEED TO KNOW THE TRUTH.
SO DO I. THE TRUTH ABOUT RUIN. AND PETE'S INNOCENCE.
I HAVE TO BELIEVE THAT MY FAITH IN AT LEAST ONE OF MY FRIENDS IS TRUE.

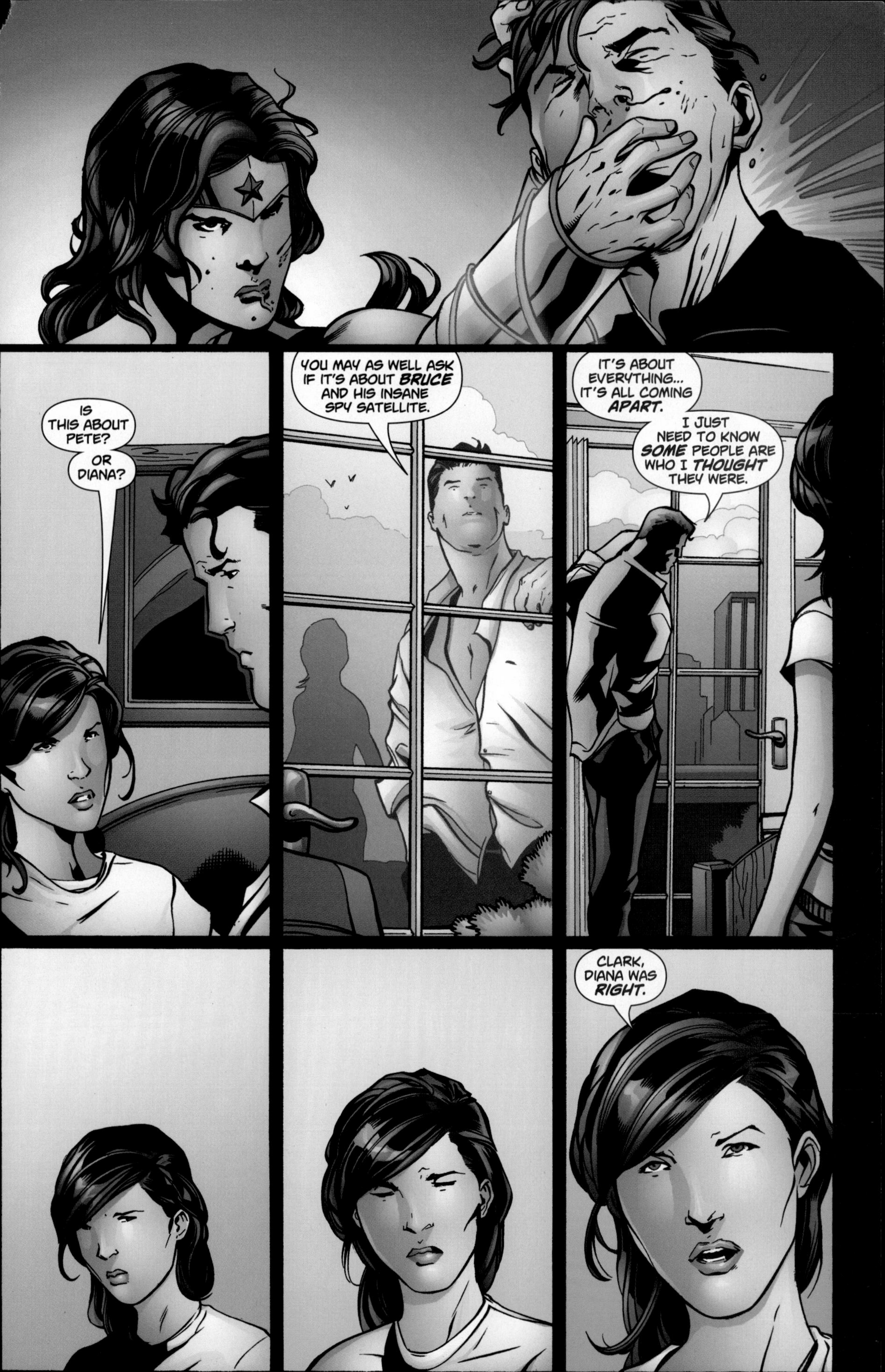
IS THIS ABOUT PETE? OR DIANA?
YOU MAY AS WELL ASK IF IT'S ABOUT BRUCE AND HIS INSANE SPY SATELLITE.
IT'S ABOUT EVERYTHING... IT'S ALL COMING APART.
I JUST NEED TO KNOW SOME PEOPLE ARE WHO I THOUGHT THEY WERE.
CLARK, DIANA WAS RIGHT.

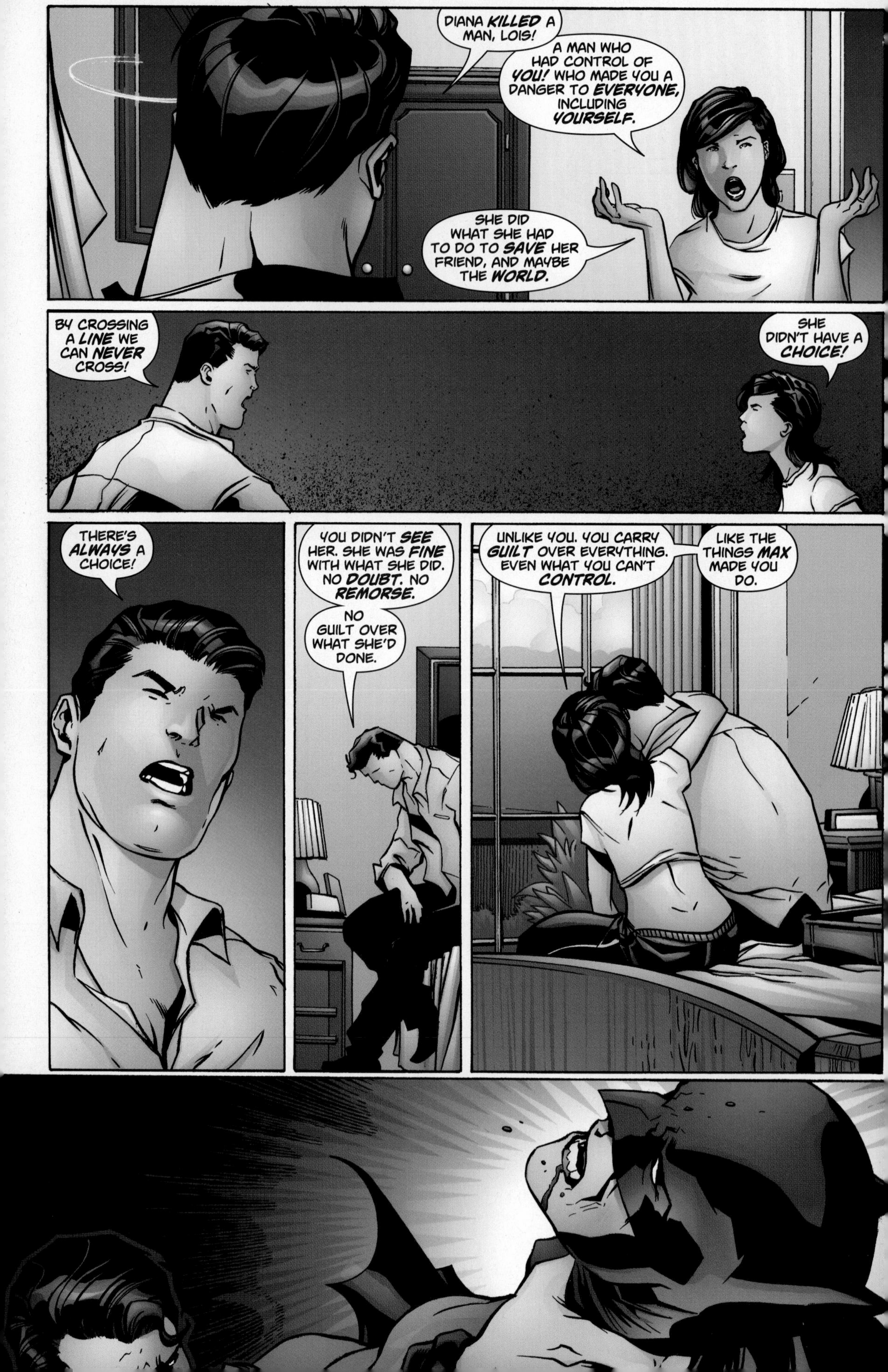
DIANA KILLED A MAN, LOIS!
A MAN WHO HAD CONTROL OF YOU! WHO MADE YOU A DANGER TO EVERYONE, INCLUDING YOURSELF.
SHE DID WHAT SHE HAD TO DO TO SAVE HER FRIEND, AND MAYBE THE WORLD.
BY CROSSING A LINE WE CAN NEVER CROSS!
SHE DIDN'T HAVE A CHOICE!
THERE'S ALWAYS A CHOICE!
YOU DIDN'T SEE HER. SHE WAS FINE WITH WHAT SHE DID. NO DOUBT. NO REMORSE.
NO GUILT OVER WHAT SHE'D DONE.
UNLIKE YOU. YOU CARRY GUILT OVER EVERYTHING. EVEN WHAT YOU CAN'T CONTROL.
LIKE THE THINGS MAX MADE YOU DO.

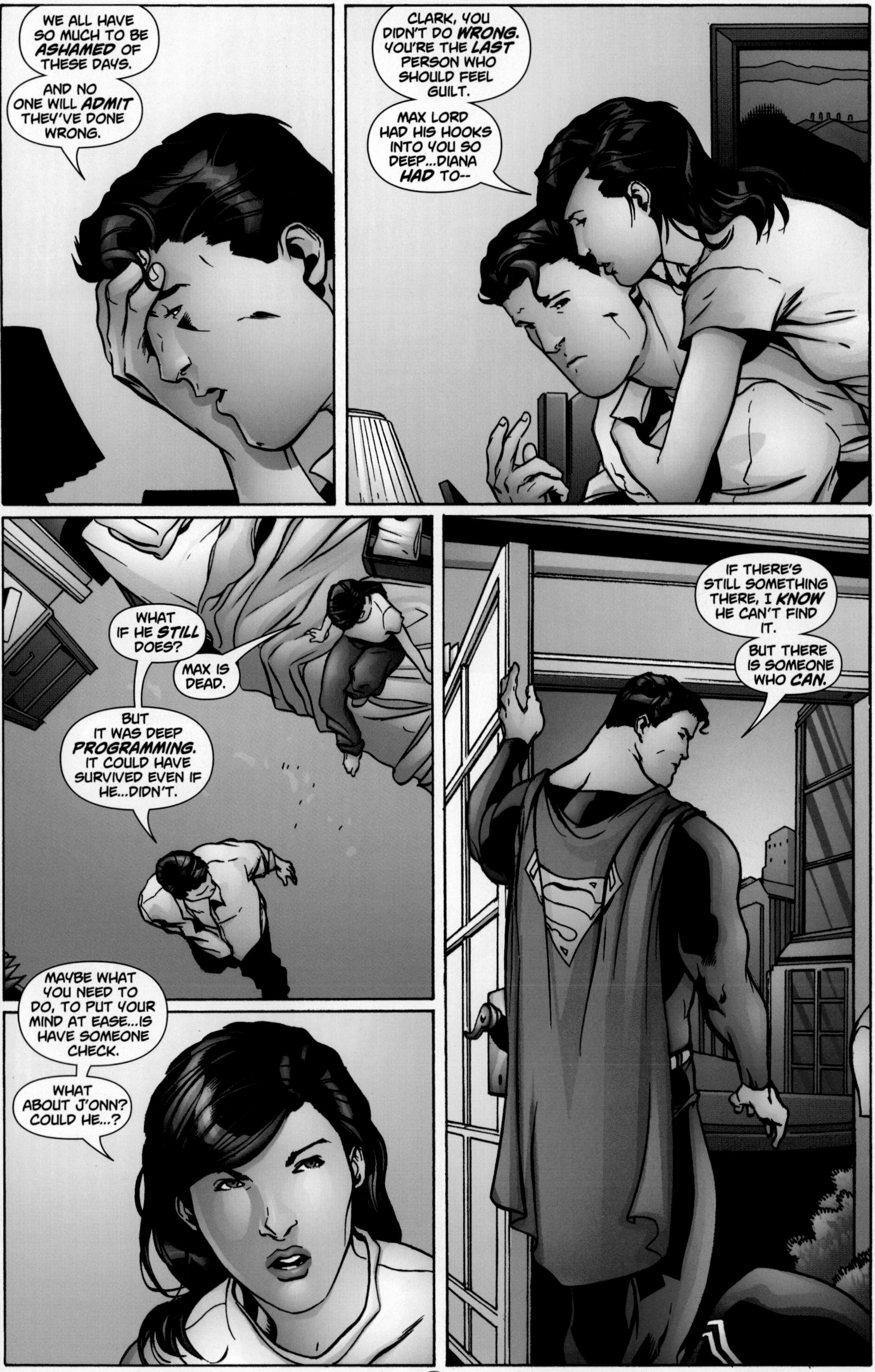
WE ALL HAVE SO MUCH TO BE ASHAMED OF THESE DAYS.
AND NO ONE WILL ADMIT THEY'VE DONE WRONG.
CLARK, YOU DIDN'T DO WRONG. YOU'RE THE LAST PERSON WHO SHOULD FEEL GUILT.
MAX LORD HAD HIS HOOKS INTO YOU SO DEEP...DIANA HAD TO--
WHAT IF HE STILL DOES?
MAX IS DEAD.
BUT IT WAS DEEP PROGRAMMING. IT COULD HAVE SURVIVED EVEN IF HE...DIDN'T.
MAYBE WHAT YOU NEED TO DO, TO PUT YOUR MIND AT EASE...IS HAVE SOMEONE CHECK.
WHAT ABOUT J'ONN? COULD HE...?
IF THERE'S STILL SOMETHING THERE, I KNOW HE CAN'T FIND IT.
BUT THERE IS SOMEONE WHO CAN.

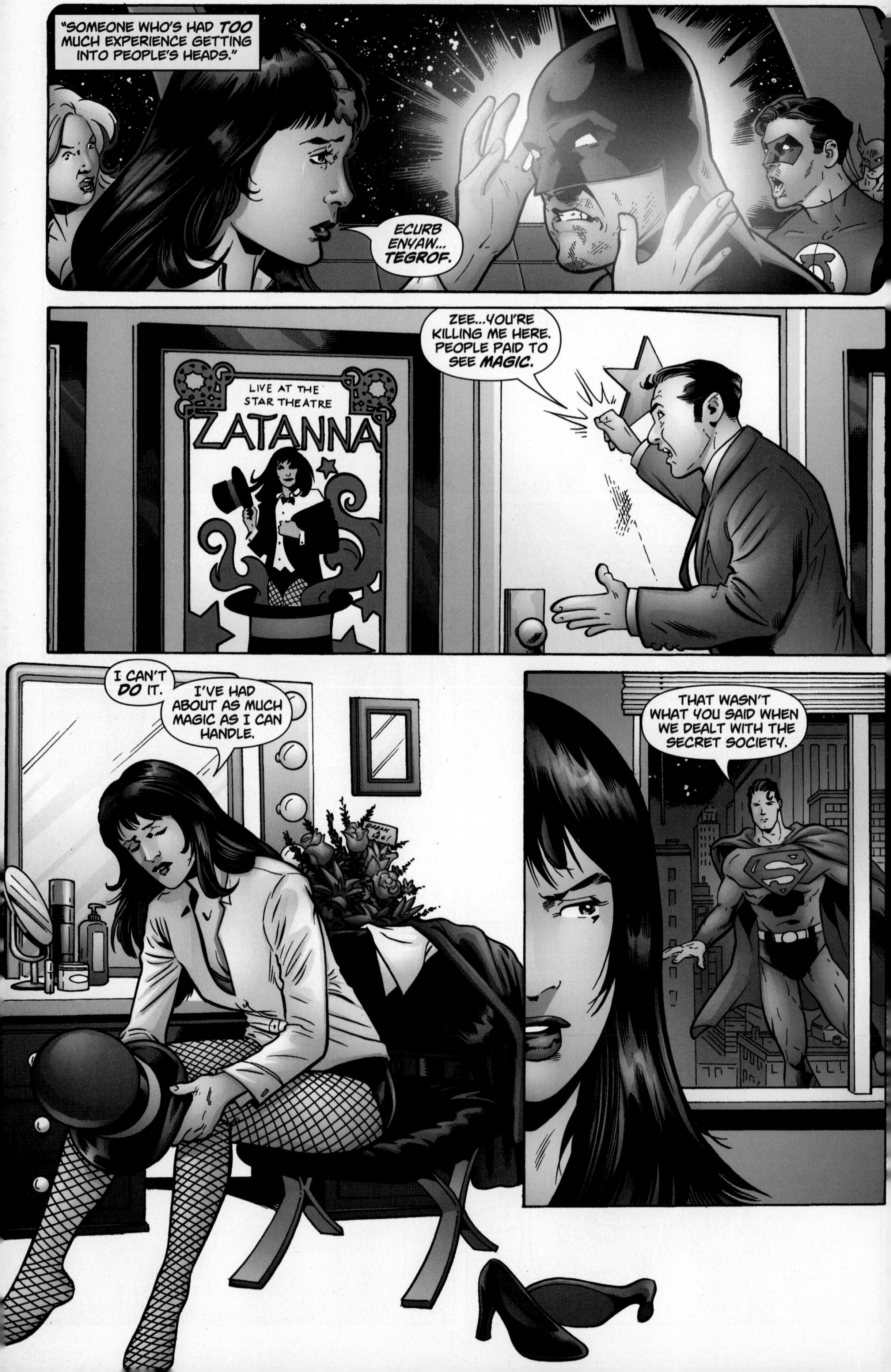
"SOMEONE WHO'S HAD TOO MUCH EXPERIENCE GETTING INTO PEOPLE'S HEADS."
ECURB ENYAW... TEGROF.
ZEE...YOU'RE KILLING ME HERE. PEOPLE PAID TO SEE MAGIC.
LIVE AT THE STAR THEATRE
ZATANNA
I CAN'T DO IT.
I'VE HAD ABOUT AS MUCH MAGIC AS I CAN HANDLE.
THAT WASN'T WHAT YOU SAID WHEN WE DEALT WITH THE SECRET SOCIETY.

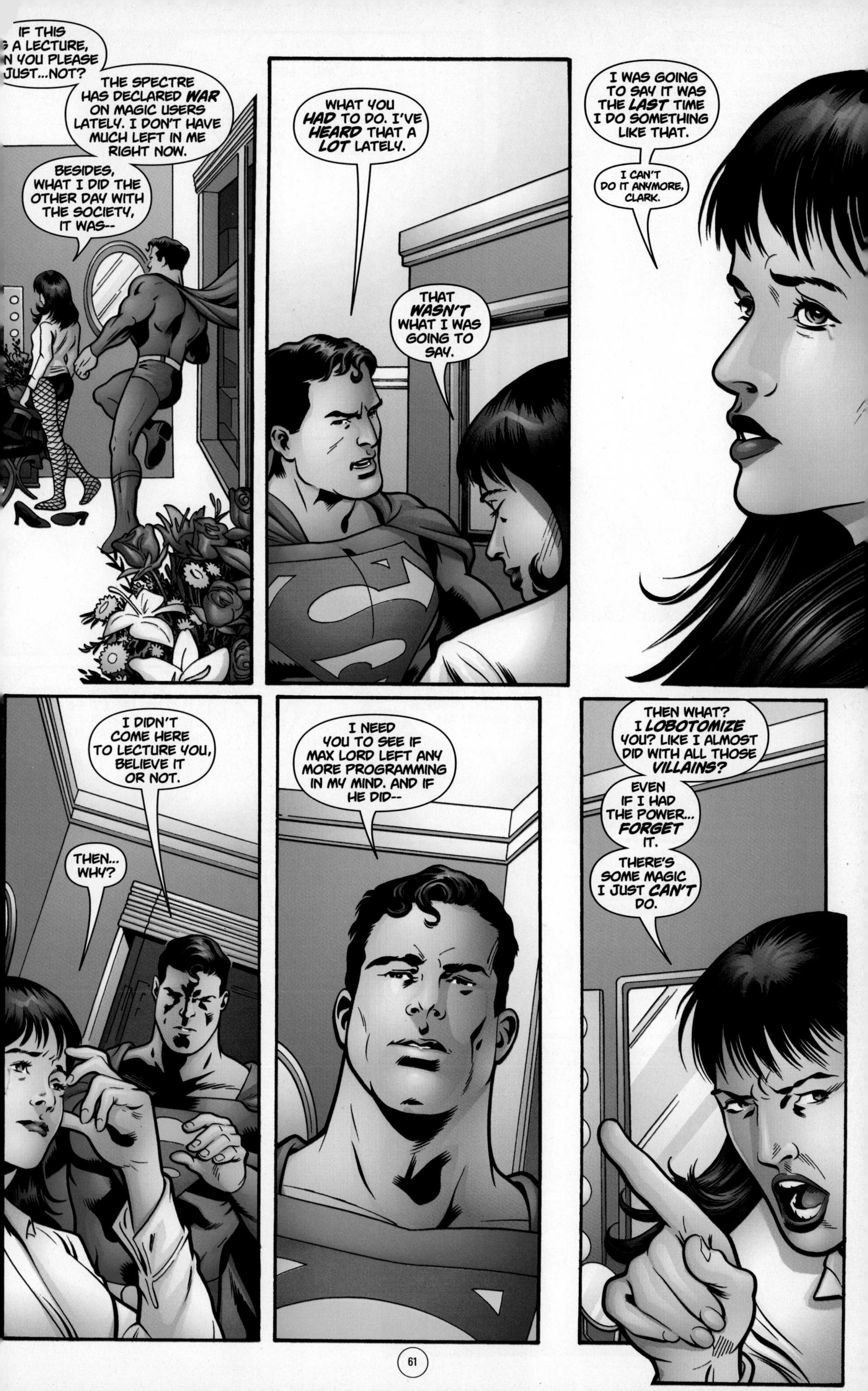
IF THIS
G A LECTURE,
N YOU PLEASE
JUST...NOT?
THE SPECTRE HAS DECLARED WAR ON MAGIC USERS LATELY. I DON'T HAVE MUCH LEFT IN ME RIGHT NOW.
BESIDES, WHAT I DID THE OTHER DAY WITH THE SOCIETY, IT WAS--
WHAT YOU HAD TO DO. I'VE HEARD THAT A LOT LATELY.
THAT WASN'T WHAT I WAS GOING TO SAY.
I WAS GOING TO SAY IT WAS THE LAST TIME I DO SOMETHING LIKE THAT.
I CAN'T DO IT ANYMORE, CLARK.
I DIDN'T COME HERE TO LECTURE YOU, BELIEVE IT OR NOT.
THEN... WHY?
I NEED YOU TO SEE IF MAX LORD LEFT ANY MORE PROGRAMMING IN MY MIND. AND IF HE DID--
THEN WHAT? I LOBOTOMIZE YOU? LIKE I ALMOST DID WITH ALL THOSE VILLAINS?
EVEN IF I HAD THE POWER... FORGET IT.
THERE'S SOME MAGIC I JUST CAN'T DO.

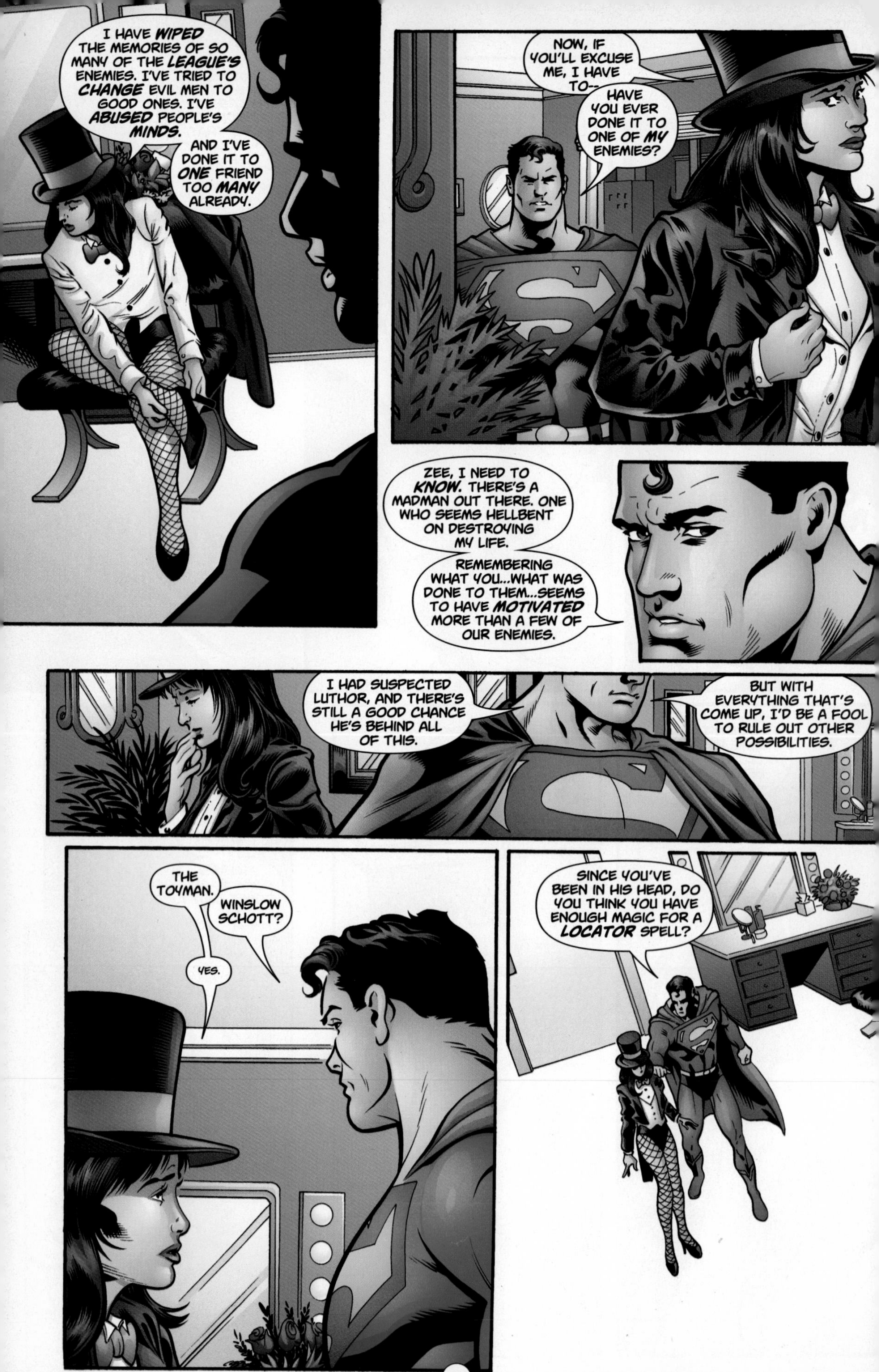
I HAVE WIPED THE MEMORIES OF SO MANY OF THE LEAGUE'S ENEMIES. I'VE TRIED TO CHANGE EVIL MEN TO GOOD ONES. I'VE ABUSED PEOPLE'S MINDS.
AND I'VE DONE IT TO ONE FRIEND TOO MANY ALREADY.
NOW, IF YOU'LL EXCUSE ME, I HAVE TO--
HAVE YOU EVER DONE IT TO ONE OF MY ENEMIES?
ZEE, I NEED TO KNOW. THERE'S A MADMAN OUT THERE. ONE WHO SEEMS HELLBENT ON DESTROYING MY LIFE.
REMEMBERING WHAT YOU...WHAT WAS DONE TO THEM...SEEMS TO HAVE MOTIVATED MORE THAN A FEW OF OUR ENEMIES.
I HAD SUSPECTED LUTHOR, AND THERE'S STILL A GOOD CHANCE HE'S BEHIND ALL OF THIS.
BUT WITH EVERYTHING THAT'S COME UP, I'D BE A FOOL TO RULE OUT OTHER POSSIBILITIES.
THE TOYMAN.
WINSLOW SCHOTT?
YES.
SINCE YOU'VE BEEN IN HIS HEAD, DO YOU THINK YOU HAVE ENOUGH MAGIC FOR A LOCATOR SPELL?

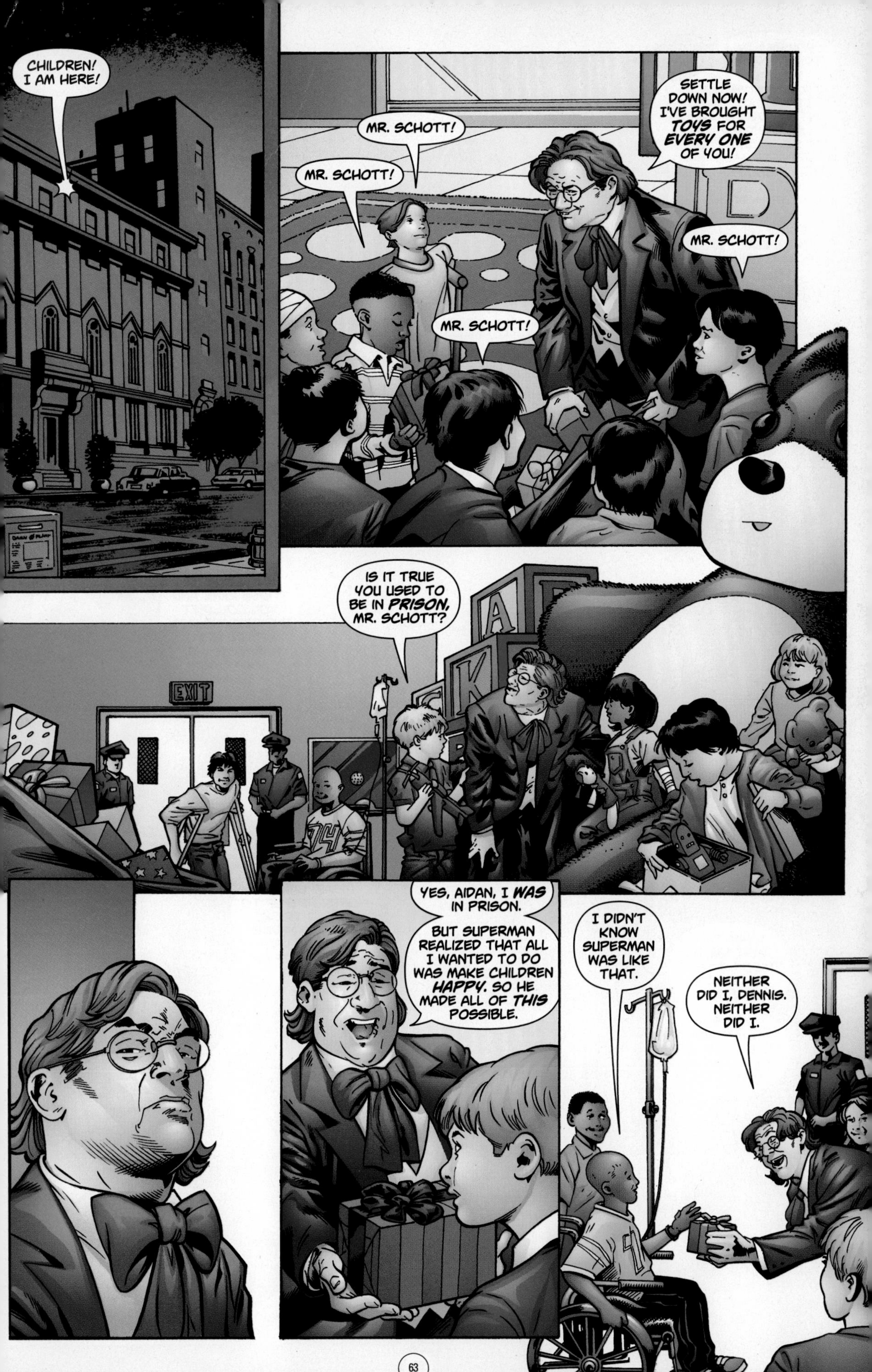
CHILDREN! I AM HERE!
MR. SCHOTT!
MR. SCHOTT!
SETTLE DOWN NOW! I'VE BROUGHT TOYS FOR EVERY ONE OF YOU!
MR. SCHOTT!
MR. SCHOTT!
IS IT TRUE YOU USED TO BE IN PRISON, MR. SCHOTT?
EXIT
YES, AIDAN, I WAS IN PRISON.
BUT SUPERMAN REALIZED THAT ALL I WANTED TO DO WAS MAKE CHILDREN HAPPY. SO HE MADE ALL OF THIS POSSIBLE.
I DIDN'T KNOW SUPERMAN WAS LIKE THAT.
NEITHER DID I, DENNIS. NEITHER DID I.

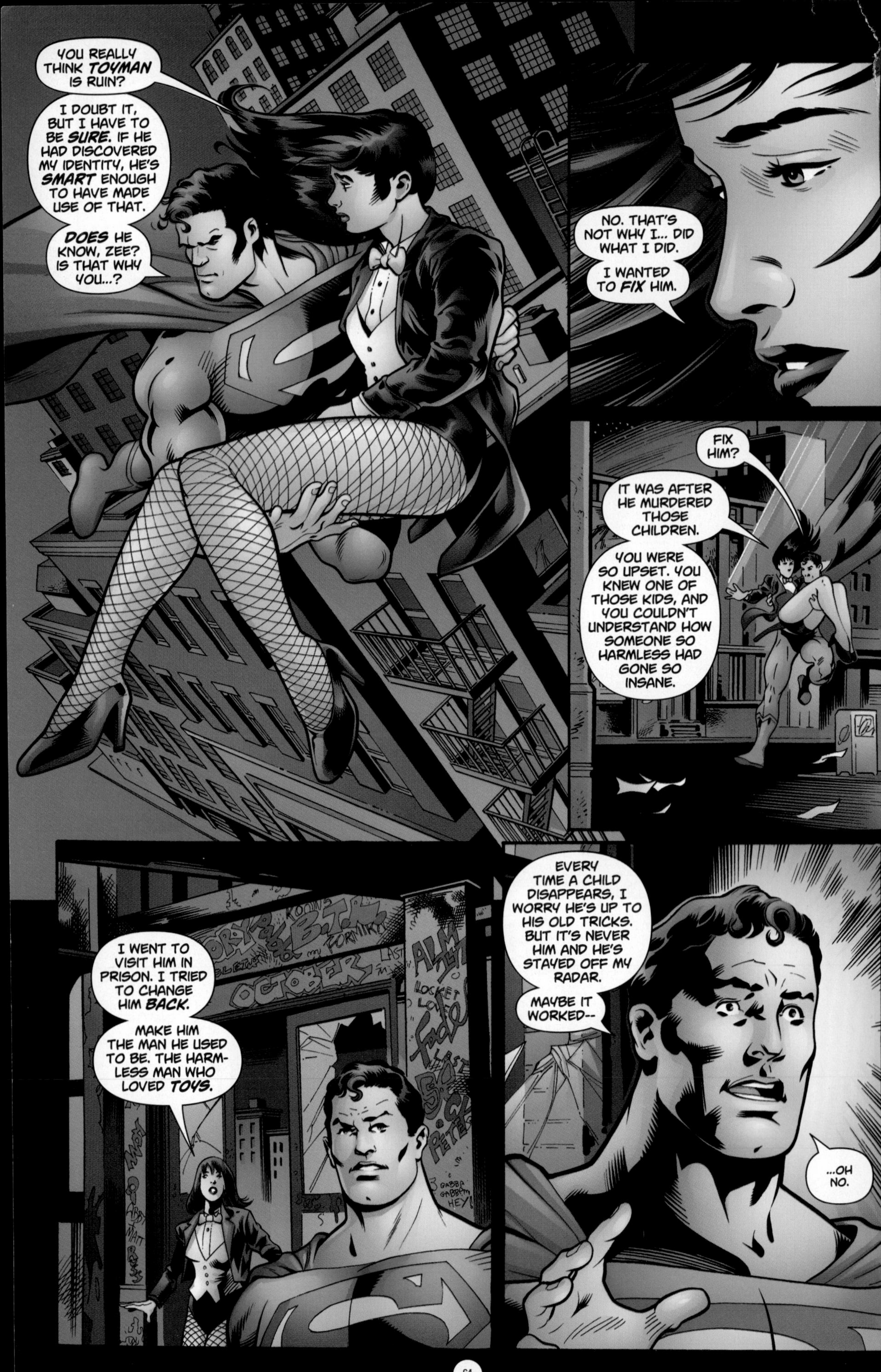
YOU REALLY THINK TOYMAN IS RUIN?
I DOUBT IT, BUT I HAVE TO BE SURE. IF HE HAD DISCOVERED MY IDENTITY, HE'S SMART ENOUGH TO HAVE MADE USE OF THAT.
DOES HE KNOW, ZEE? IS THAT WHY YOU...?
NO. THAT'S NOT WHY I... DID WHAT I DID.
I WANTED TO FIX HIM.
FIX HIM?
IT WAS AFTER HE MURDERED THOSE CHILDREN.
YOU WERE SO UPSET. YOU KNEW ONE OF THOSE KIDS, AND YOU COULDN'T UNDERSTAND HOW SOMEONE SO HARMLESS HAD GONE SO INSANE.
I WENT TO VISIT HIM IN PRISON. I TRIED TO CHANGE HIM BACK.
MAKE HIM THE MAN HE USED TO BE. THE HARM-LESS MAN WHO LOVED TOYS.
EVERY TIME A CHILD DISAPPEARS, I WORRY HE'S UP TO HIS OLD TRICKS. BUT IT'S NEVER HIM AND HE'S STAYED OFF MY RADAR.
MAYBE IT WORKED--
...OH NO.

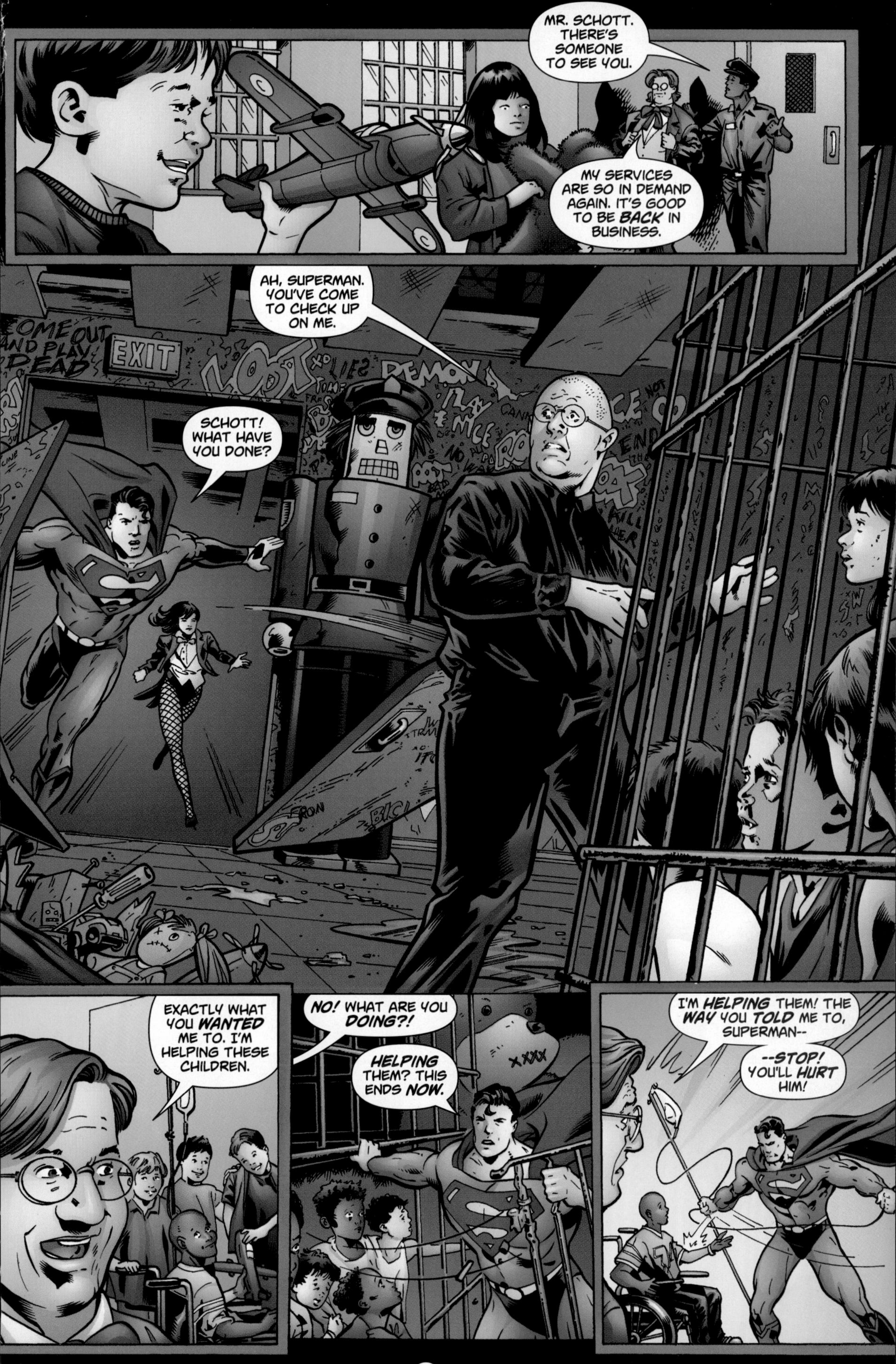

MR. SCHOTT. THERE'S SOMEONE TO SEE YOU.
MY SERVICES ARE SO IN DEMAND AGAIN. IT'S GOOD TO BE BACK IN BUSINESS.
AH, SUPERMAN. YOU'VE COME TO CHECK UP ON ME.
SCHOTT! WHAT HAVE YOU DONE?
COME OUT AND PLAY DEAD
EXIT
EXACTLY WHAT YOU WANTED ME TO. I'M HELPING THESE CHILDREN.
NO! WHAT ARE YOU DOING?!
HELPING THEM? THIS ENDS NOW.
I'M HELPING THEM! THE WAY YOU TOLD ME TO, SUPERMAN--
--STOP! YOU'LL HURT HIM!

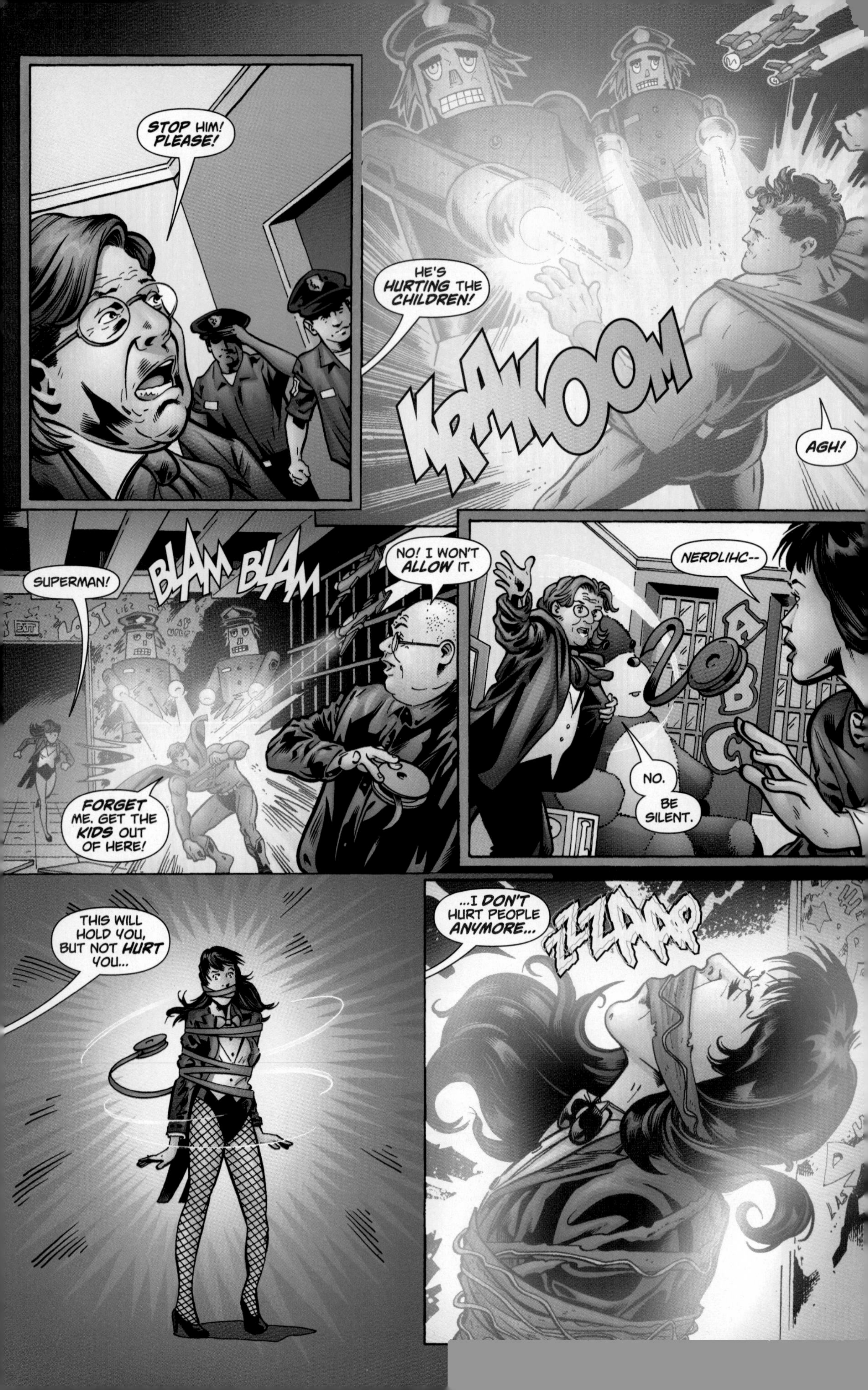
STOP HIM! PLEASE!
HE'S HURTING THE CHILDREN!
KRAKOOM
AGH!
SUPERMAN!
BLAM BLAM
NO! I WON'T ALLOW IT.
FORGET ME. GET THE KIDS OUT OF HERE!
NERDLIHC--
NO.
BE SILENT.
THIS WILL HOLD YOU, BUT NOT HURT YOU...
...I DON'T HURT PEOPLE ANYMORE...
ZZZAAP

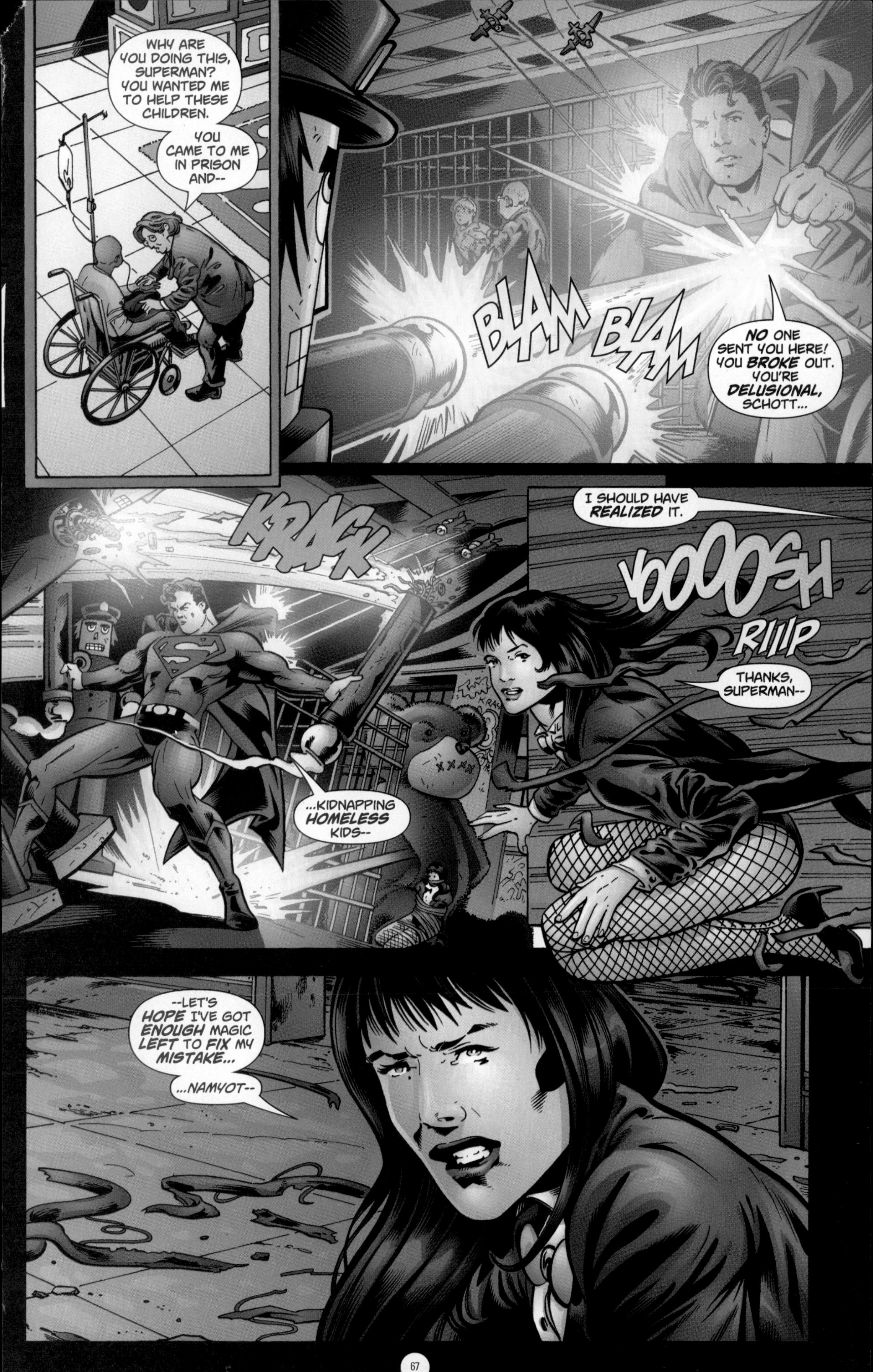
WHY ARE YOU DOING THIS, SUPERMAN? YOU WANTED ME TO HELP THESE CHILDREN.
YOU CAME TO ME IN PRISON AND--
BLAM BLAM
NO ONE SENT YOU HERE! YOU BROKE OUT. YOU'RE DELUSIONAL, SCHOTT...
KRACK
...KIDNAPPING HOMELESS KIDS--
I SHOULD HAVE REALIZED IT.
VOOOOSH
RIIIP
THANKS, SUPERMAN--
--LET'S HOPE I'VE GOT ENOUGH MAGIC LEFT TO FIX MY MISTAKE...
...NAMYOT--

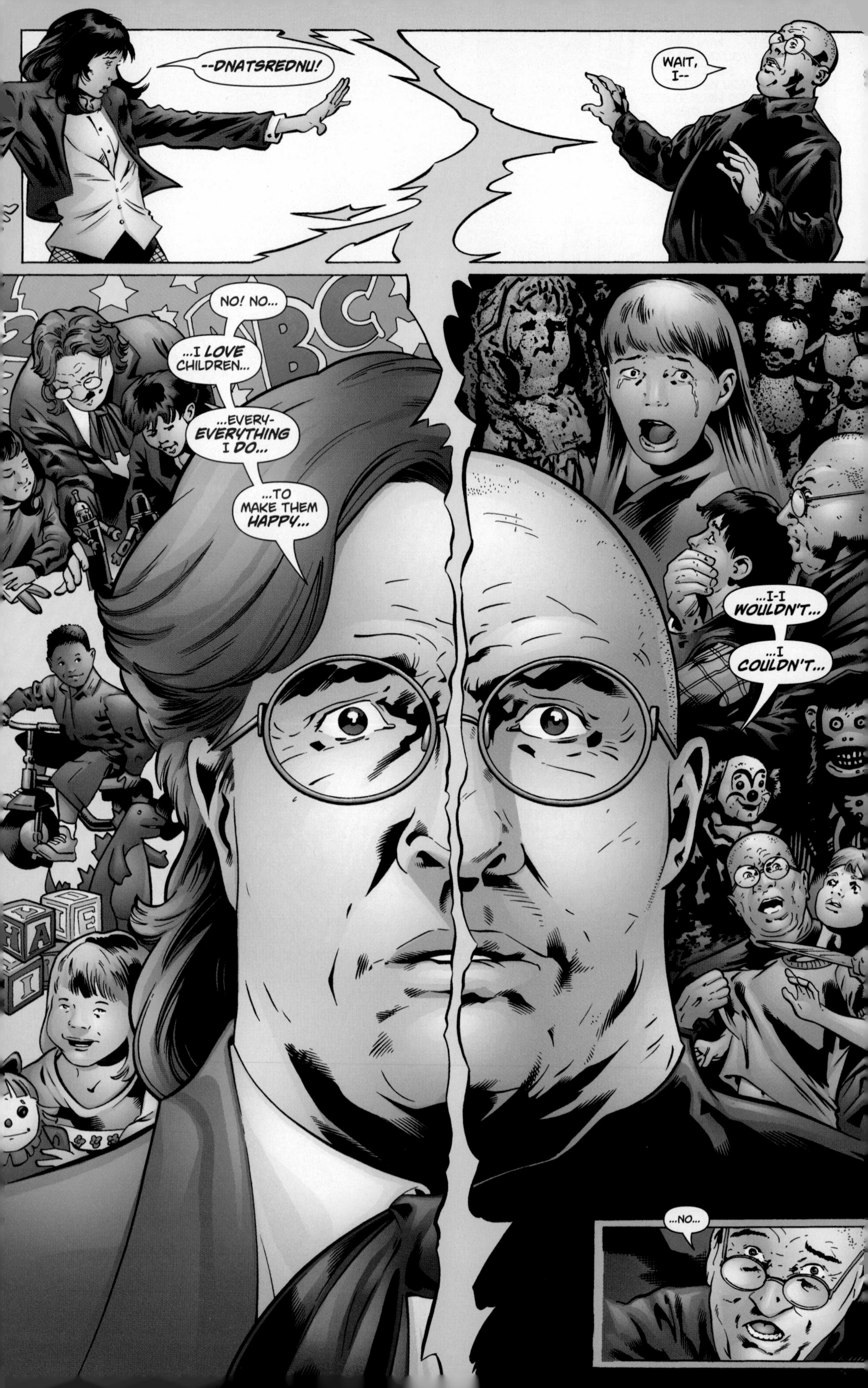
--DNATSREDNU!
WAIT, I--
NO! NO...
...I LOVE CHILDREN...
...EVERY- EVERYTHING I DO...
...TO MAKE THEM HAPPY...
...I-I WOULDN'T...
...I COULDN'T...
...NO...

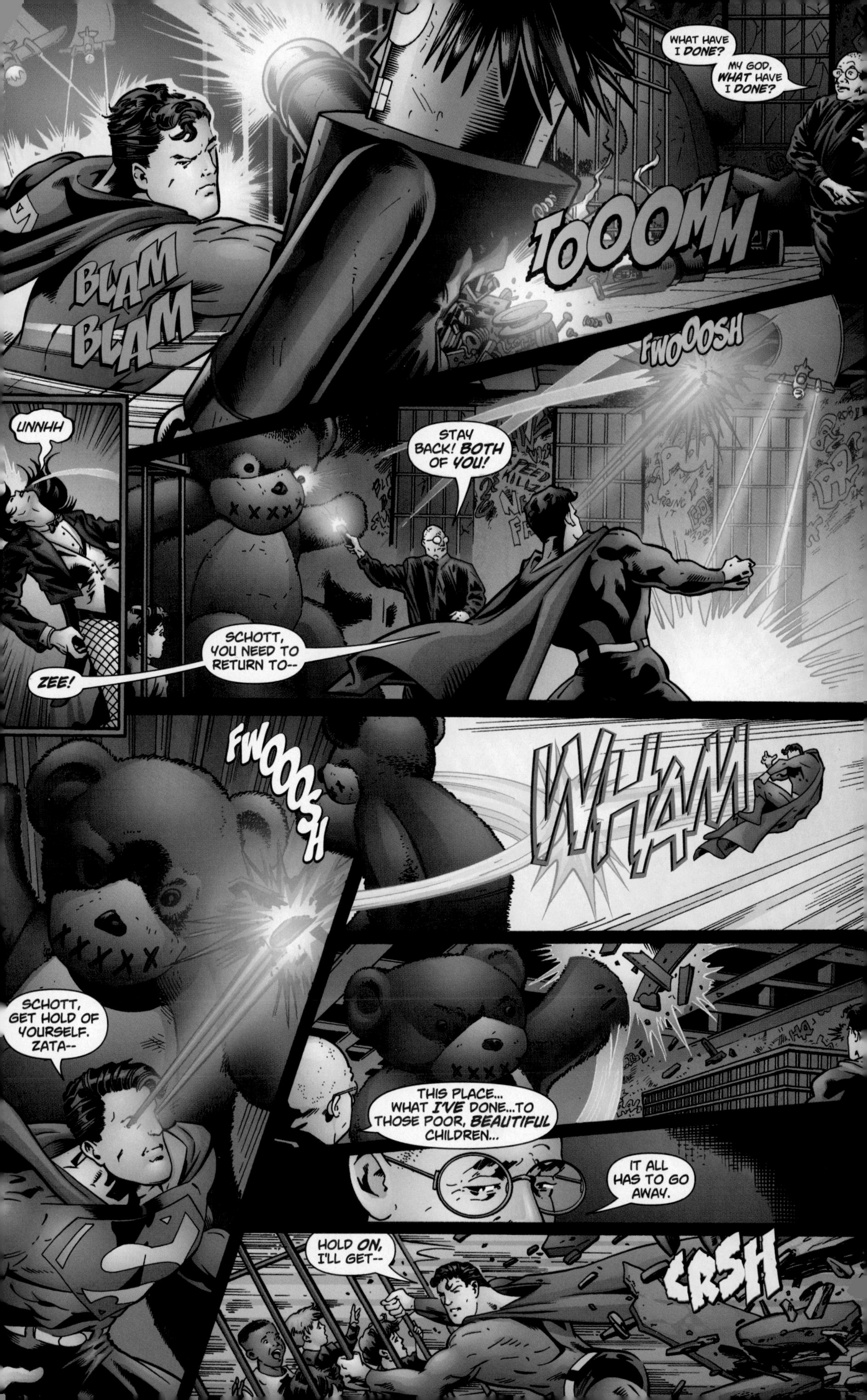
WHAT HAVE I DONE?
MY GOD, WHAT HAVE I DONE?
BLAM BLAM
TOOOMM
FWOOOSH
UNNHH
STAY BACK! BOTH OF YOU!
SCHOTT, YOU NEED TO RETURN TO--
ZEE!
FWOOOSH
WHAM
SCHOTT, GET HOLD OF YOURSELF. ZATA--
THIS PLACE... WHAT I'VE DONE...TO THOSE POOR, BEAUTIFUL CHILDREN...
IT ALL HAS TO GO AWAY.
HOLD ON, I'LL GET--
CRSH

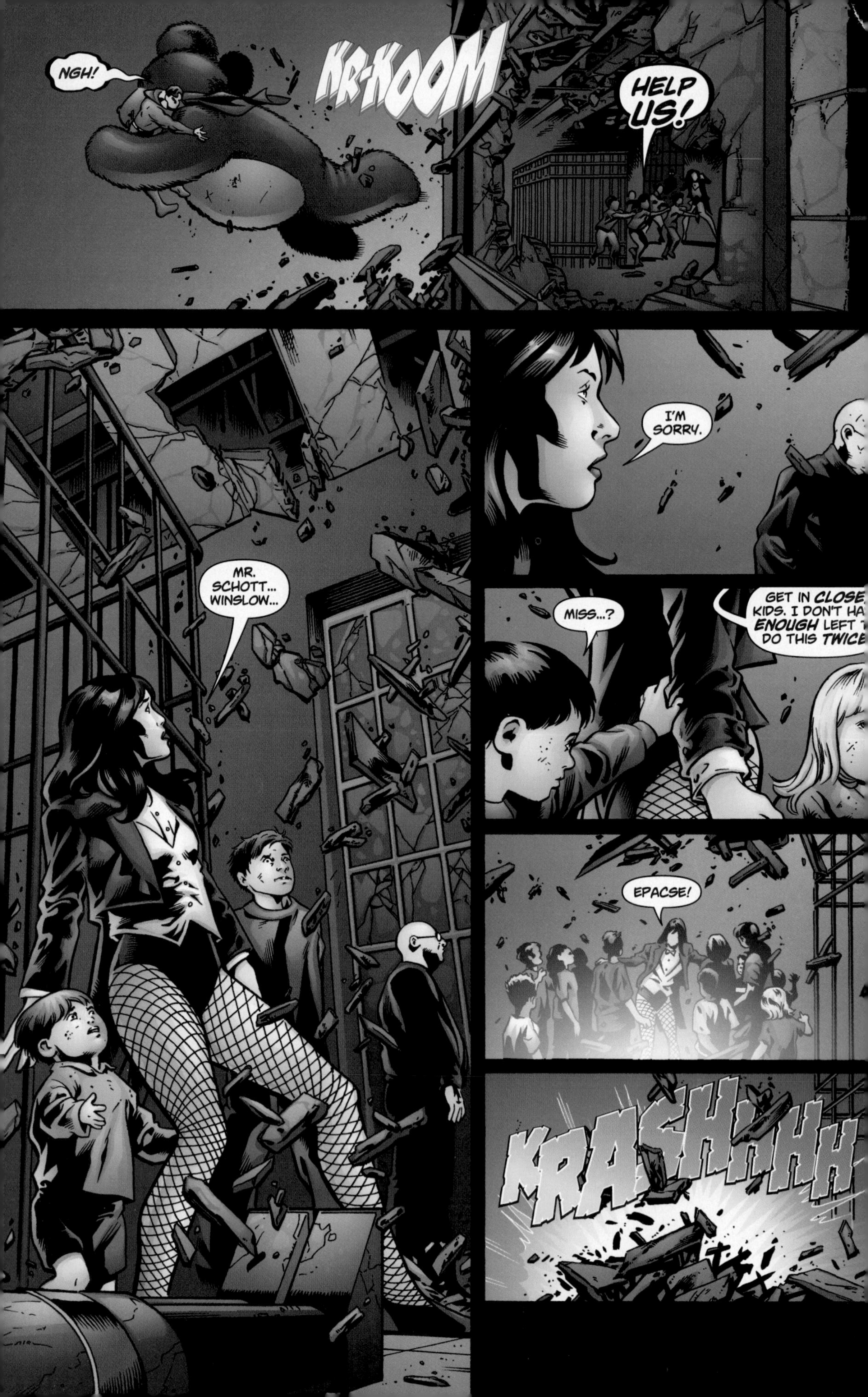
NGH!
KR-KOOM
HELP US!
MR. SCHOTT... WINSLOW...
I'M SORRY.
MISS...?
GET IN CLOSE, KIDS. I DON'T HA ENOUGH LEFT DO THIS TWICE
EPACSE!
KRASHHHH

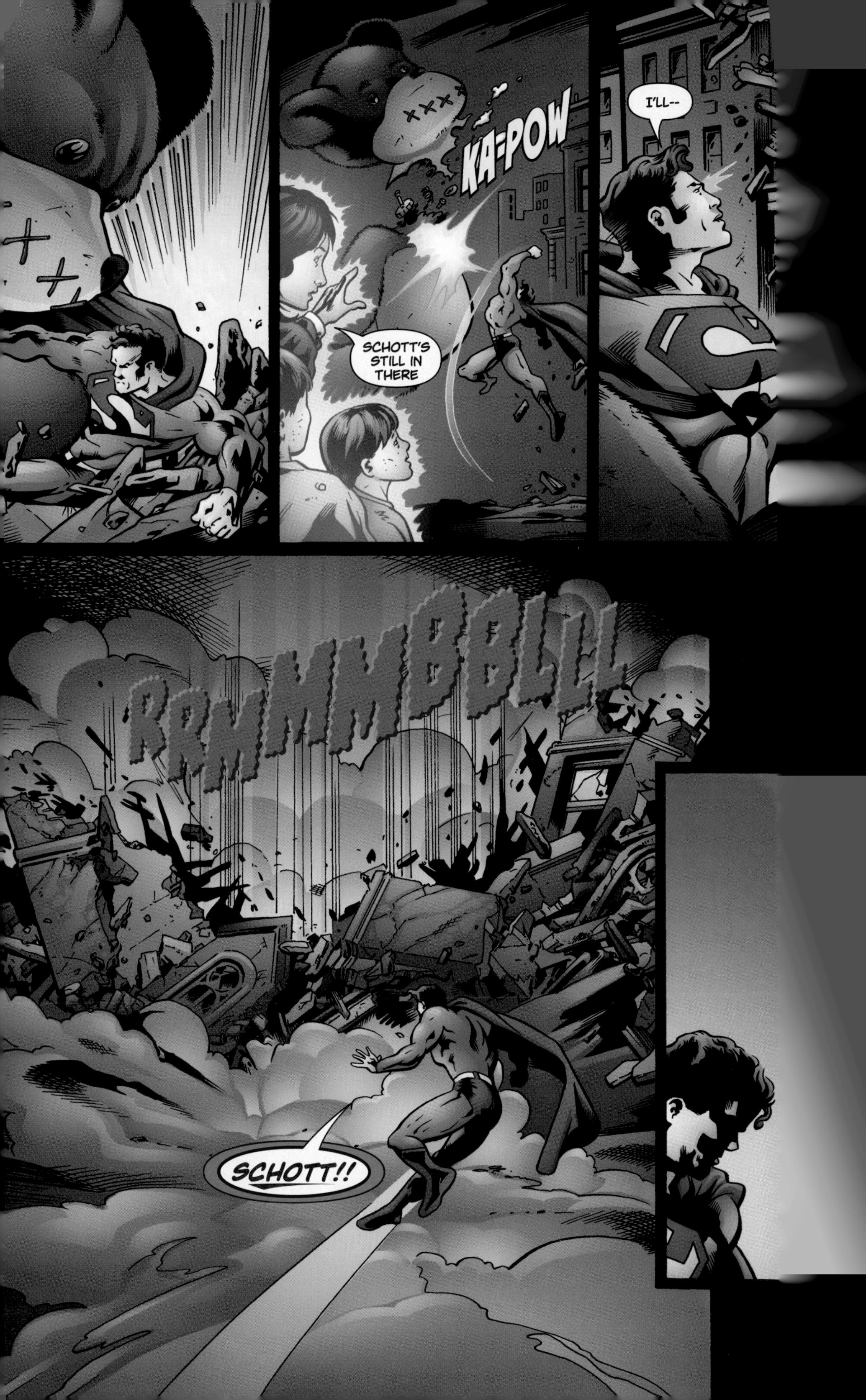
KA-POW
SCHOTT'S STILL IN THERE
I'LL--
RRMMMBBLLL
SCHOTT!!

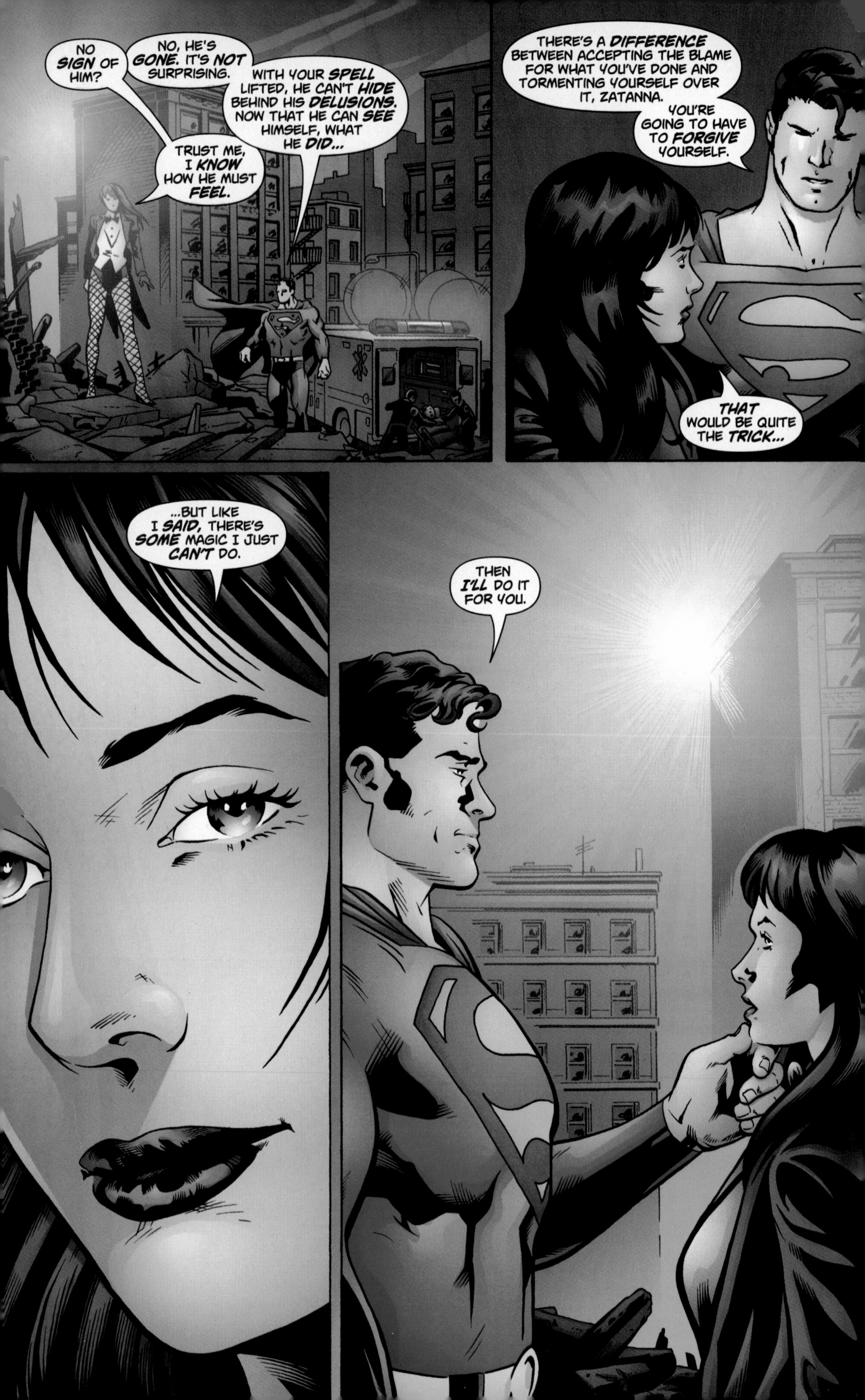
NO SIGN OF HIM?
NO, HE'S GONE. IT'S NOT SURPRISING.
TRUST ME, I KNOW HOW HE MUST FEEL.
WITH YOUR SPELL LIFTED, HE CAN'T HIDE BEHIND HIS DELUSIONS. NOW THAT HE CAN SEE HIMSELF, WHAT HE DID...
THERE'S A DIFFERENCE BETWEEN ACCEPTING THE BLAME FOR WHAT YOU'VE DONE AND TORMENTING YOURSELF OVER IT, ZATANNA.
YOU'RE GOING TO HAVE TO FORGIVE YOURSELF.
THAT WOULD BE QUITE THE TRICK...
...BUT LIKE I SAID, THERE'S SOME MAGIC I JUST CAN'T DO.
THEN I'LL DO IT FOR YOU.

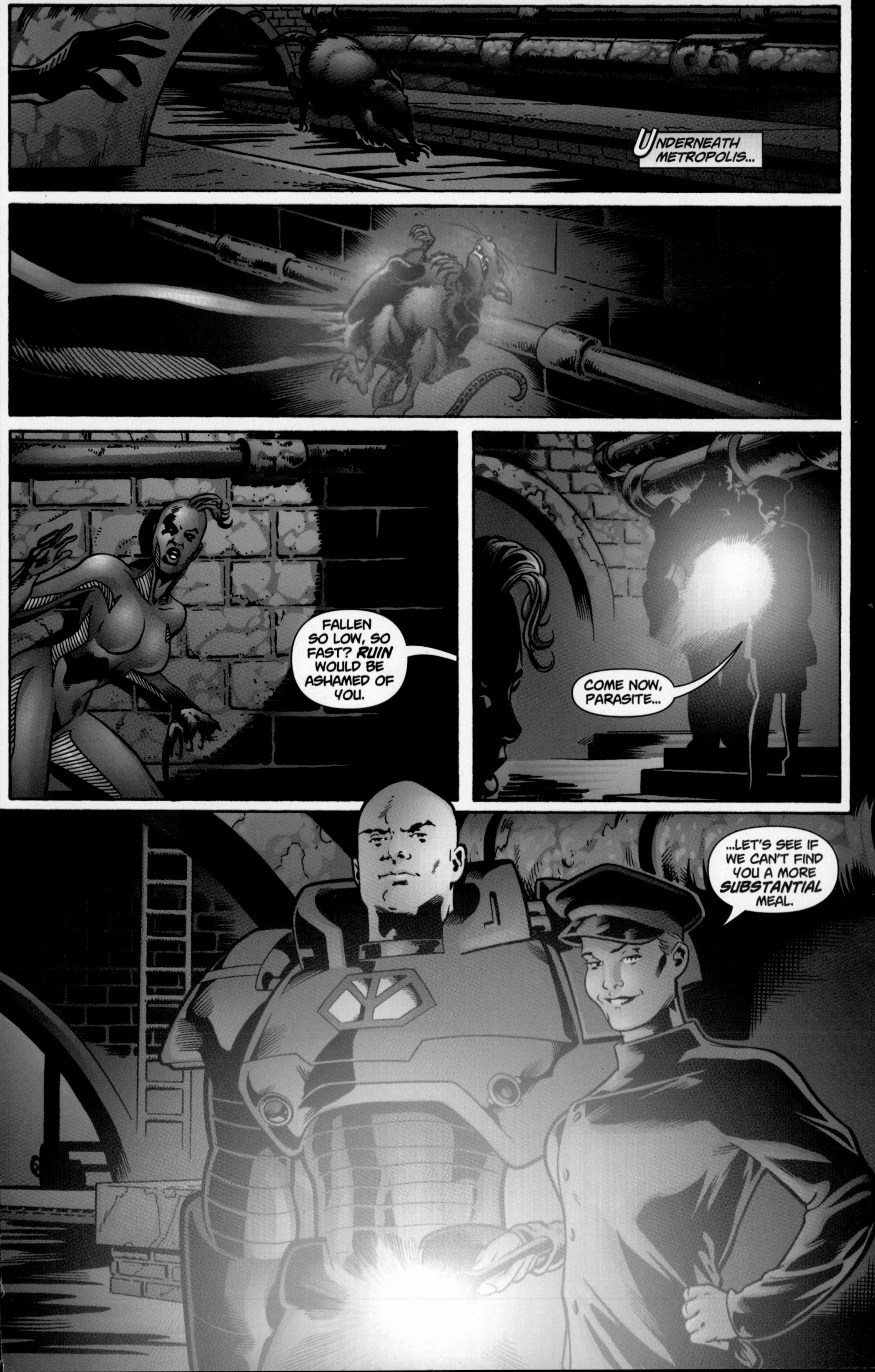
UNDERNEATH METROPOLIS...
FALLEN SO LOW, SO FAST? RUIN WOULD BE ASHAMED OF YOU.
COME NOW, PARASITE...
...LET'S SEE IF WE CAN'T FIND YOU A MORE SUBSTANTIAL MEAL.

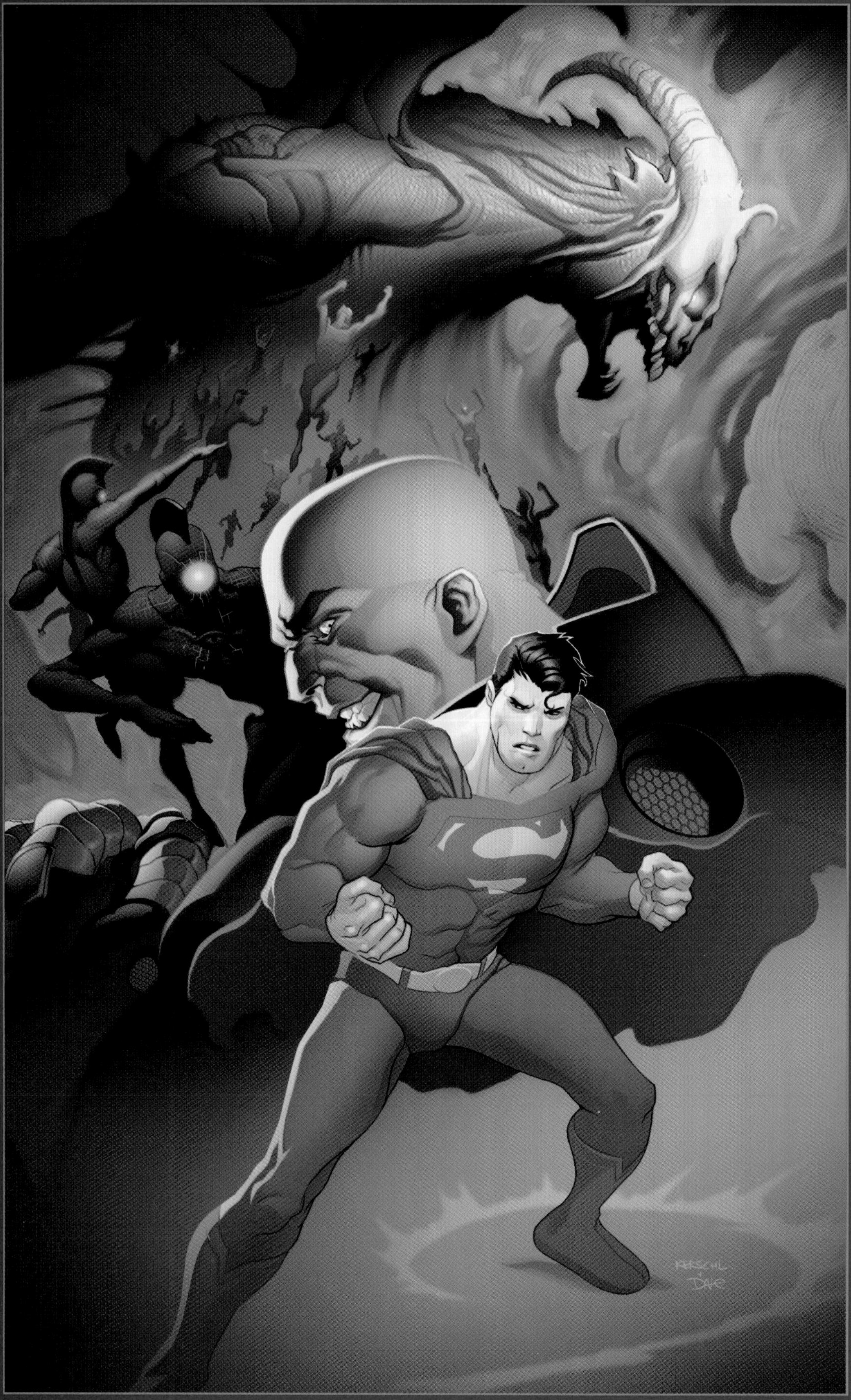

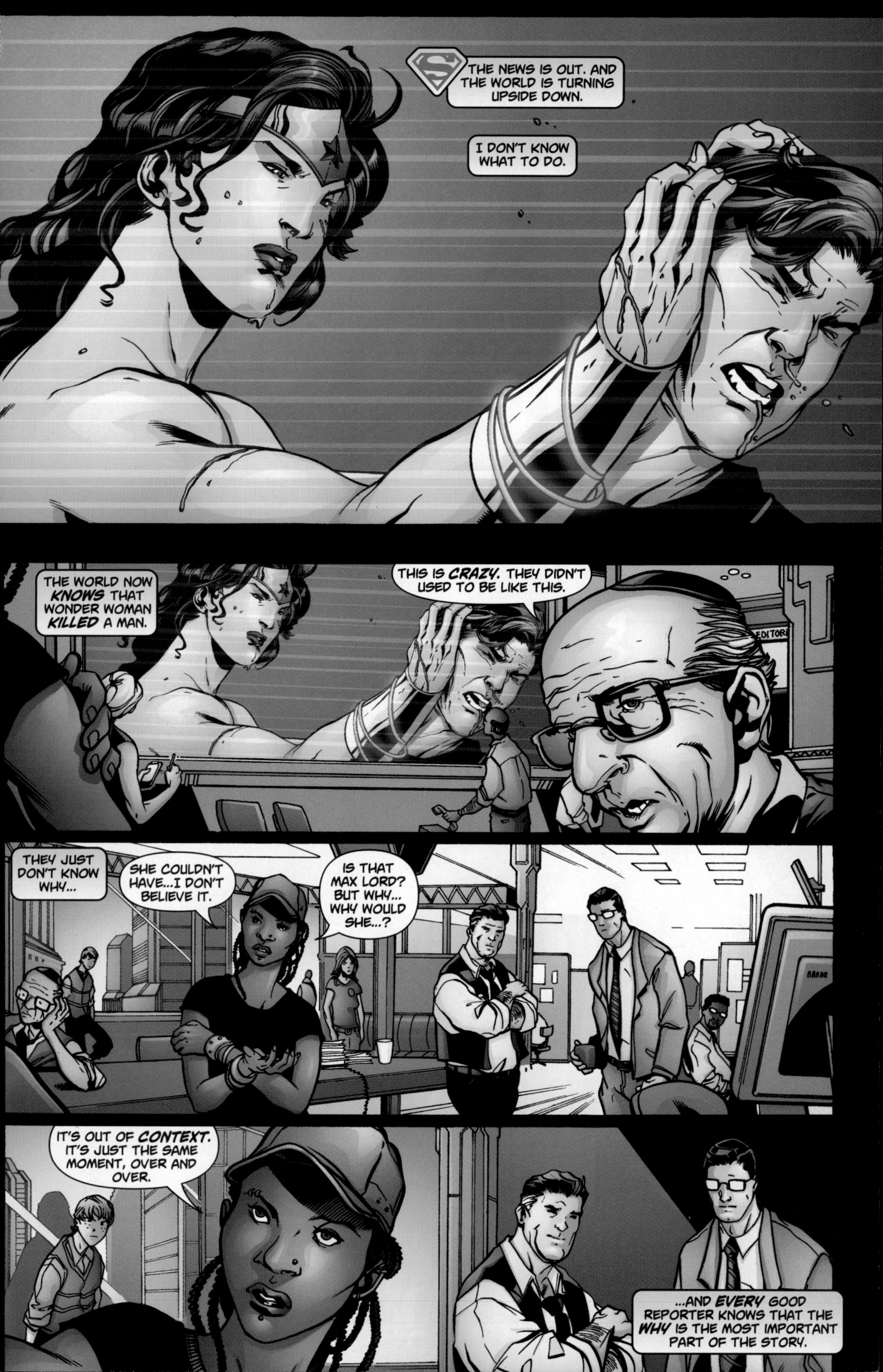
THE NEWS IS OUT. AND THE WORLD IS TURNING UPSIDE DOWN.
I DON'T KNOW WHAT TO DO.
THE WORLD NOW KNOWS THAT WONDER WOMAN KILLED A MAN.
THIS IS CRAZY. THEY DIDN'T USED TO BE LIKE THIS.
EDITOR
THEY JUST DON'T KNOW WHY...
SHE COULDN'T HAVE...I DON'T BELIEVE IT.
IS THAT MAX LORD? BUT WHY... WHY WOULD SHE...?
IT'S OUT OF CONTEXT. IT'S JUST THE SAME MOMENT, OVER AND OVER.
...AND EVERY GOOD REPORTER KNOWS THAT THE WHY IS THE MOST IMPORTANT PART OF THE STORY.

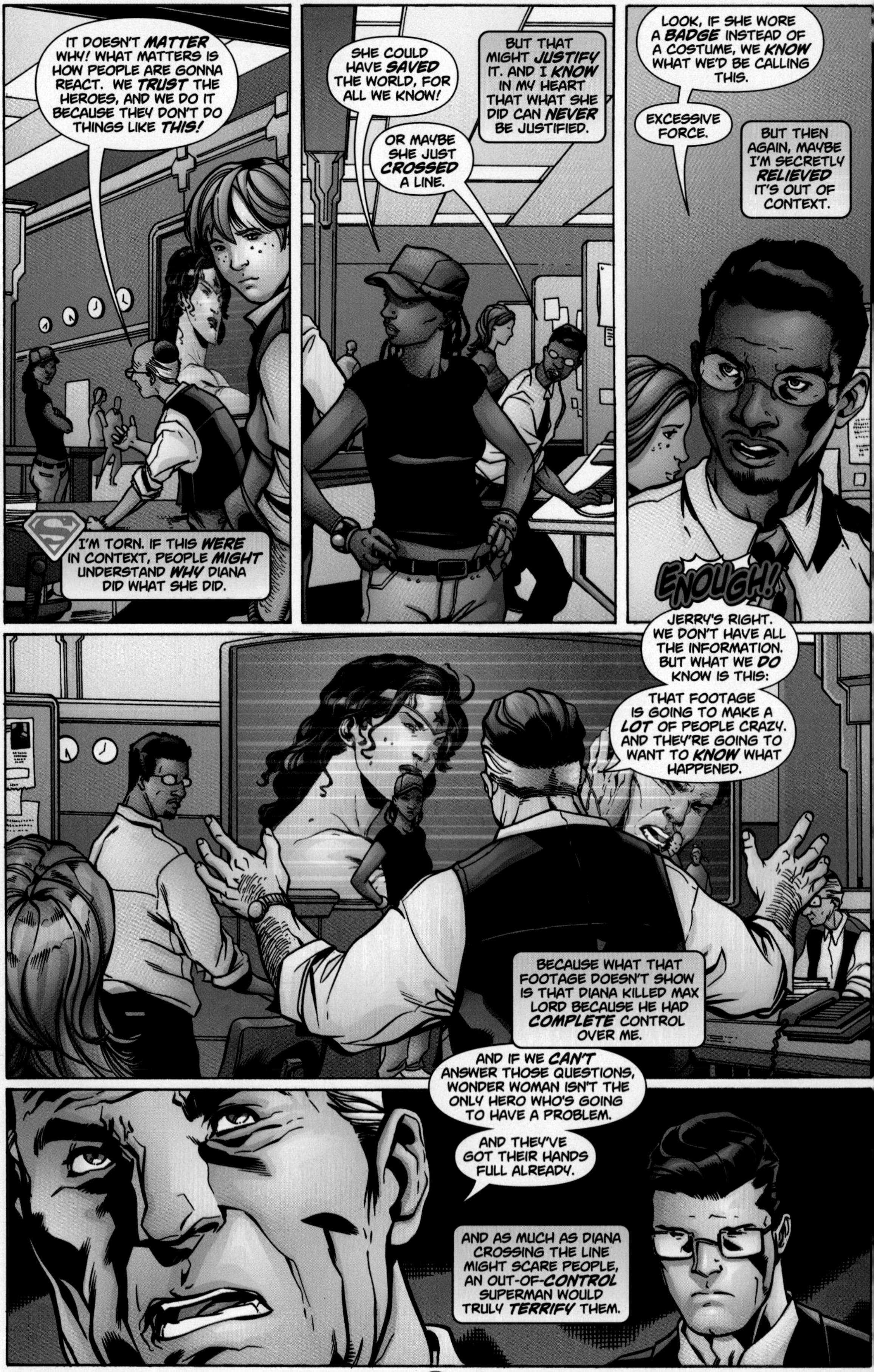
IT DOESN'T MATTER WHY! WHAT MATTERS IS HOW PEOPLE ARE GONNA REACT. WE TRUST THE HEROES, AND WE DO IT BECAUSE THEY DON'T DO THINGS LIKE THIS!
I'M TORN. IF THIS WERE IN CONTEXT, PEOPLE MIGHT UNDERSTAND WHY DIANA DID WHAT SHE DID.
SHE COULD HAVE SAVED THE WORLD, FOR ALL WE KNOW!
OR MAYBE SHE JUST CROSSED A LINE.
BUT THAT MIGHT JUSTIFY IT. AND I KNOW IN MY HEART THAT WHAT SHE DID CAN NEVER BE JUSTIFIED.
LOOK, IF SHE WORE A BADGE INSTEAD OF A COSTUME, WE KNOW WHAT WE'D BE CALLING THIS.
EXCESSIVE FORCE.
BUT THEN AGAIN, MAYBE I'M SECRETLY RELIEVED IT'S OUT OF CONTEXT.
ENOUGH!
JERRY'S RIGHT. WE DON'T HAVE ALL THE INFORMATION. BUT WHAT WE DO KNOW IS THIS:
THAT FOOTAGE IS GOING TO MAKE A LOT OF PEOPLE CRAZY. AND THEY'RE GOING TO WANT TO KNOW WHAT HAPPENED.
BECAUSE WHAT THAT FOOTAGE DOESN'T SHOW IS THAT DIANA KILLED MAX LORD BECAUSE HE HAD COMPLETE CONTROL OVER ME.
AND IF WE CAN'T ANSWER THOSE QUESTIONS, WONDER WOMAN ISN'T THE ONLY HERO WHO'S GOING TO HAVE A PROBLEM.
AND THEY'VE GOT THEIR HANDS FULL ALREADY.
AND AS MUCH AS DIANA CROSSING THE LINE MIGHT SCARE PEOPLE, AN OUT-OF-CONTROL SUPERMAN WOULD TRULY TERRIFY THEM.

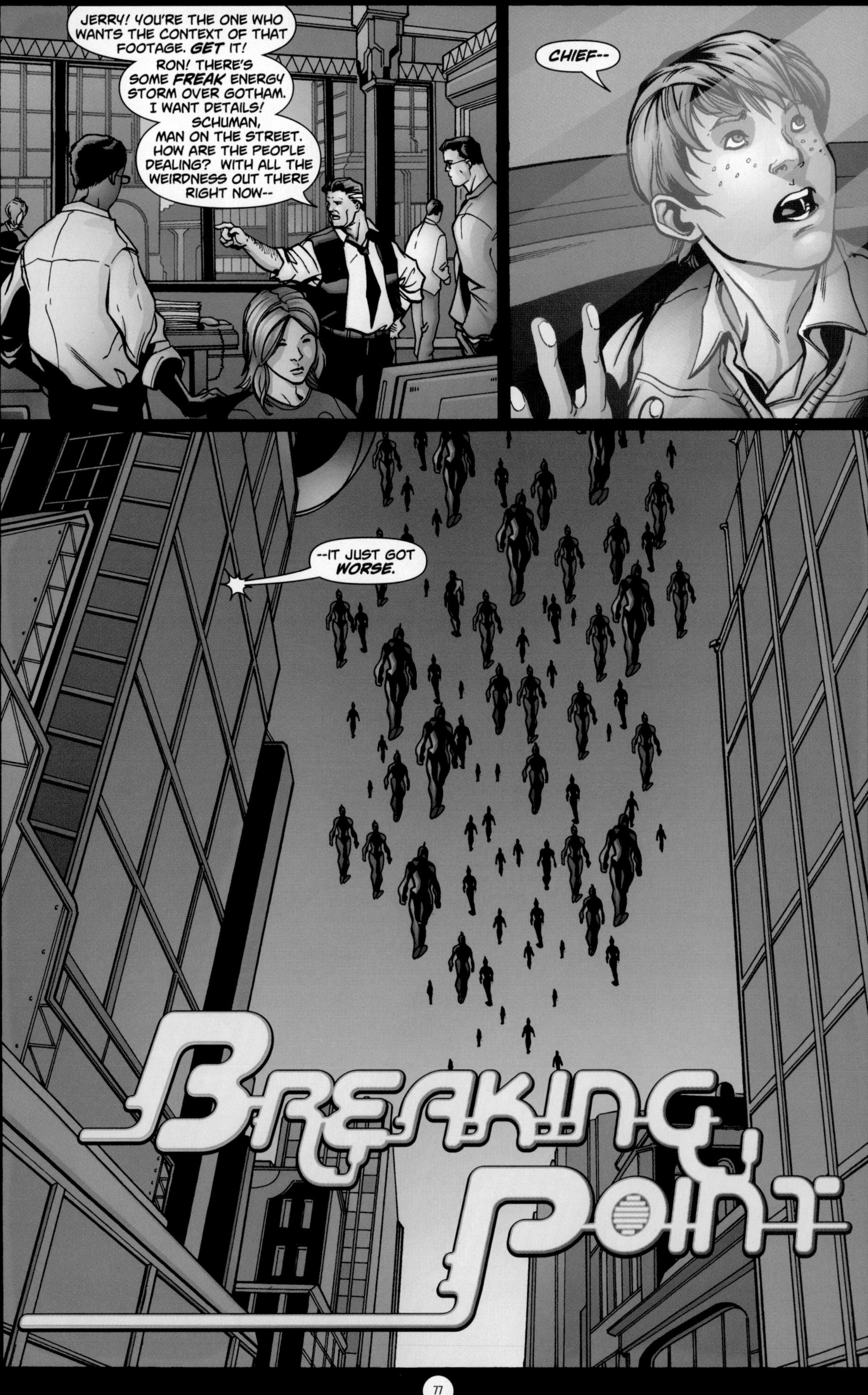

JERRY! YOU'RE THE ONE WHO WANTS THE CONTEXT OF THAT FOOTAGE. GET IT!
RON! THERE'S SOME FREAK ENERGY STORM OVER GOTHAM. I WANT DETAILS!
SCHUMAN, MAN ON THE STREET. HOW ARE THE PEOPLE DEALING? WITH ALL THE WEIRDNESS OUT THERE RIGHT NOW--
CHIEF--
--IT JUST GOT WORSE.
BREAKING POINT

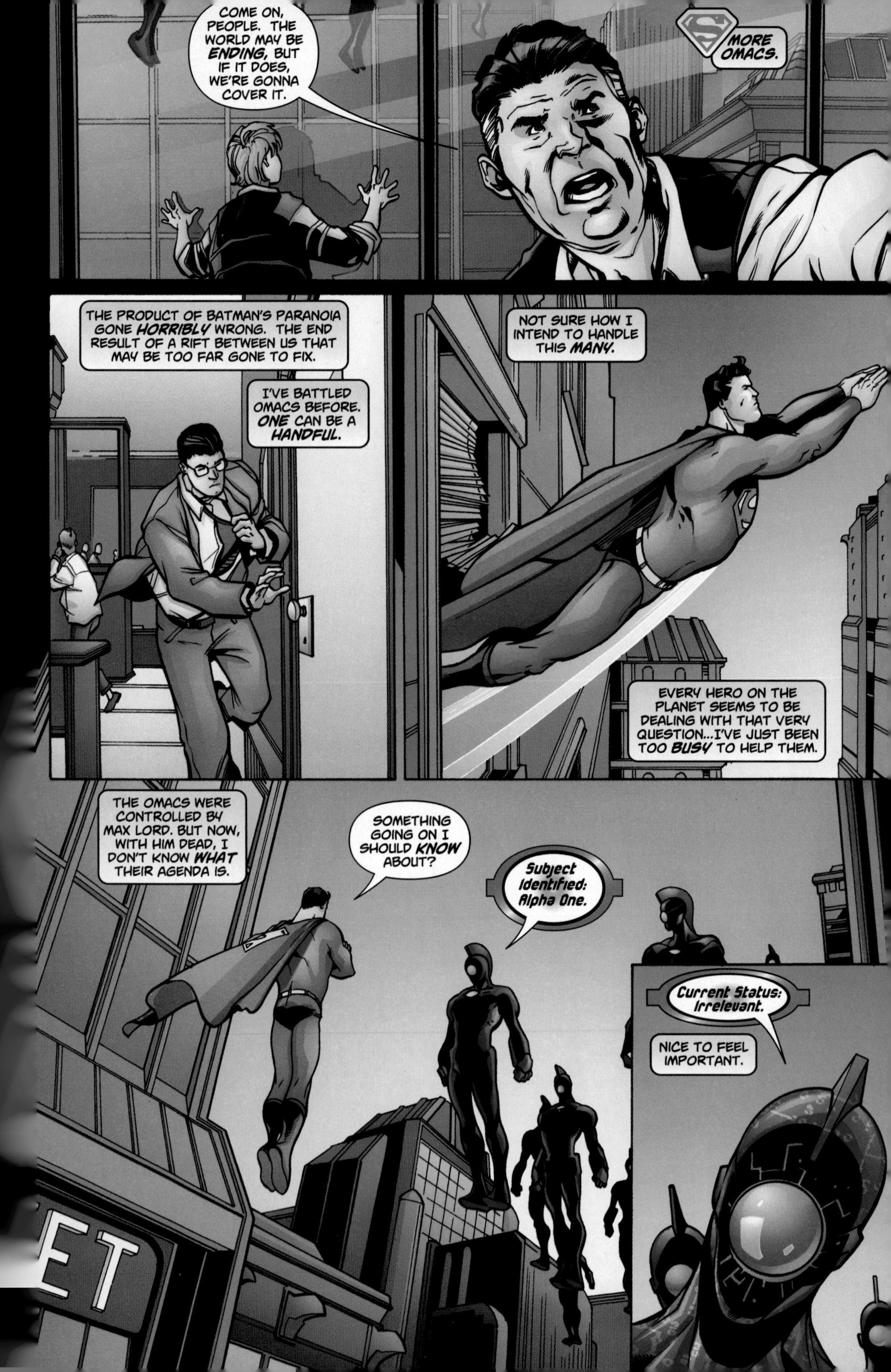
COME ON, PEOPLE. THE WORLD MAY BE ENDING, BUT IF IT DOES, WE'RE GONNA COVER IT.
MORE OMACS.
THE PRODUCT OF BATMAN'S PARANOIA GONE HORRIBLY WRONG. THE END RESULT OF A RIFT BETWEEN US THAT MAY BE TOO FAR GONE TO FIX.
I'VE BATTLED OMACS BEFORE. ONE CAN BE A HANDFUL.
NOT SURE HOW I INTEND TO HANDLE THIS MANY.
EVERY HERO ON THE PLANET SEEMS TO BE DEALING WITH THAT VERY QUESTION...I'VE JUST BEEN TOO BUSY TO HELP THEM.
THE OMACS WERE CONTROLLED BY MAX LORD. BUT NOW, WITH HIM DEAD, I DON'T KNOW WHAT THEIR AGENDA IS.
SOMETHING GOING ON I SHOULD KNOW ABOUT?
Subject Identified: Alpha One.
Current Status: Irrelevant.
NICE TO FEEL IMPORTANT.
ET

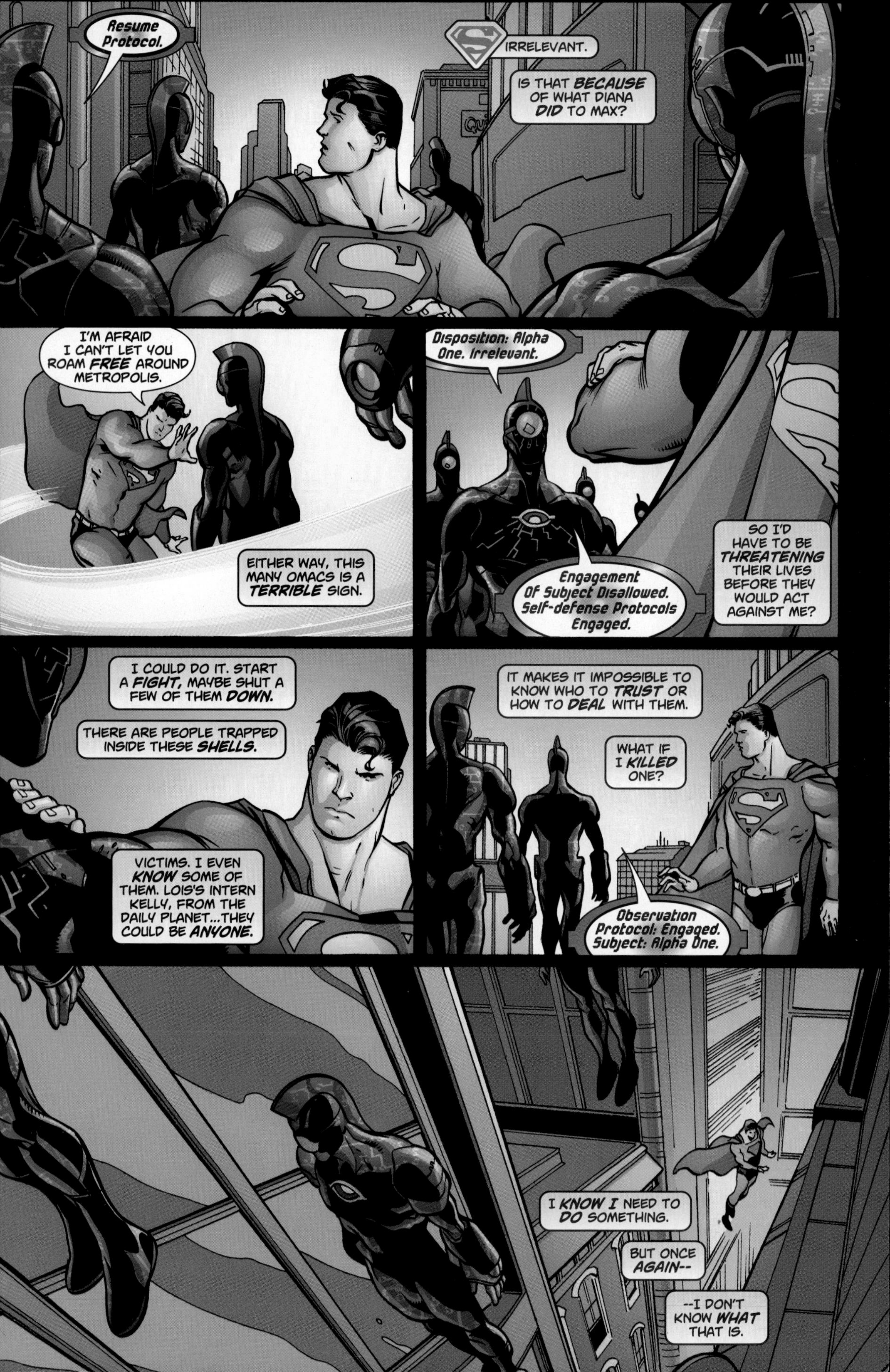
Resume Protocol.
IRRELEVANT.
IS THAT BECAUSE OF WHAT DIANA DID TO MAX?
I'M AFRAID I CAN'T LET YOU ROAM FREE AROUND METROPOLIS.
EITHER WAY, THIS MANY OMACS IS A TERRIBLE SIGN.
Disposition: Alpha One. Irrelevant.
Engagement Of Subject Disallowed. Self-defense Protocols Engaged.
SO I'D HAVE TO BE THREATENING THEIR LIVES BEFORE THEY WOULD ACT AGAINST ME?
I COULD DO IT. START A FIGHT, MAYBE SHUT A FEW OF THEM DOWN.
THERE ARE PEOPLE TRAPPED INSIDE THESE SHELLS.
VICTIMS. I EVEN KNOW SOME OF THEM. LOIS'S INTERN KELLY, FROM THE DAILY PLANET...THEY COULD BE ANYONE.
IT MAKES IT IMPOSSIBLE TO KNOW WHO TO TRUST OR HOW TO DEAL WITH THEM.
WHAT IF I KILLED ONE?
Observation Protocol: Engaged. Subject: Alpha One.
I KNOW I NEED TO DO SOMETHING.
BUT ONCE AGAIN--
--I DON'T KNOW WHAT THAT IS.

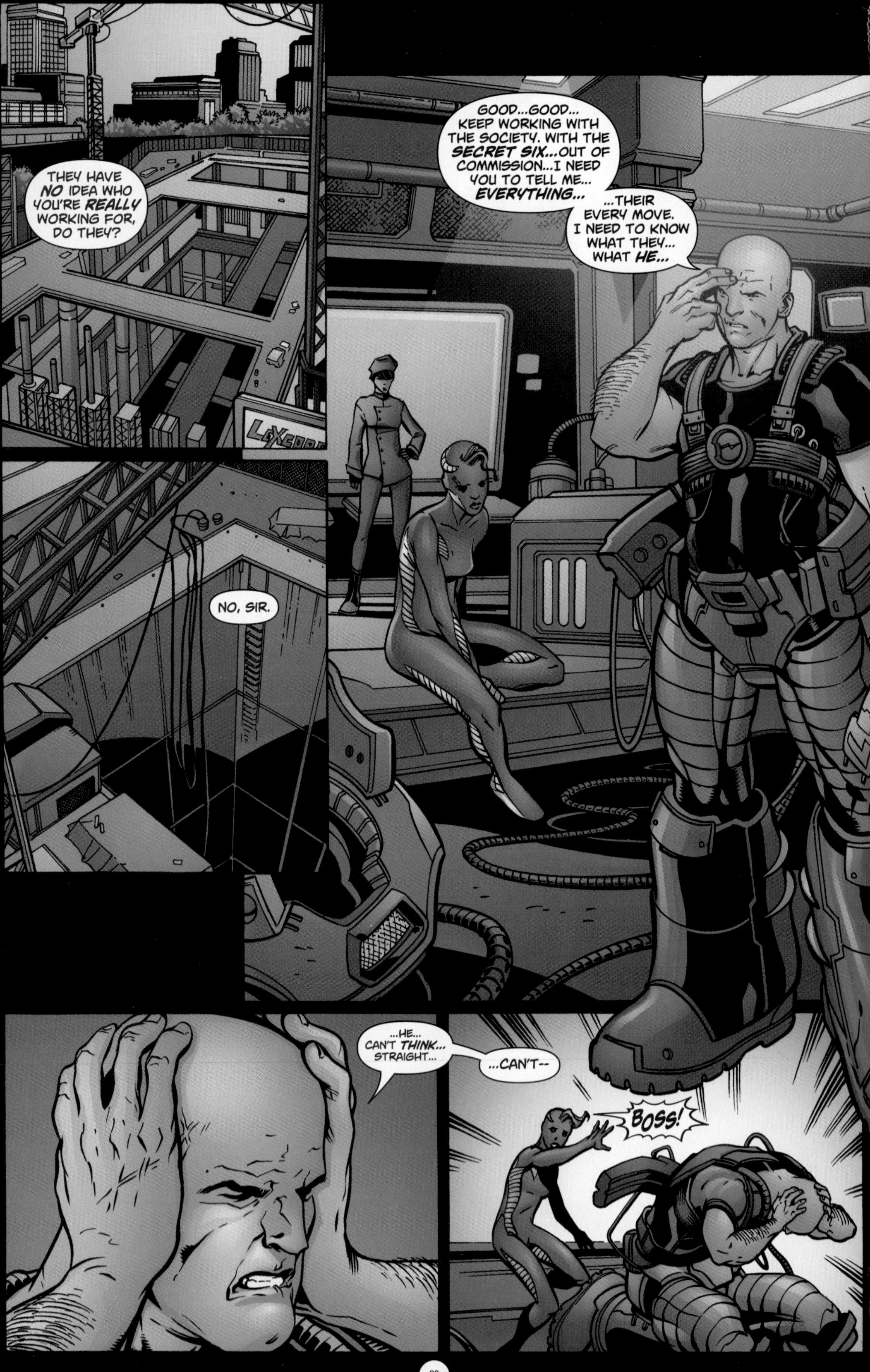
THEY HAVE NO IDEA WHO YOU'RE REALLY WORKING FOR, DO THEY?
NO, SIR.
GOOD...GOOD... KEEP WORKING WITH THE SOCIETY. WITH THE SECRET SIX...OUT OF COMMISSION...I NEED YOU TO TELL ME... EVERYTHING...
...THEIR EVERY MOVE. I NEED TO KNOW WHAT THEY... WHAT HE...
...HE... CAN'T THINK... STRAIGHT...
...CAN'T--
BOSS!

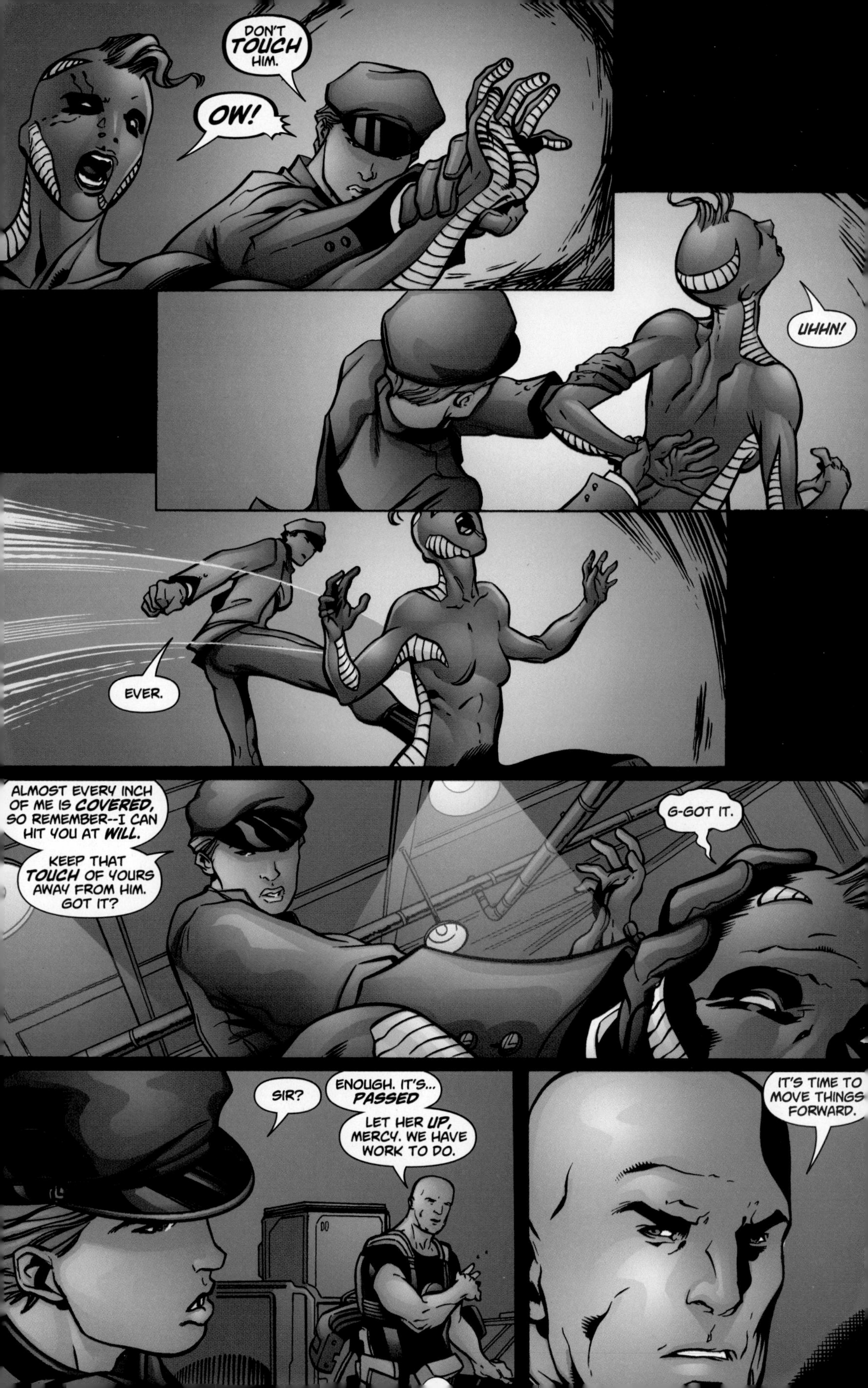
DON'T TOUCH HIM.
OW!
UHHN!
EVER.
ALMOST EVERY INCH OF ME IS COVERED, SO REMEMBER--I CAN HIT YOU AT WILL.
KEEP THAT TOUCH OF YOURS AWAY FROM HIM. GOT IT?
G-GOT IT.
SIR?
ENOUGH. IT'S... PASSED
LET HER UP, MERCY. WE HAVE WORK TO DO.
IT'S TIME TO MOVE THINGS FORWARD.

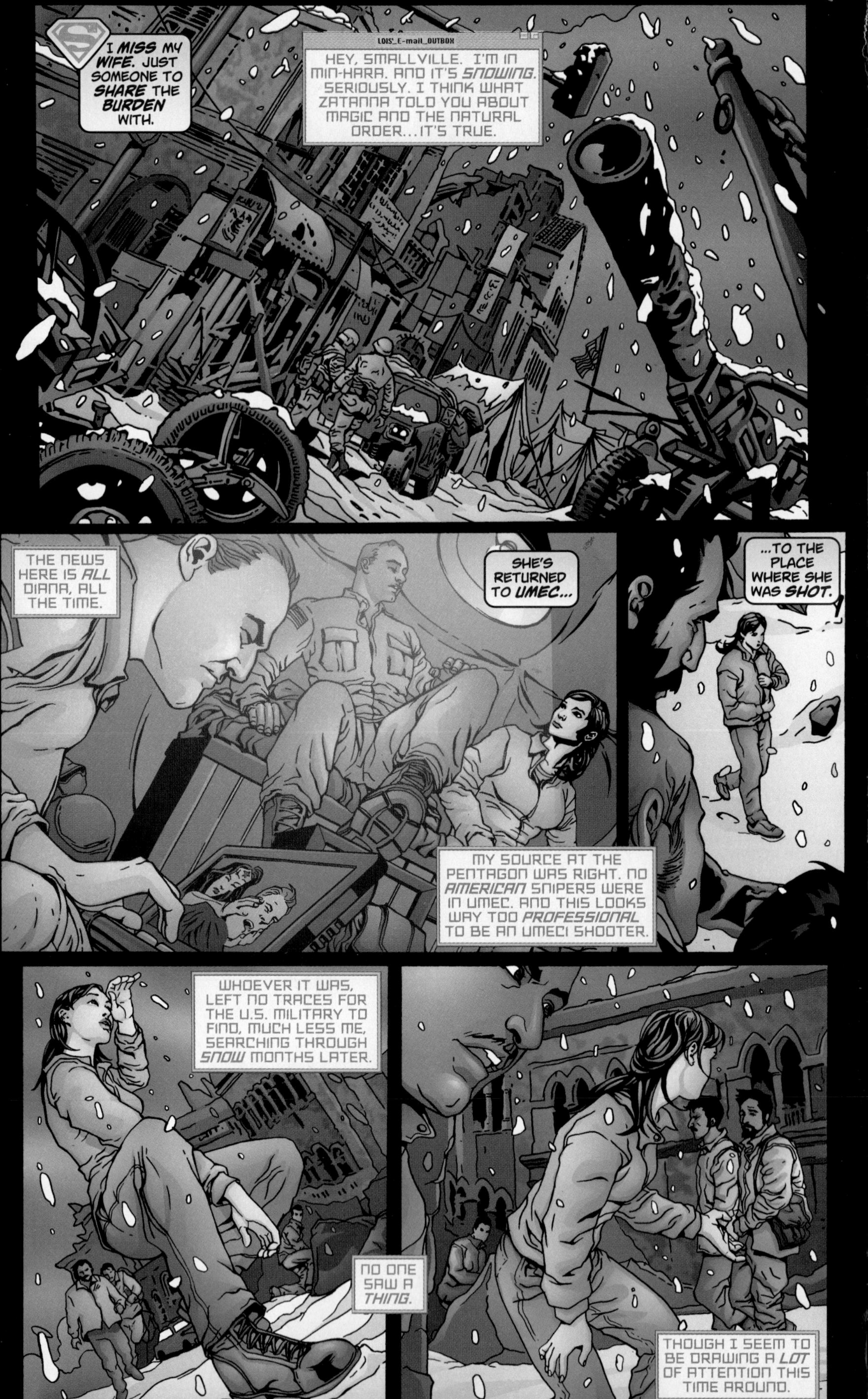
I MISS MY WIFE. JUST SOMEONE TO SHARE THE BURDEN WITH.
LOIS'_E-mail_OUTBOX
HEY, SMALLVILLE. I'M IN MIN-HARA. AND IT'S SNOWING. SERIOUSLY. I THINK WHAT ZATANNA TOLD YOU ABOUT MAGIC AND THE NATURAL ORDER... IT'S TRUE.
THE NEWS HERE IS ALL DIANA, ALL THE TIME.
SHE'S RETURNED TO UMEC...
...TO THE PLACE WHERE SHE WAS SHOT.
MY SOURCE AT THE PENTAGON WAS RIGHT. NO AMERICAN SNIPERS WERE IN UMEC. AND THIS LOOKS WAY TOO PROFESSIONAL TO BE AN UMECI SHOOTER.
WHOEVER IT WAS, LEFT NO TRACES FOR THE U.S. MILITARY TO FIND, MUCH LESS ME, SEARCHING THROUGH SNOW MONTHS LATER.
NO ONE SAW A THING.
THOUGH I SEEM TO BE DRAWING A LOT OF ATTENTION THIS TIME AROUND.

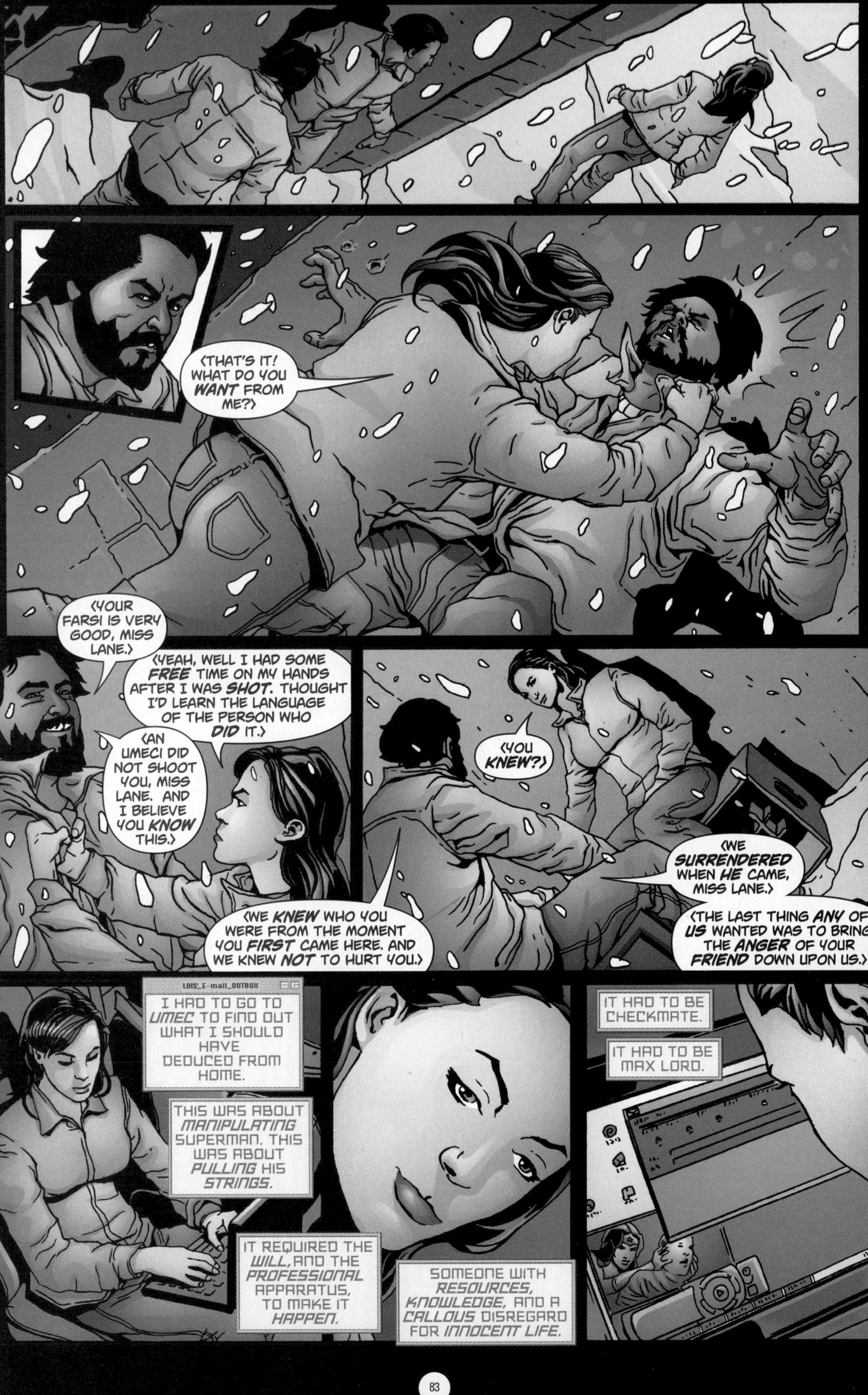

(THAT'S IT! WHAT DO YOU WANT FROM ME?)
(YOUR FARSI IS VERY GOOD, MISS LANE.)
(YEAH, WELL I HAD SOME FREE TIME ON MY HANDS AFTER I WAS SHOT. THOUGHT I'D LEARN THE LANGUAGE OF THE PERSON WHO DID IT.)
(AN UMECI DID NOT SHOOT YOU, MISS LANE. AND I BELIEVE YOU KNOW THIS.)
(YOU KNEW?)
(WE KNEW WHO YOU WERE FROM THE MOMENT YOU FIRST CAME HERE. AND WE KNEW NOT TO HURT YOU.)
(WE SURRENDERED WHEN HE CAME, MISS LANE.)
(THE LAST THING ANY OF US WANTED WAS TO BRING THE ANGER OF YOUR FRIEND DOWN UPON US.)
LOIS_E-mail_OUTBOX
I HAD TO GO TO UMEC TO FIND OUT WHAT I SHOULD HAVE DEDUCED FROM HOME.
THIS WAS ABOUT MANIPULATING SUPERMAN. THIS WAS ABOUT PULLING HIS STRINGS.
IT REQUIRED THE WILL, AND THE PROFESSIONAL APPARATUS, TO MAKE IT HAPPEN.
SOMEONE WITH RESOURCES, KNOWLEDGE, AND A CALLOUS DISREGARD FOR INNOCENT LIFE.
IT HAD TO BE CHECKMATE.
IT HAD TO BE MAX LORD.

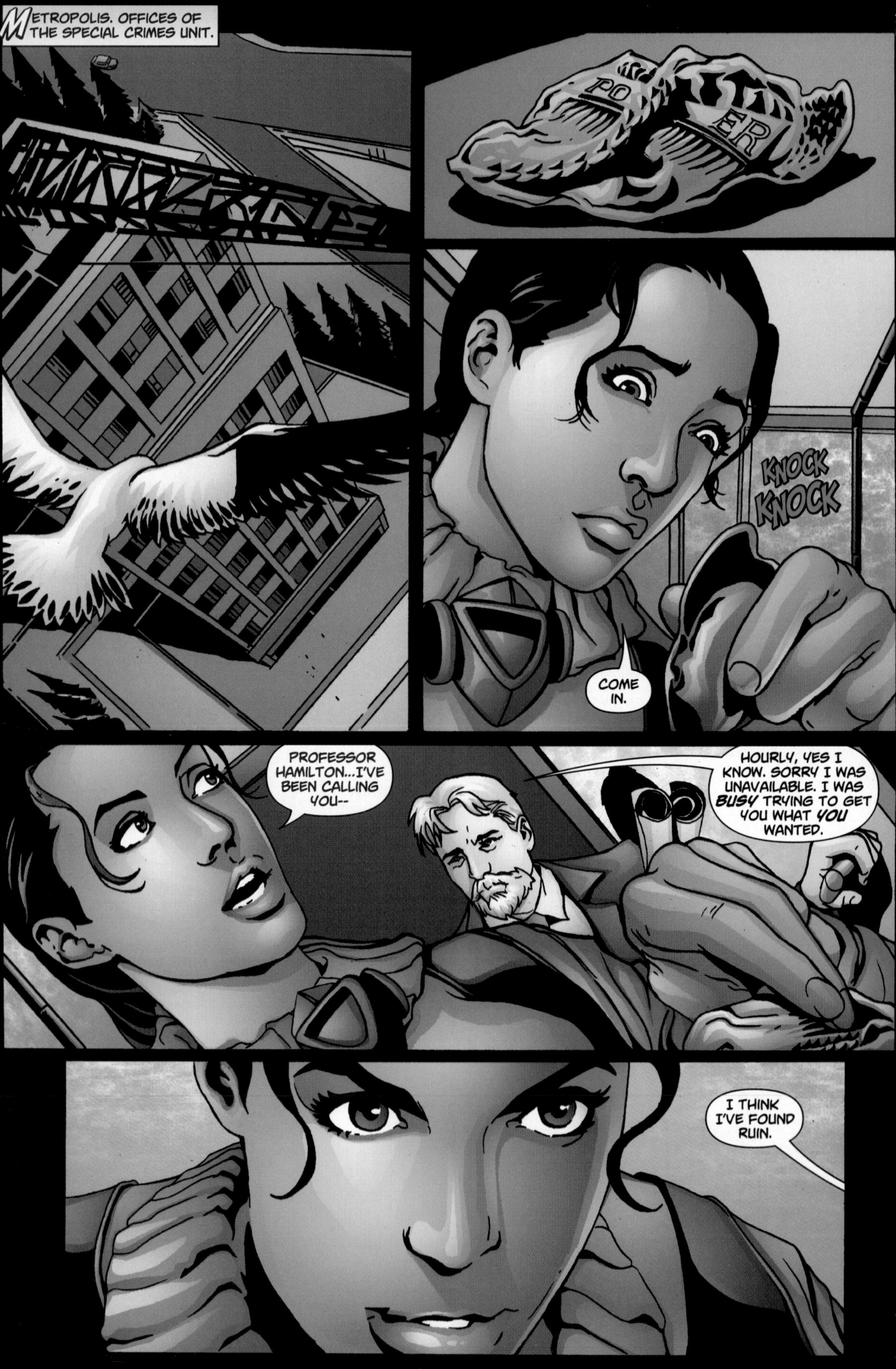
METROPOLIS. OFFICES OF THE SPECIAL CRIMES UNIT.
PO ER
KNOCK KNOCK
COME IN.
PROFESSOR HAMILTON...I'VE BEEN CALLING YOU--
HOURLY, YES I KNOW. SORRY I WAS UNAVAILABLE. I WAS BUSY TRYING TO GET YOU WHAT YOU WANTED.
I THINK I'VE FOUND RUIN.

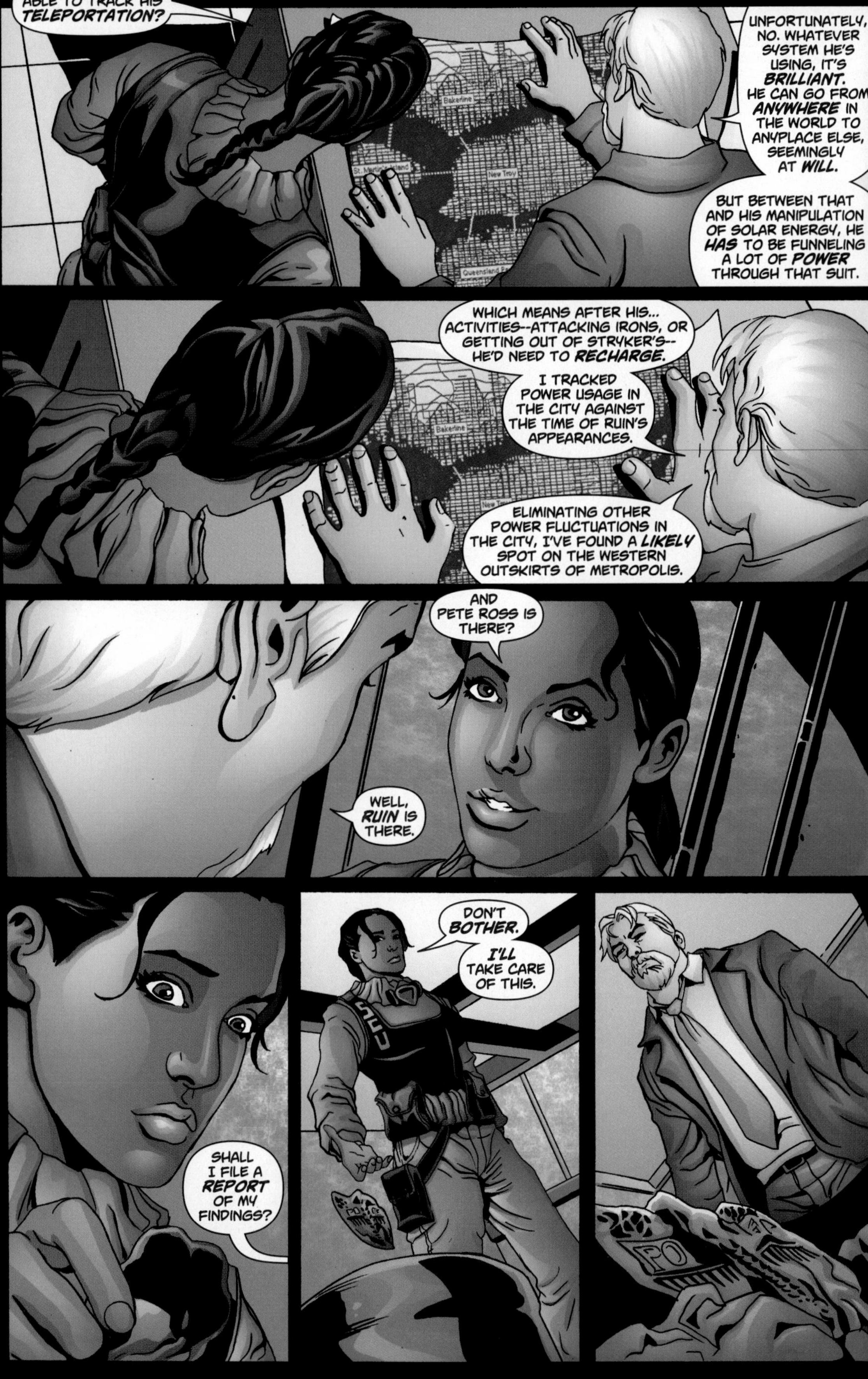

YOU'RE ABLE TO TRACK HIS TELEPORTATION?
UNFORTUNATELY, NO. WHATEVER SYSTEM HE'S USING, IT'S BRILLIANT. HE CAN GO FROM ANYWHERE IN THE WORLD TO ANYPLACE ELSE, SEEMINGLY AT WILL.
BUT BETWEEN THAT AND HIS MANIPULATION OF SOLAR ENERGY, HE HAS TO BE FUNNELING A LOT OF POWER THROUGH THAT SUIT.
Bakerline
St. Martin's Island
New Troy
WHICH MEANS AFTER HIS... ACTIVITIES--ATTACKING IRONS, OR GETTING OUT OF STRYKER'S--HE'D NEED TO RECHARGE.
I TRACKED POWER USAGE IN THE CITY AGAINST THE TIME OF RUIN'S APPEARANCES.
Bakerline
ELIMINATING OTHER POWER FLUCTUATIONS IN THE CITY, I'VE FOUND A LIKELY SPOT ON THE WESTERN OUTSKIRTS OF METROPOLIS.
AND PETE ROSS IS THERE?
WELL, RUIN IS THERE.
SHALL I FILE A REPORT OF MY FINDINGS?
DON'T BOTHER.
I'LL TAKE CARE OF THIS.

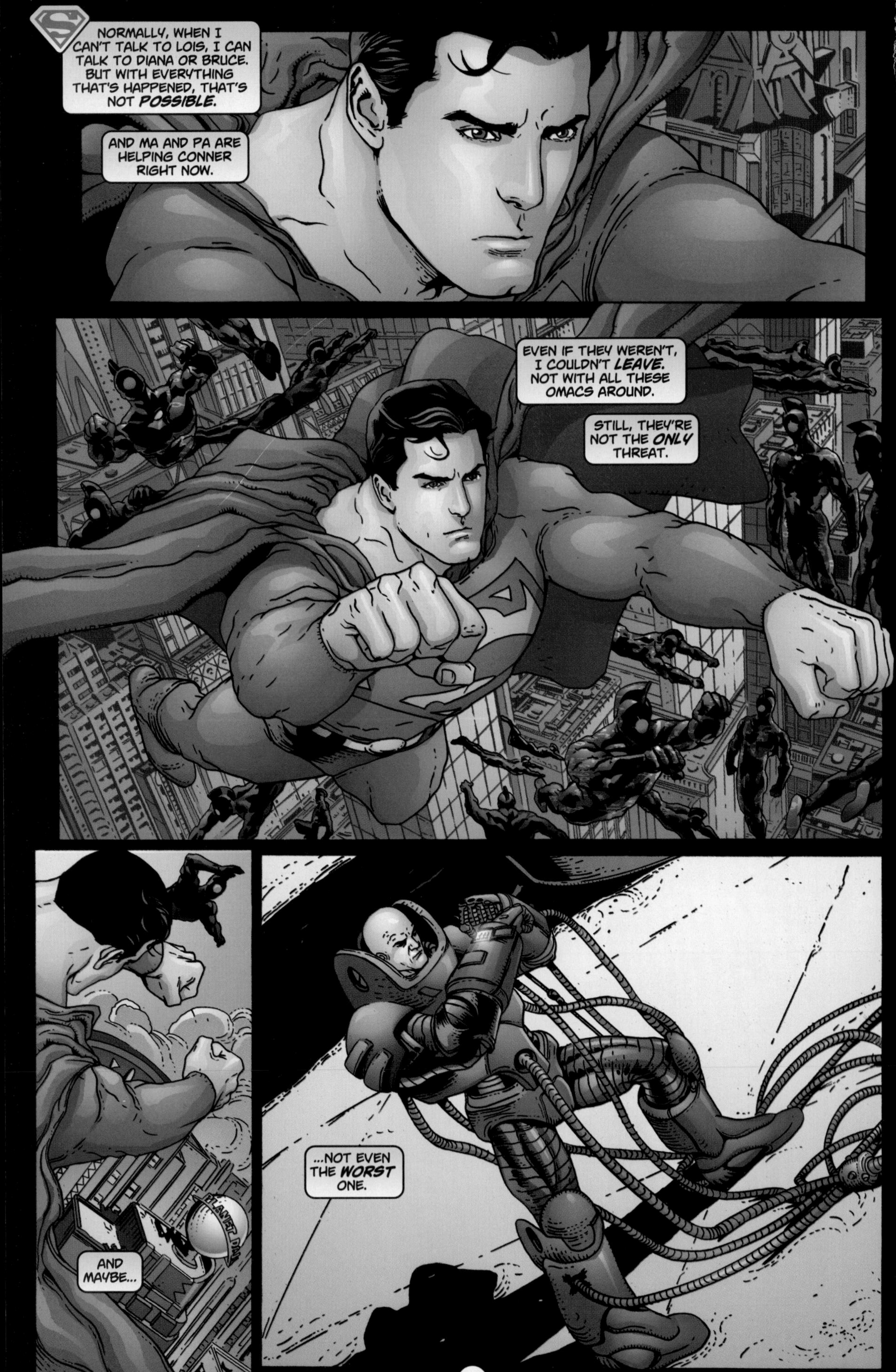
NORMALLY, WHEN I CAN'T TALK TO LOIS, I CAN TALK TO DIANA OR BRUCE. BUT WITH EVERYTHING THAT'S HAPPENED, THAT'S NOT POSSIBLE.
AND MA AND PA ARE HELPING CONNER RIGHT NOW.
EVEN IF THEY WEREN'T, I COULDN'T LEAVE. NOT WITH ALL THESE OMACS AROUND.
STILL, THEY'RE NOT THE ONLY THREAT.
AND MAYBE...
...NOT EVEN THE WORST ONE.

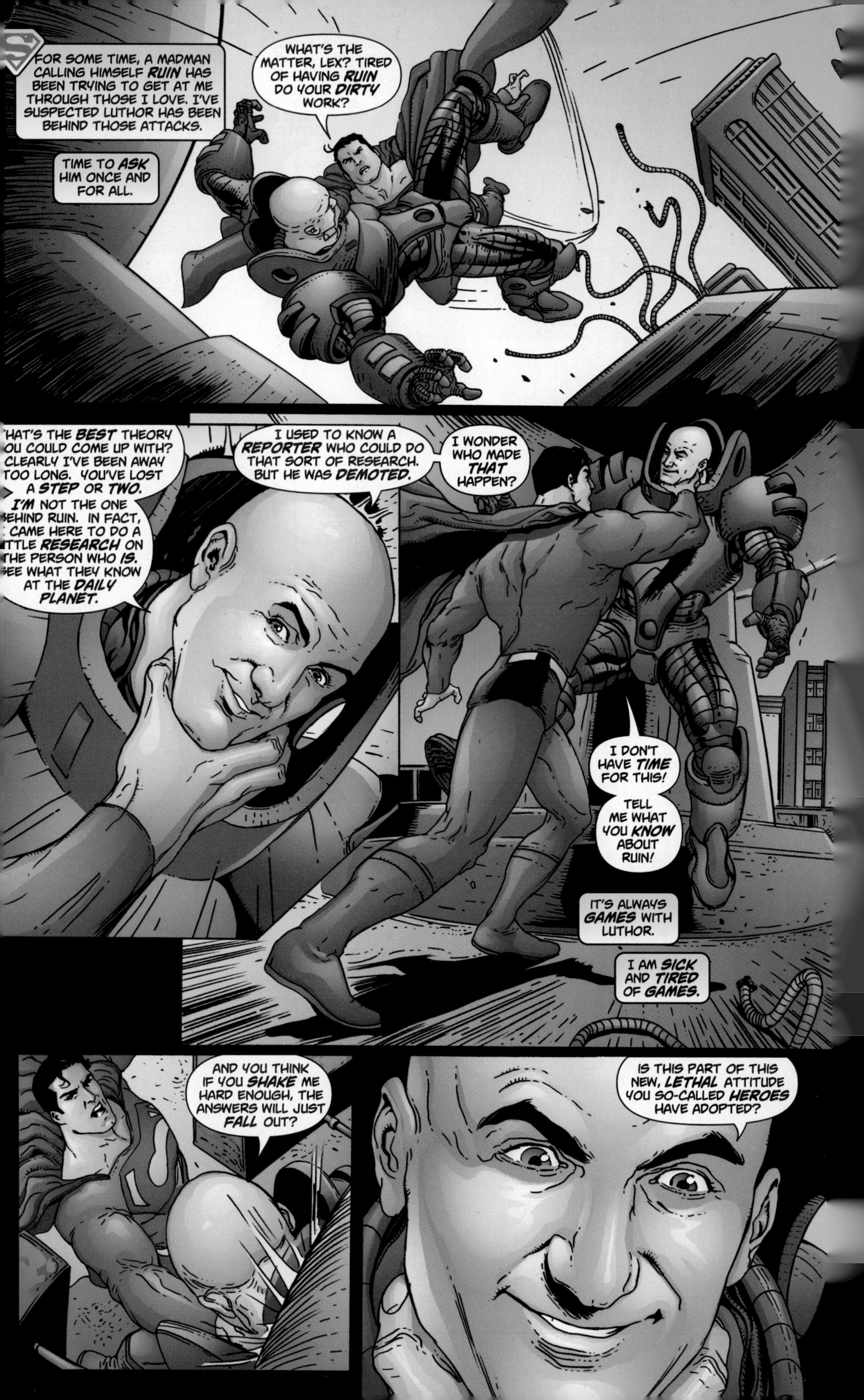
FOR SOME TIME, A MADMAN CALLING HIMSELF RUIN HAS BEEN TRYING TO GET AT ME THROUGH THOSE I LOVE. I'VE SUSPECTED LUTHOR HAS BEEN BEHIND THOSE ATTACKS.
TIME TO ASK HIM ONCE AND FOR ALL.
WHAT'S THE MATTER, LEX? TIRED OF HAVING RUIN DO YOUR DIRTY WORK?
HAT'S THE BEST THEORY OU COULD COME UP WITH? CLEARLY I'VE BEEN AWAY TOO LONG. YOU'VE LOST A STEP OR TWO.
I'M NOT THE ONE BEHIND RUIN. IN FACT, CAME HERE TO DO A TTLE RESEARCH ON THE PERSON WHO IS. EE WHAT THEY KNOW AT THE DAILY PLANET.
I USED TO KNOW A REPORTER WHO COULD DO THAT SORT OF RESEARCH. BUT HE WAS DEMOTED.
I WONDER WHO MADE THAT HAPPEN?
I DON'T HAVE TIME FOR THIS!
TELL ME WHAT YOU KNOW ABOUT RUIN!
IT'S ALWAYS GAMES WITH LUTHOR.
I AM SICK AND TIRED OF GAMES.
AND YOU THINK IF YOU SHAKE ME HARD ENOUGH, THE ANSWERS WILL JUST FALL OUT?
IS THIS PART OF THIS NEW, LETHAL ATTITUDE YOU SO-CALLED HEROES HAVE ADOPTED?

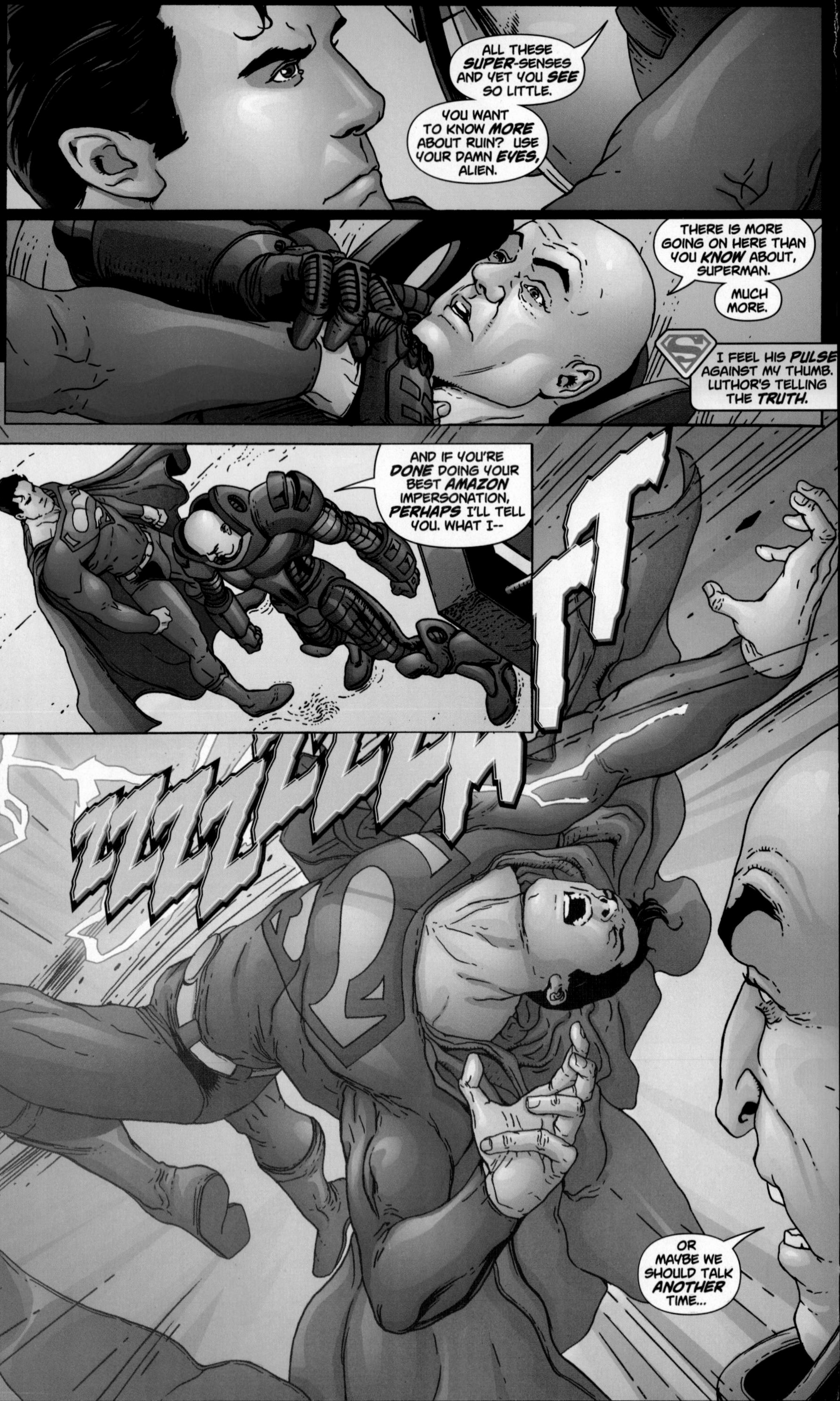
ALL THESE SUPER-SENSES AND YET YOU SEE SO LITTLE.
YOU WANT TO KNOW MORE ABOUT RUIN? USE YOUR DAMN EYES, ALIEN.
THERE IS MORE GOING ON HERE THAN YOU KNOW ABOUT, SUPERMAN.
MUCH MORE.
I FEEL HIS PULSE AGAINST MY THUMB. LUTHOR'S TELLING THE TRUTH.
AND IF YOU'RE DONE DOING YOUR BEST AMAZON IMPERSONATION, PERHAPS I'LL TELL YOU. WHAT I--
ZZZZZZZZT
OR MAYBE WE SHOULD TALK ANOTHER TIME...

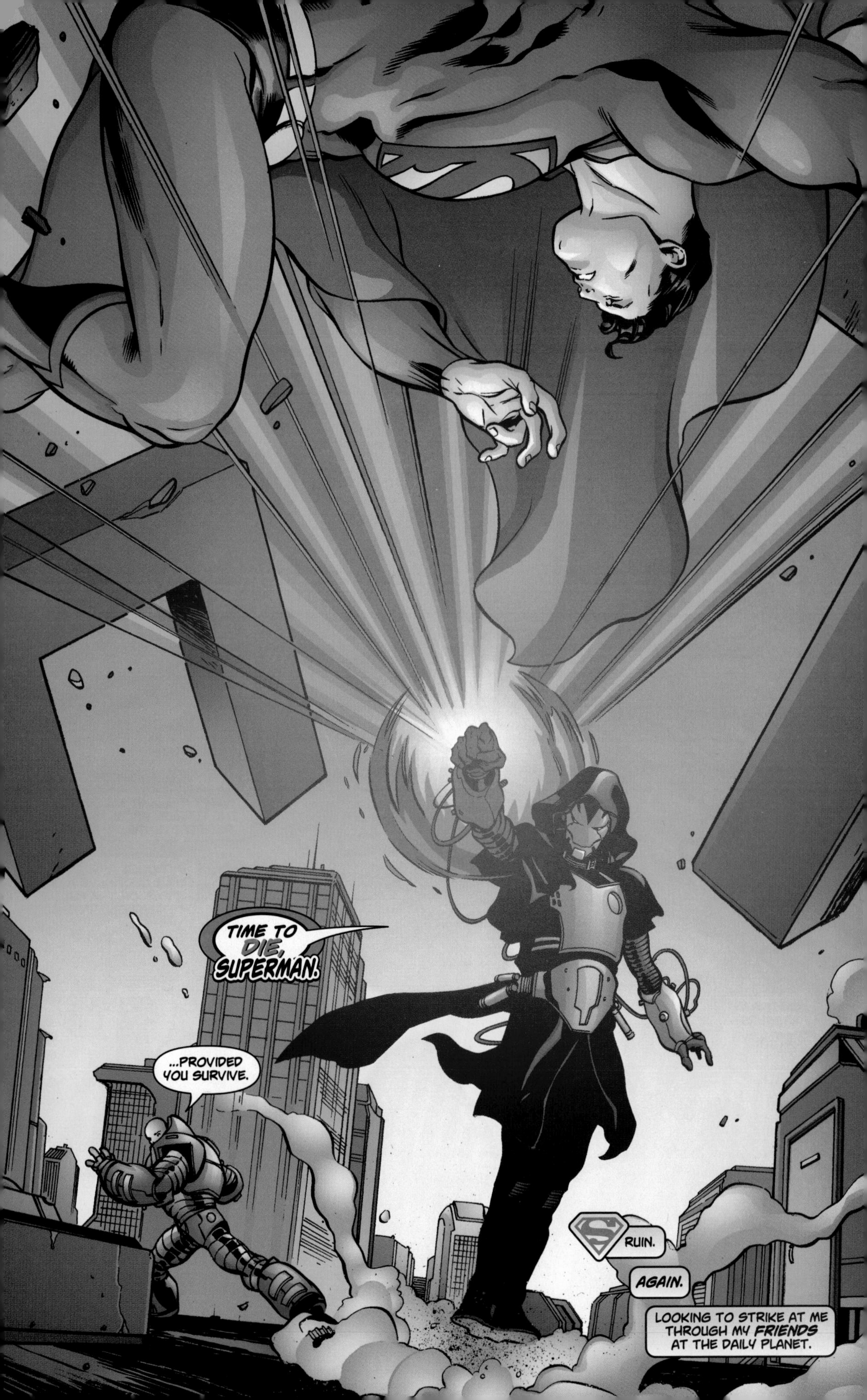
TIME TO DIE, SUPERMAN.
...PROVIDED YOU SURVIVE.
RUIN.
AGAIN.
LOOKING TO STRIKE AT ME THROUGH MY FRIENDS AT THE DAILY PLANET.

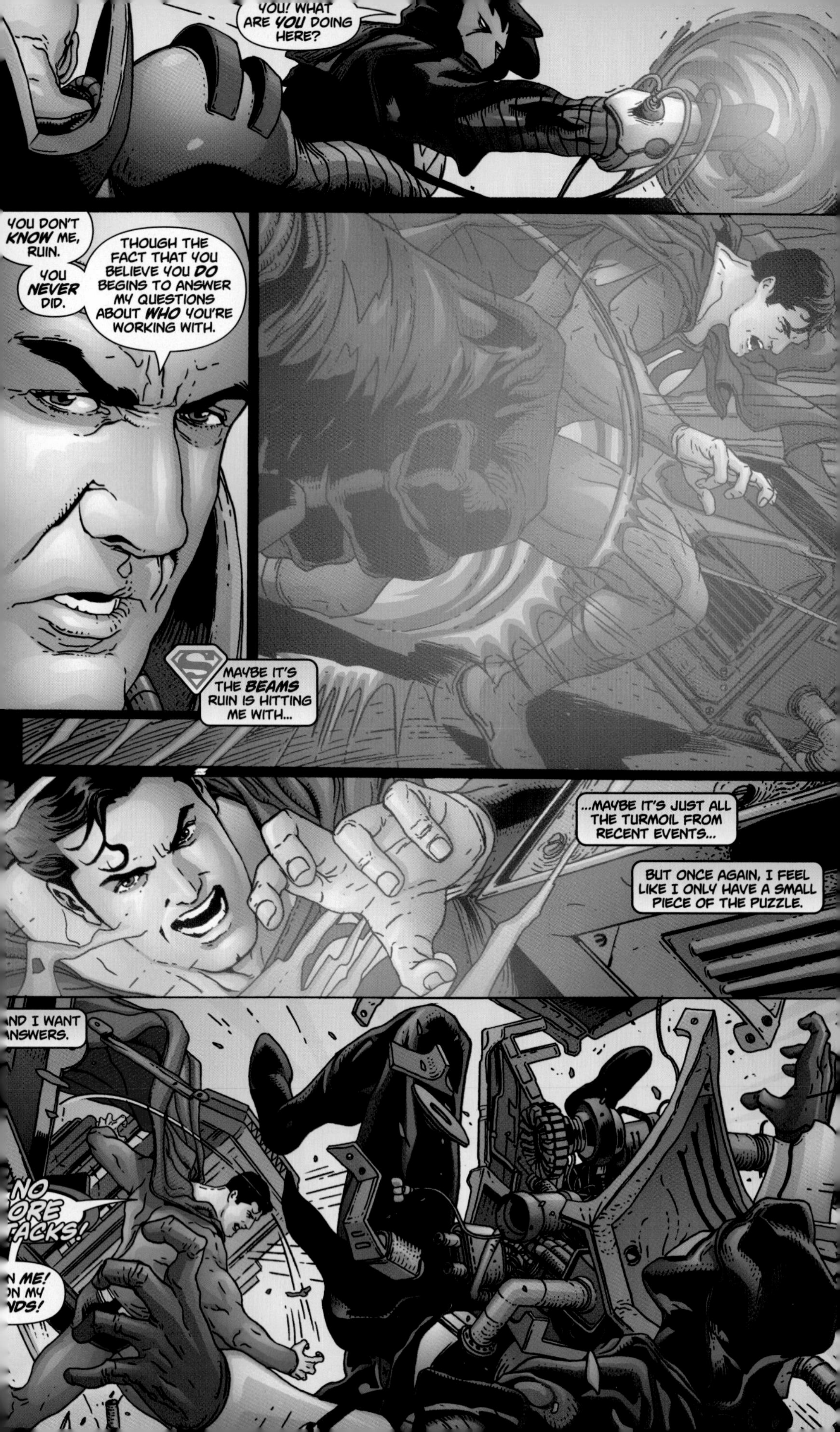
YOU! WHAT ARE YOU DOING HERE?
YOU DON'T KNOW ME, RUIN.
YOU NEVER DID.
THOUGH THE FACT THAT YOU BELIEVE YOU DO BEGINS TO ANSWER MY QUESTIONS ABOUT WHO YOU'RE WORKING WITH.
MAYBE IT'S THE BEAMS RUIN IS HITTING ME WITH...
...MAYBE IT'S JUST ALL THE TURMOIL FROM RECENT EVENTS...
BUT ONCE AGAIN, I FEEL LIKE I ONLY HAVE A SMALL PIECE OF THE PUZZLE.
ND I WANT NSWERS.
NO ORE TACKS!
N ME! ON MY NDS!

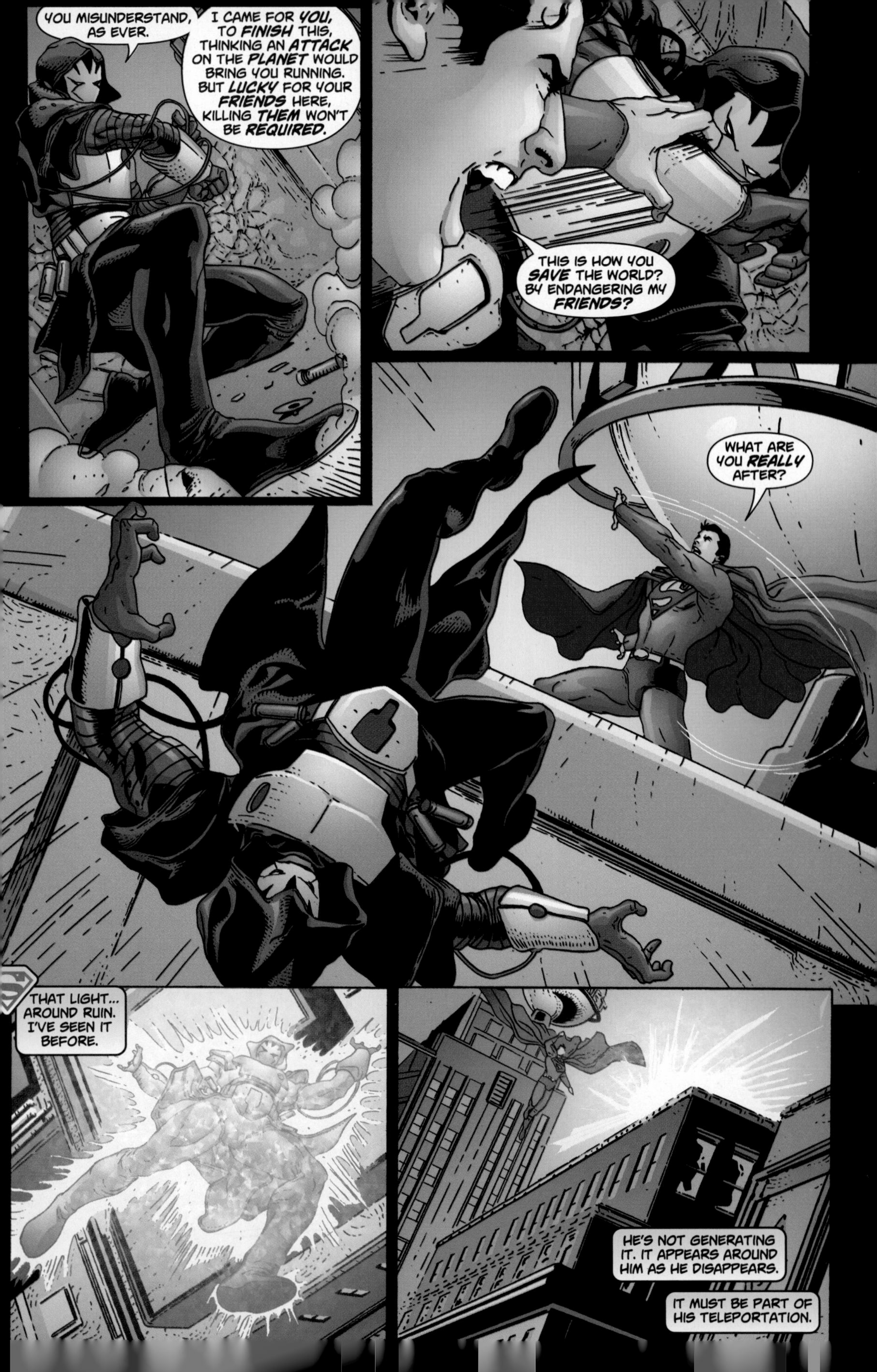

YOU MISUNDERSTAND, AS EVER.
I CAME FOR YOU, TO FINISH THIS, THINKING AN ATTACK ON THE PLANET WOULD BRING YOU RUNNING. BUT LUCKY FOR YOUR FRIENDS HERE, KILLING THEM WON'T BE REQUIRED.
THIS IS HOW YOU SAVE THE WORLD? BY ENDANGERING MY FRIENDS?
WHAT ARE YOU REALLY AFTER?
THAT LIGHT... AROUND RUIN. I'VE SEEN IT BEFORE.
HE'S NOT GENERATING IT. IT APPEARS AROUND HIM AS HE DISAPPEARS.
IT MUST BE PART OF HIS TELEPORTATION.

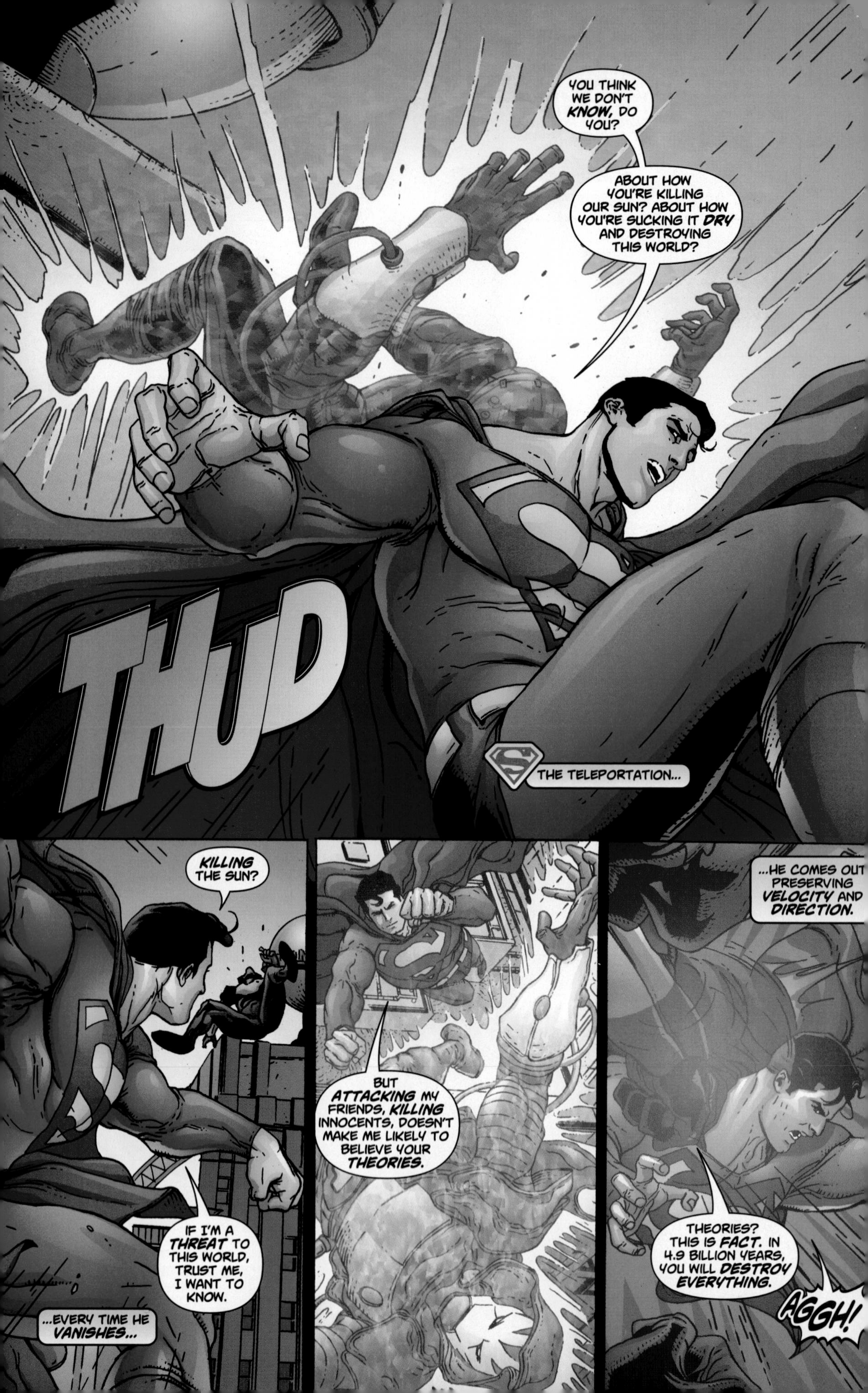
YOU THINK WE DON'T KNOW, DO YOU?
ABOUT HOW YOU'RE KILLING OUR SUN? ABOUT HOW YOU'RE SUCKING IT DRY AND DESTROYING THIS WORLD?
THUD
THE TELEPORTATION...
KILLING THE SUN?
IF I'M A THREAT TO THIS WORLD, TRUST ME, I WANT TO KNOW.
...EVERY TIME HE VANISHES...
BUT ATTACKING MY FRIENDS, KILLING INNOCENTS, DOESN'T MAKE ME LIKELY TO BELIEVE YOUR THEORIES.
...HE COMES OUT PRESERVING VELOCITY AND DIRECTION.
THEORIES? THIS IS FACT. IN 4.9 BILLION YEARS, YOU WILL DESTROY EVERYTHING.
AGGH!

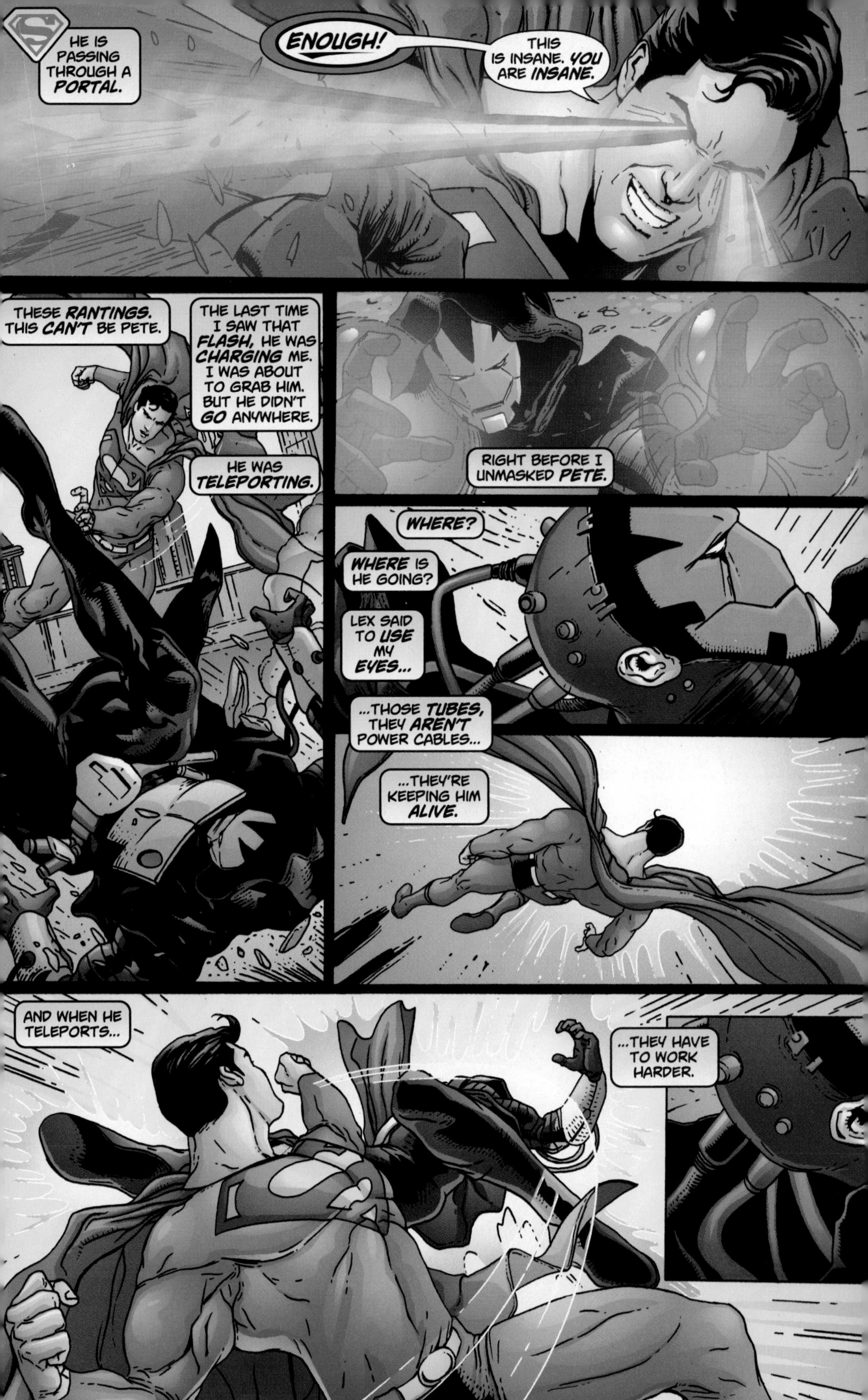

HE IS PASSING THROUGH A PORTAL.
ENOUGH!
THIS IS INSANE. YOU ARE INSANE.
THESE RANTINGS. THIS CAN'T BE PETE.
THE LAST TIME I SAW THAT FLASH, HE WAS CHARGING ME. I WAS ABOUT TO GRAB HIM. BUT HE DIDN'T GO ANYWHERE.
HE WAS TELEPORTING.
RIGHT BEFORE I UNMASKED PETE.
WHERE?
WHERE IS HE GOING?
LEX SAID TO USE MY EYES...
...THOSE TUBES, THEY AREN'T POWER CABLES...
...THEY'RE KEEPING HIM ALIVE.
AND WHEN HE TELEPORTS...
...THEY HAVE TO WORK HARDER.

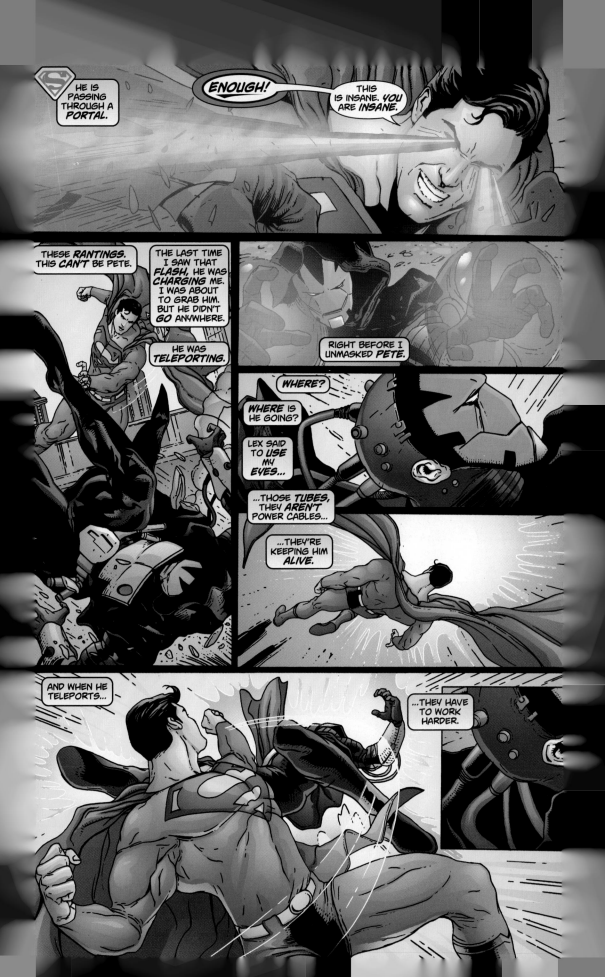

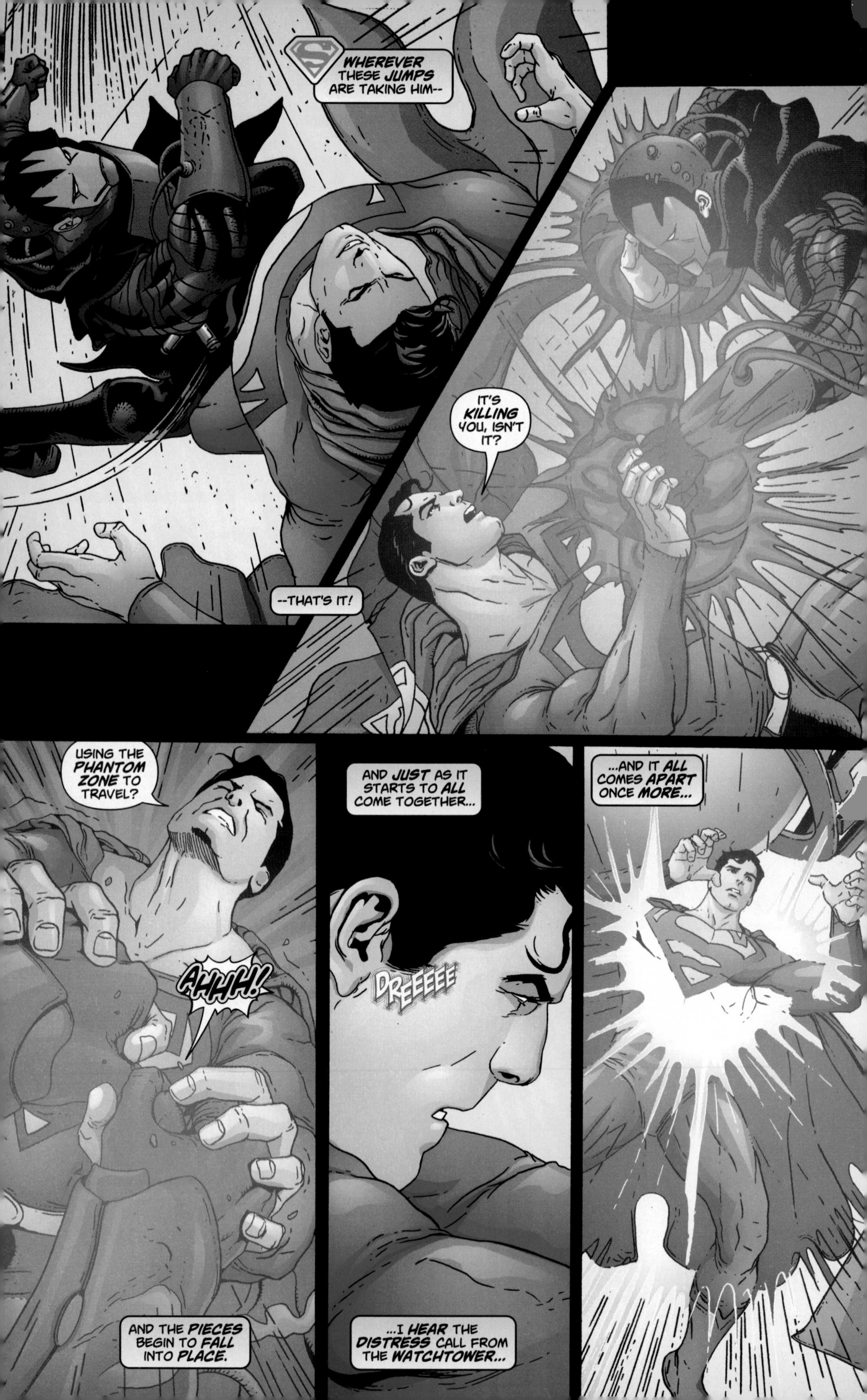
WHEREVER THESE JUMPS ARE TAKING HIM--
IT'S KILLING YOU, ISN'T IT?
--THAT'S IT!
USING THE PHANTOM ZONE TO TRAVEL?
AHHH!
AND THE PIECES BEGIN TO FALL INTO PLACE.
AND JUST AS IT STARTS TO ALL COME TOGETHER...
DREEEEE
...I HEAR THE DISTRESS CALL FROM THE WATCHTOWER...
...AND IT ALL COMES APART ONCE MORE...

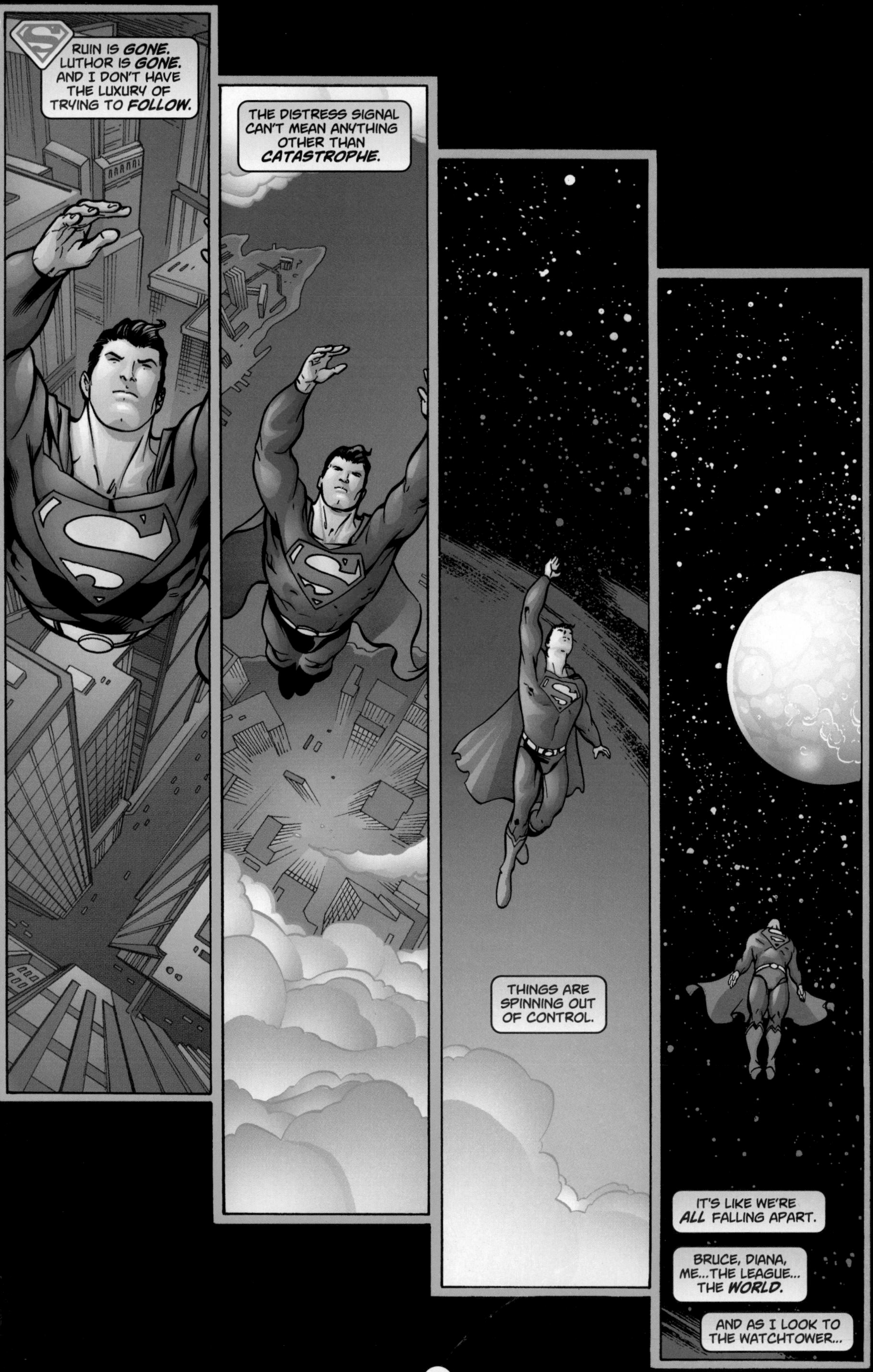
RUIN IS GONE. LUTHOR IS GONE. AND I DON'T HAVE THE LUXURY OF TRYING TO FOLLOW.
THE DISTRESS SIGNAL CAN'T MEAN ANYTHING OTHER THAN CATASTROPHE.
THINGS ARE SPINNING OUT OF CONTROL.
IT'S LIKE WE'RE ALL FALLING APART.
BRUCE, DIANA, ME...THE LEAGUE... THE WORLD.
AND AS I LOOK TO THE WATCHTOWER...

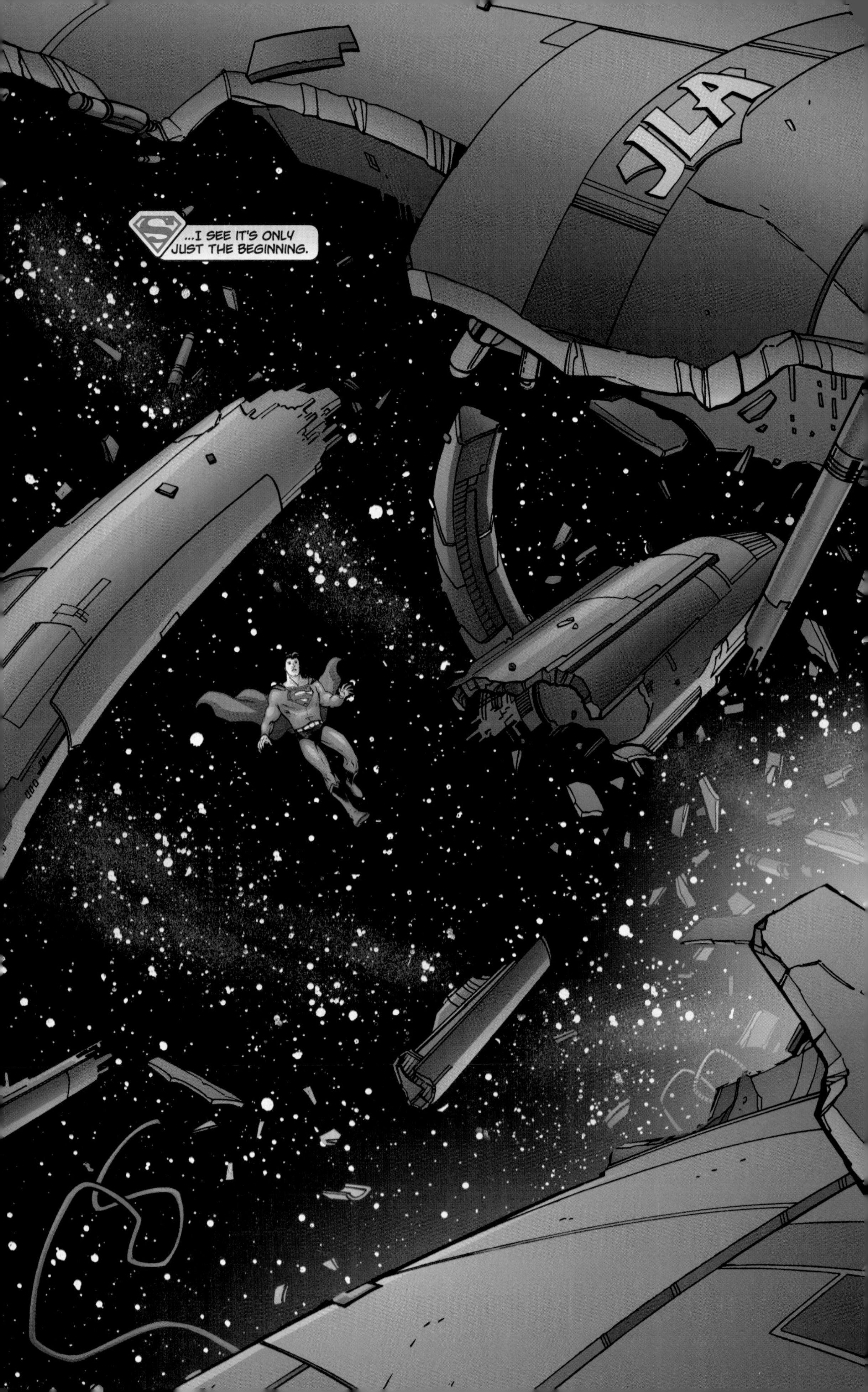
...I SEE IT'S ONLY JUST THE BEGINNING.
JLA

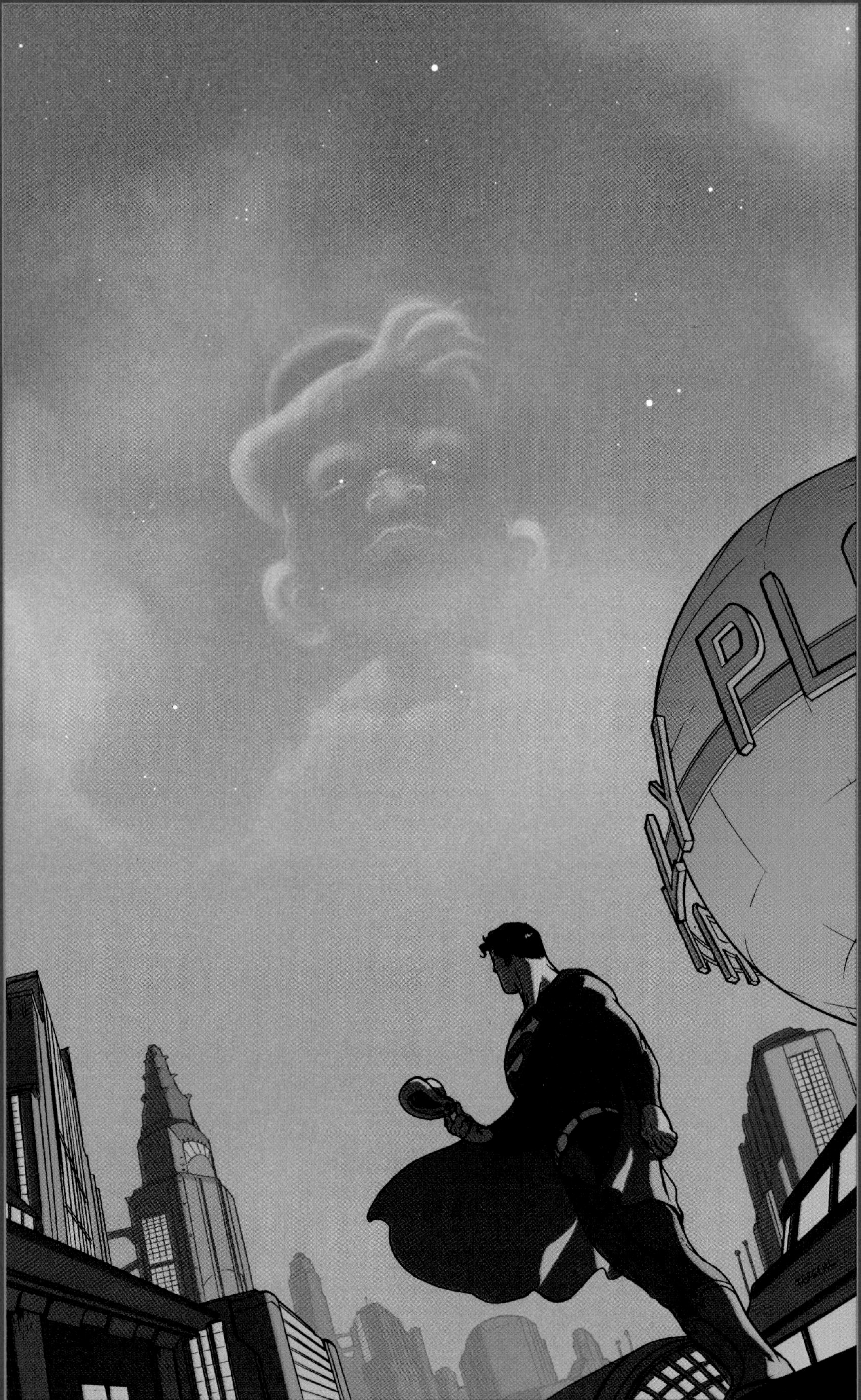

A distress call from the JLA's moon-based Watchtower was sent by the Martian Manhunter, who was attacked and taken just as the complex was destroyed. Superman, Batman and Wonder Woman, still harboring hard feelings toward one another, sifted through the wreckage in an attempt to understand what had happened. Upon hearing that the JLA's headquarters had been destroyed, the would-be galactic conqueror Mongul arrived to recover a mysterious artifact that belonged to his father.

The heroic trio battled Mongul amid the wreckage of the JLA's trophy room, and when he had nearly been defeated, Superman stopped the Amazon Princess from delivering what seemed to be a killing blow. As they argued over principles, Mongul escaped. Both Wonder Woman and Batman confronted the Man of Steel, claiming he had lost his way and had stopped being the example against which every other costumed champion was measured.

Shaken to his core, Superman returned to Metropolis, hung up his cape, and tried to sort things out. He realized, however, that there would be little time for reflection, given the Society's growing actions around the globe, the absence of the Martian Manhunter, and the dissolution of the Justice League. Yet he could not ignore his own more personal problems, such as the escaped Parasite Alison Allston and the continued threat from Ruin.

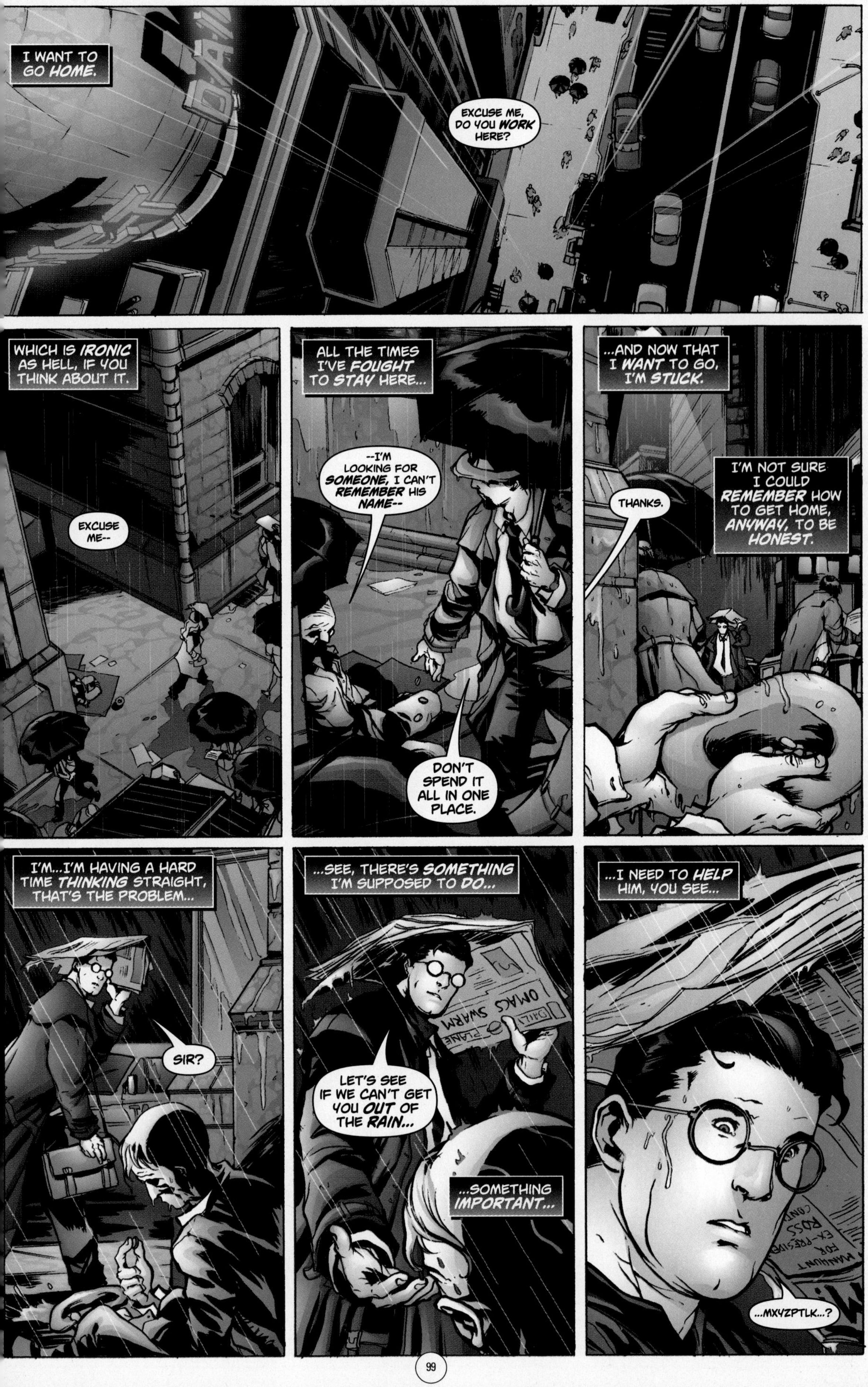
I WANT TO GO HOME.
EXCUSE ME, DO YOU WORK HERE?
WHICH IS IRONIC AS HELL, IF YOU THINK ABOUT IT.
EXCUSE ME--
ALL THE TIMES I'VE FOUGHT TO STAY HERE...
--I'M LOOKING FOR SOMEONE, I CAN'T REMEMBER HIS NAME--
DON'T SPEND IT ALL IN ONE PLACE.
...AND NOW THAT I WANT TO GO, I'M STUCK.
THANKS.
I'M NOT SURE I COULD REMEMBER HOW TO GET HOME, ANYWAY, TO BE HONEST.
I'M...I'M HAVING A HARD TIME THINKING STRAIGHT, THAT'S THE PROBLEM...
SIR?
...SEE, THERE'S SOMETHING I'M SUPPOSED TO DO...
LET'S SEE IF WE CAN'T GET YOU OUT OF THE RAIN...
...SOMETHING IMPORTANT...
...I NEED TO HELP HIM, YOU SEE...
...MXYZPTLK...?

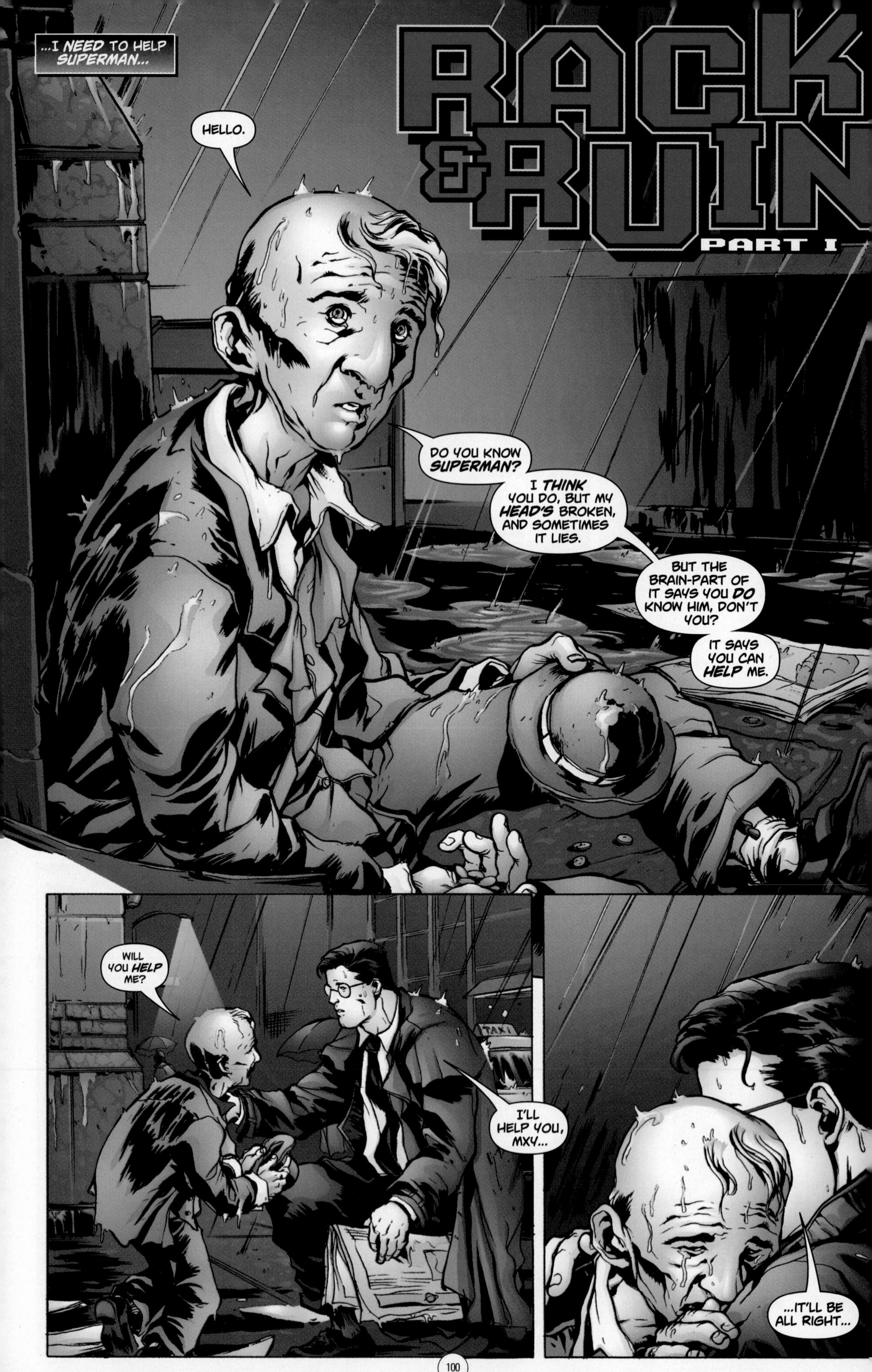
...I NEED TO HELP SUPERMAN...
RACK & RUIN
PART I
HELLO.
DO YOU KNOW SUPERMAN?
I THINK YOU DO, BUT MY HEAD'S BROKEN, AND SOMETIMES IT LIES.
BUT THE BRAIN-PART OF IT SAYS YOU DO KNOW HIM, DON'T YOU?
IT SAYS YOU CAN HELP ME.
WILL YOU HELP ME?
TAXI
I'LL HELP YOU, MXY...
...IT'LL BE ALL RIGHT...

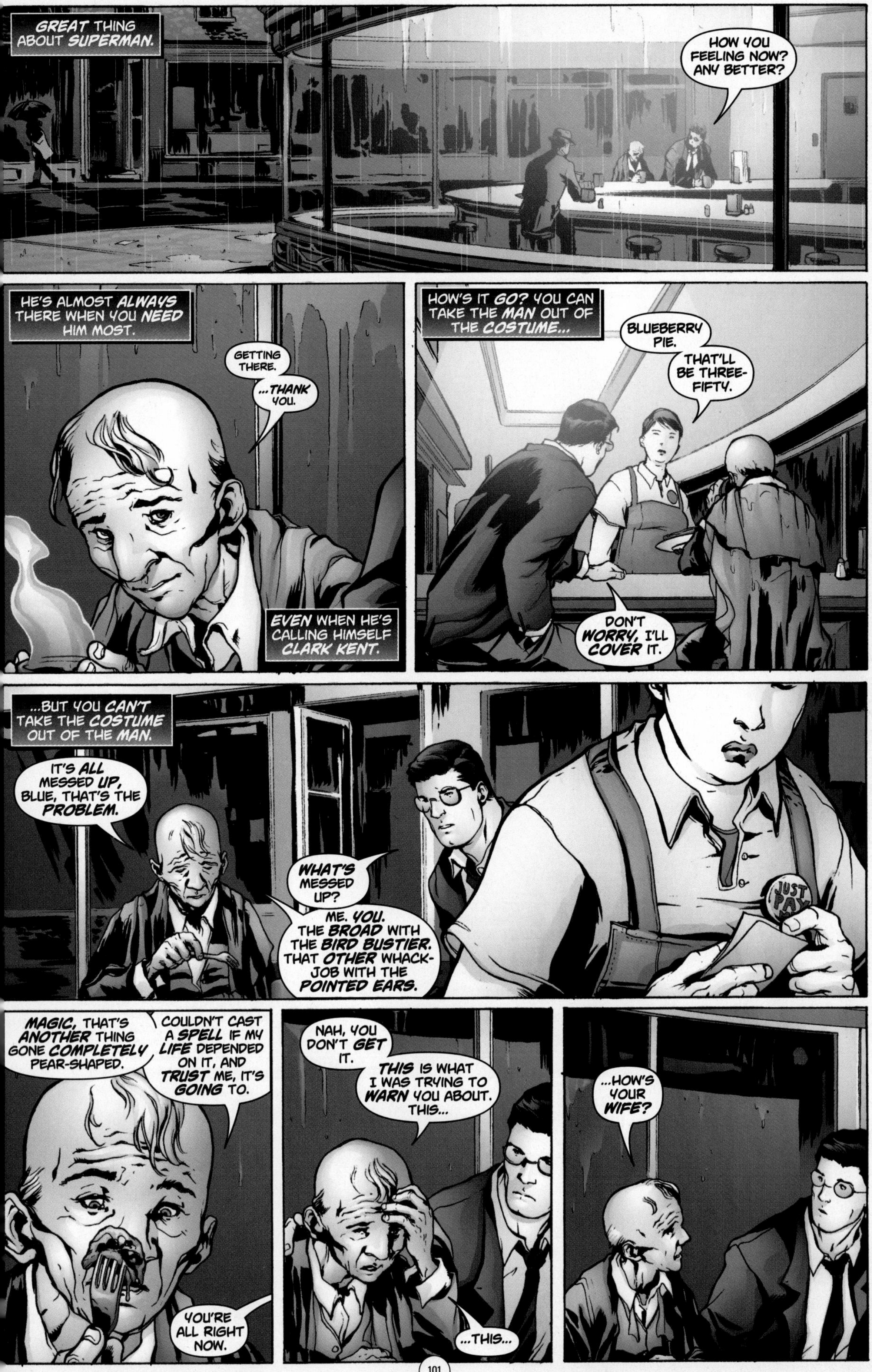
GREAT THING ABOUT SUPERMAN.
HOW YOU FEELING NOW? ANY BETTER?
HE'S ALMOST ALWAYS THERE WHEN YOU NEED HIM MOST.
GETTING THERE.
...THANK YOU.
EVEN WHEN HE'S CALLING HIMSELF CLARK KENT.
HOW'S IT GO? YOU CAN TAKE THE MAN OUT OF THE COSTUME...
BLUEBERRY PIE.
THAT'LL BE THREE-FIFTY.
DON'T WORRY, I'LL COVER IT.
...BUT YOU CAN'T TAKE THE COSTUME OUT OF THE MAN.
IT'S ALL MESSED UP, BLUE, THAT'S THE PROBLEM.
WHAT'S MESSED UP?
ME. YOU. THE BROAD WITH THE BIRD BUSTIER. THAT OTHER WHACK-JOB WITH THE POINTED EARS.
MAGIC, THAT'S ANOTHER THING GONE COMPLETELY PEAR-SHAPED.
COULDN'T CAST A SPELL IF MY LIFE DEPENDED ON IT, AND TRUST ME, IT'S GOING TO.
YOU'RE ALL RIGHT NOW.
NAH, YOU DON'T GET IT.
THIS IS WHAT I WAS TRYING TO WARN YOU ABOUT. THIS...
...THIS...
...HOW'S YOUR WIFE?

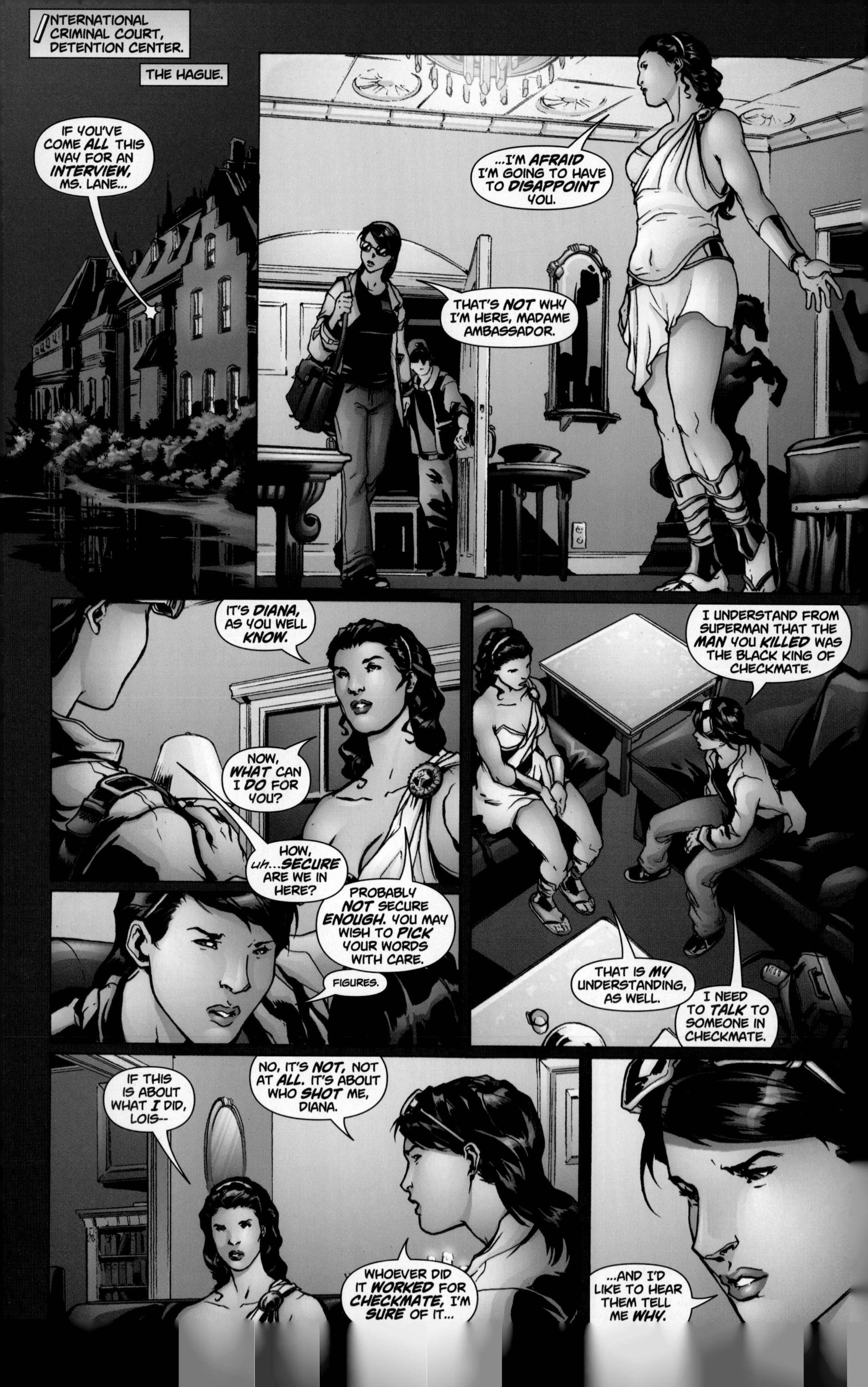
INTERNATIONAL CRIMINAL COURT, DETENTION CENTER.
THE HAGUE.
IF YOU'VE COME ALL THIS WAY FOR AN INTERVIEW, MS. LANE...
...I'M AFRAID I'M GOING TO HAVE TO DISAPPOINT YOU.
THAT'S NOT WHY I'M HERE, MADAME AMBASSADOR.
IT'S DIANA, AS YOU WELL KNOW.
NOW, WHAT CAN I DO FOR YOU?
HOW, uh...SECURE ARE WE IN HERE?
PROBABLY NOT SECURE ENOUGH. YOU MAY WISH TO PICK YOUR WORDS WITH CARE.
FIGURES.
I UNDERSTAND FROM SUPERMAN THAT THE MAN YOU KILLED WAS THE BLACK KING OF CHECKMATE.
THAT IS MY UNDERSTANDING, AS WELL.
I NEED TO TALK TO SOMEONE IN CHECKMATE.
IF THIS IS ABOUT WHAT I DID, LOIS--
NO, IT'S NOT, NOT AT ALL. IT'S ABOUT WHO SHOT ME, DIANA.
WHOEVER DID IT WORKED FOR CHECKMATE, I'M SURE OF IT...
...AND I'D LIKE TO HEAR THEM TELL ME WHY.

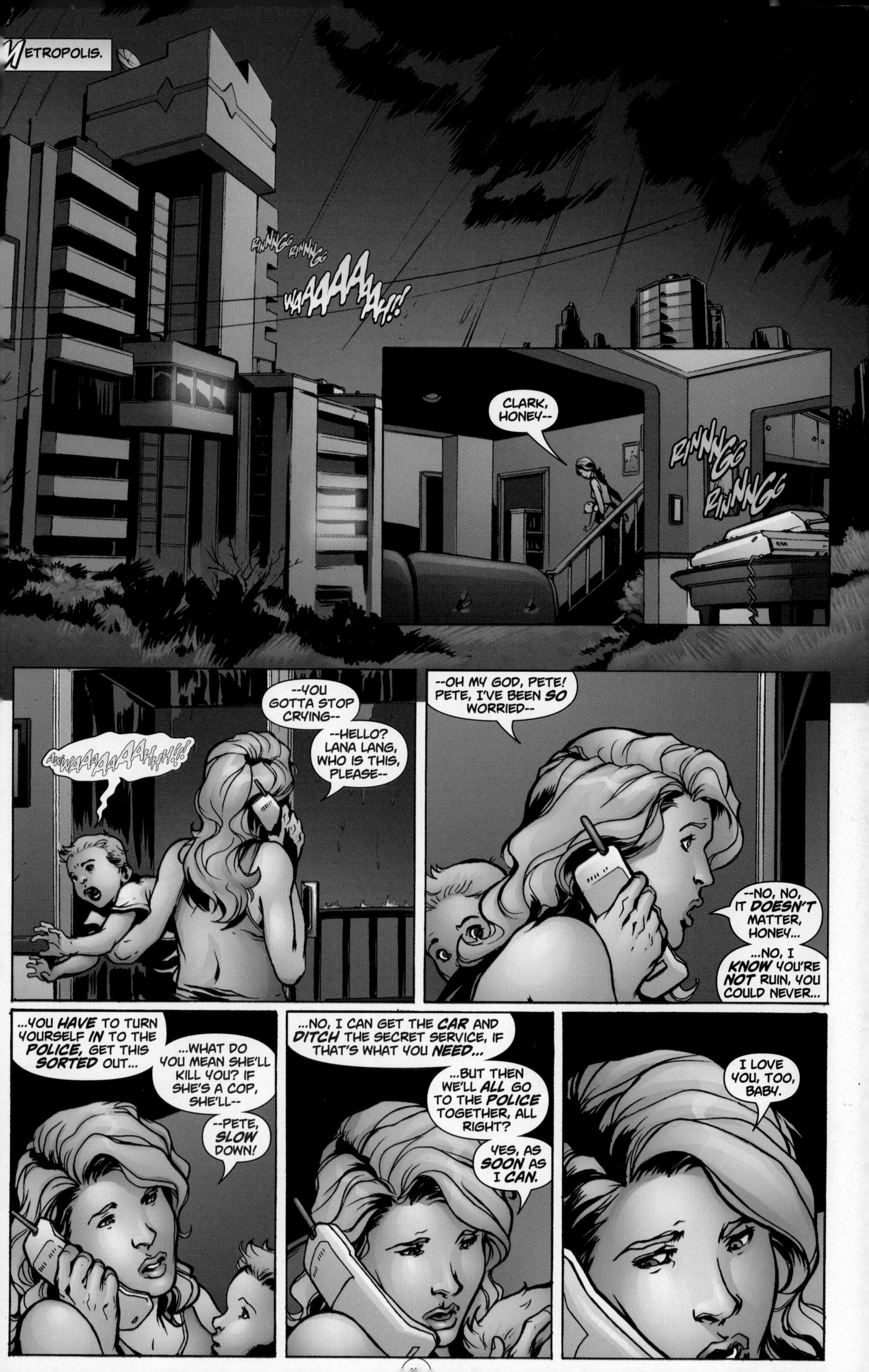
METROPOLIS.
RINNNGG RINNNGG
WAAAAAAAH!!
CLARK, HONEY--
RINNNGG RINNNGG
--YOU GOTTA STOP CRYING--
AWWAAAAAAAAHHHH!!!
--HELLO? LANA LANG, WHO IS THIS, PLEASE--
--OH MY GOD, PETE! PETE, I'VE BEEN SO WORRIED--
--NO, NO, IT DOESN'T MATTER, HONEY...
...NO, I KNOW YOU'RE NOT RUIN, YOU COULD NEVER...
...YOU HAVE TO TURN YOURSELF IN TO THE POLICE, GET THIS SORTED OUT...
...WHAT DO YOU MEAN SHE'LL KILL YOU? IF SHE'S A COP, SHE'LL--
--PETE, SLOW DOWN!
...NO, I CAN GET THE CAR AND DITCH THE SECRET SERVICE, IF THAT'S WHAT YOU NEED...
...BUT THEN WE'LL ALL GO TO THE POLICE TOGETHER, ALL RIGHT?
YES, AS SOON AS I CAN.
I LOVE YOU, TOO, BABY.

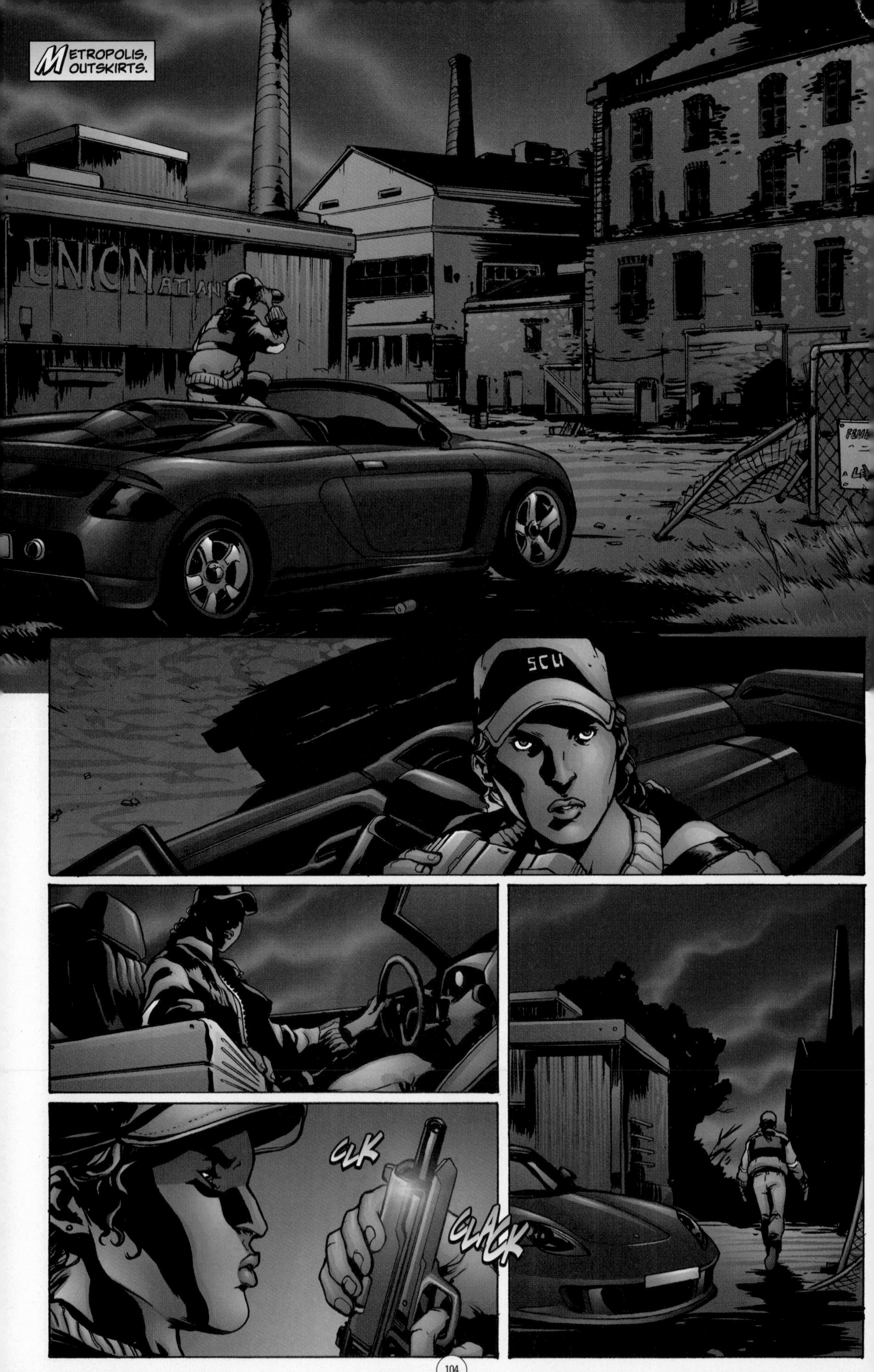

METROPOLIS, OUTSKIRTS.
UNION
ATLAN
SCU
CLK
CLACK

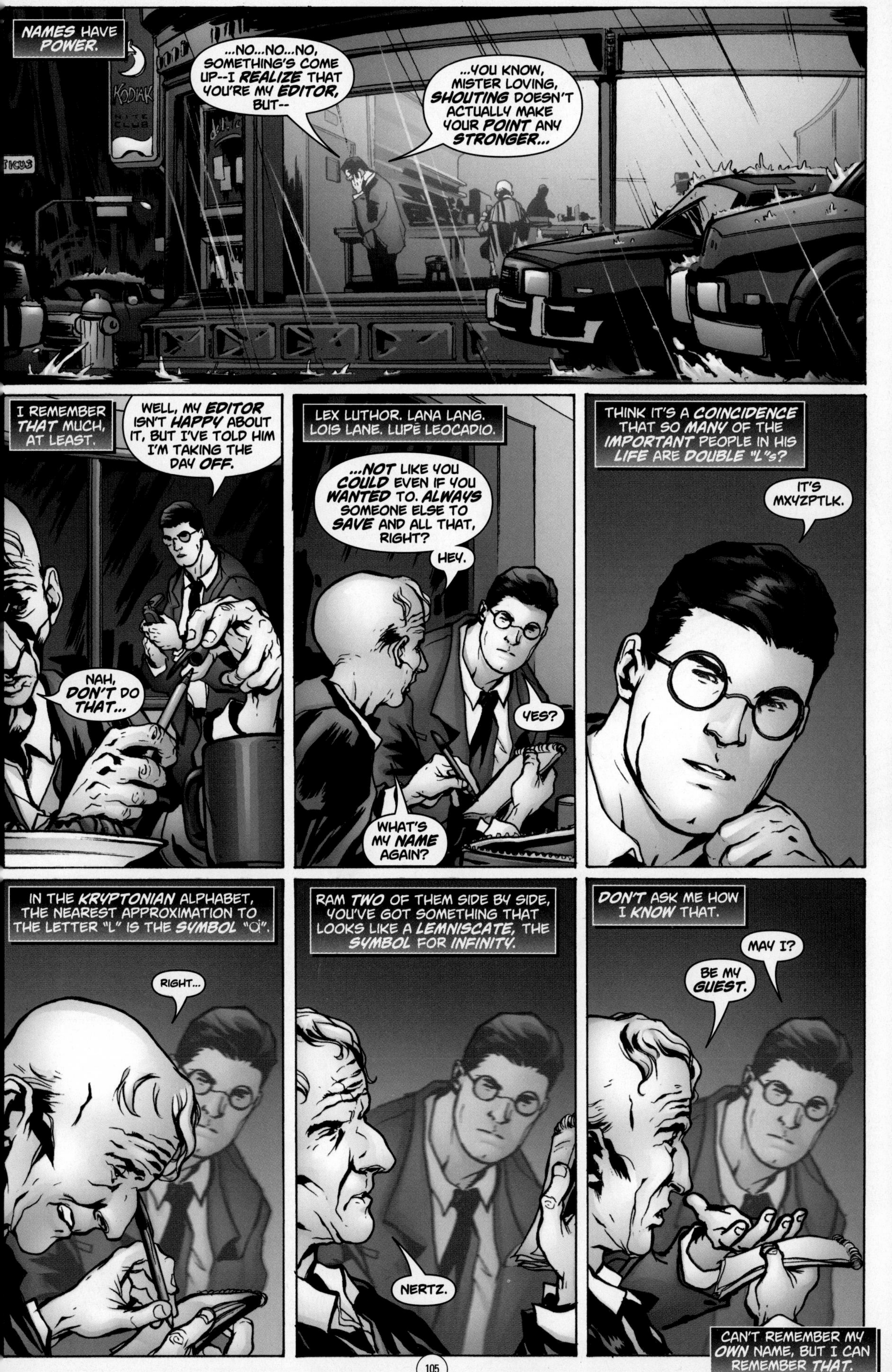
NAMES HAVE POWER.
...NO...NO...NO, SOMETHING'S COME UP--I REALIZE THAT YOU'RE MY EDITOR, BUT--
...YOU KNOW, MISTER LOVING, SHOUTING DOESN'T ACTUALLY MAKE YOUR POINT ANY STRONGER...
I REMEMBER THAT MUCH, AT LEAST.
WELL, MY EDITOR ISN'T HAPPY ABOUT IT, BUT I'VE TOLD HIM I'M TAKING THE DAY OFF.
NAH, DON'T DO THAT...
LEX LUTHOR. LANA LANG. LOIS LANE. LUPÉ LEOCADIO.
...NOT LIKE YOU COULD EVEN IF YOU WANTED TO. ALWAYS SOMEONE ELSE TO SAVE AND ALL THAT, RIGHT?
HEY.
YES?
WHAT'S MY NAME AGAIN?
THINK IT'S A COINCIDENCE THAT SO MANY OF THE IMPORTANT PEOPLE IN HIS LIFE ARE DOUBLE "L"s?
IT'S MXYZPTLK.
IN THE KRYPTONIAN ALPHABET, THE NEAREST APPROXIMATION TO THE LETTER "L" IS THE SYMBOL "ɑ̇".
RIGHT...
RAM TWO OF THEM SIDE BY SIDE, YOU'VE GOT SOMETHING THAT LOOKS LIKE A LEMNISCATE, THE SYMBOL FOR INFINITY.
NERTZ.
DON'T ASK ME HOW I KNOW THAT.
MAY I?
BE MY GUEST.
CAN'T REMEMBER MY OWN NAME, BUT I CAN REMEMBER THAT.

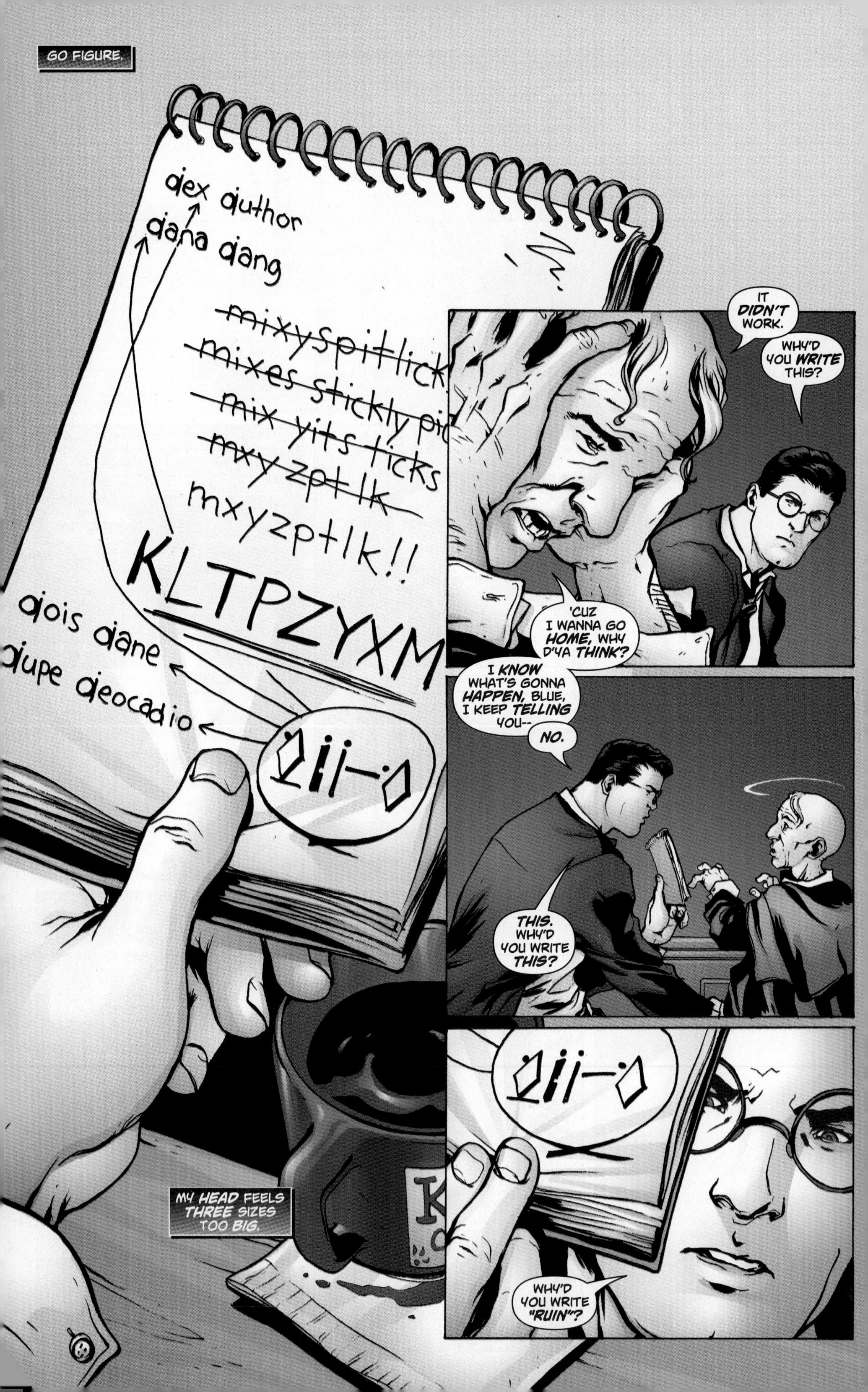
GO FIGURE.
alex authur
dana dang
mixyspitlick
mixes stickly pic
mix yits ticks
mxyzptlk
mxyzptlk
mxyzptlk!!
KLTPZYXM
alois dane
alupe aleocadio
IT DIDN'T WORK.
WHY'D YOU WRITE THIS?
'CUZ I WANNA GO HOME, WHY D'YA THINK?
I KNOW WHAT'S GONNA HAPPEN, BLUE, I KEEP TELLING YOU--
NO.
THIS. WHY'D YOU WRITE THIS?
MY HEAD FEELS THREE SIZES TOO BIG.
WHY'D YOU WRITE "RUIN"?

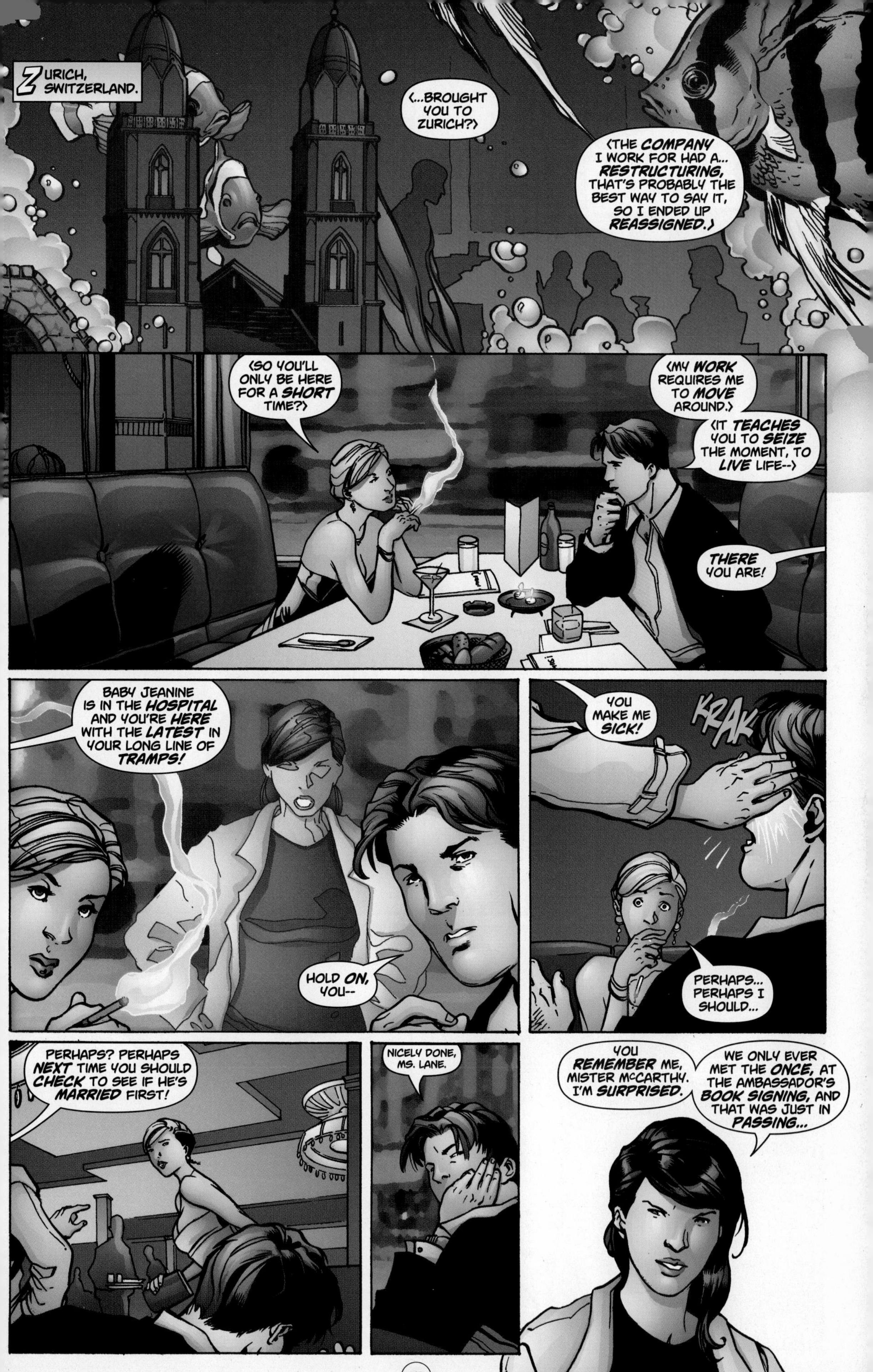
ZURICH, SWITZERLAND.
‹...BROUGHT YOU TO ZURICH?›
‹THE COMPANY I WORK FOR HAD A... RESTRUCTURING, THAT'S PROBABLY THE BEST WAY TO SAY IT, SO I ENDED UP REASSIGNED.›
‹SO YOU'LL ONLY BE HERE FOR A SHORT TIME?›
‹MY WORK REQUIRES ME TO MOVE AROUND.›
‹IT TEACHES YOU TO SEIZE THE MOMENT, TO LIVE LIFE--›
THERE YOU ARE!
BABY JEANINE IS IN THE HOSPITAL AND YOU'RE HERE WITH THE LATEST IN YOUR LONG LINE OF TRAMPS!
HOLD ON, YOU--
YOU MAKE ME SICK!
KRAK
PERHAPS... PERHAPS I SHOULD...
PERHAPS? PERHAPS NEXT TIME YOU SHOULD CHECK TO SEE IF HE'S MARRIED FIRST!
NICELY DONE, MS. LANE.
YOU REMEMBER ME, MISTER McCARTHY. I'M SURPRISED.
WE ONLY EVER MET THE ONCE, AT THE AMBASSADOR'S BOOK SIGNING, AND THAT WAS JUST IN PASSING...

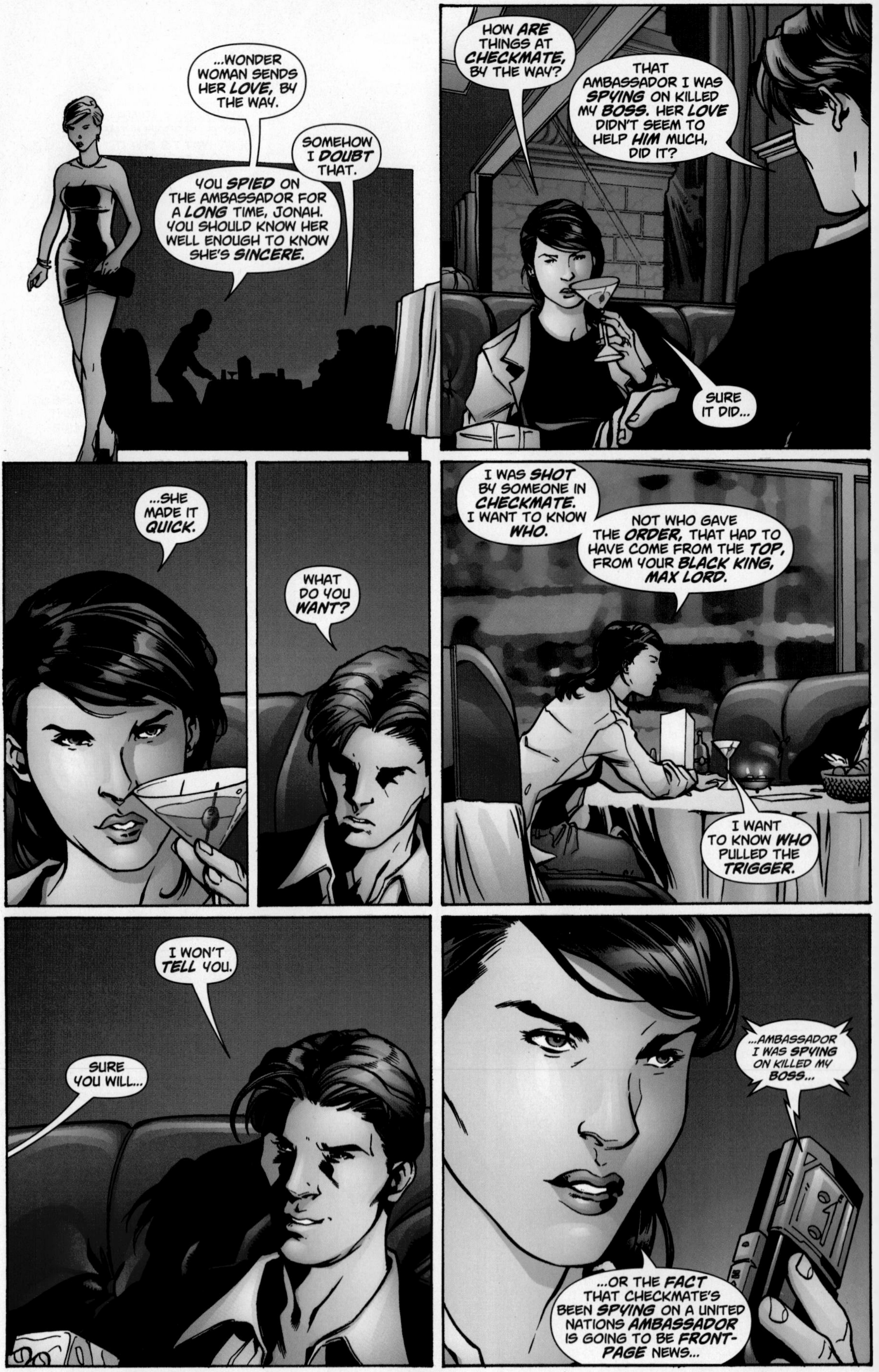
...WONDER WOMAN SENDS HER LOVE, BY THE WAY.
YOU SPIED ON THE AMBASSADOR FOR A LONG TIME, JONAH. YOU SHOULD KNOW HER WELL ENOUGH TO KNOW SHE'S SINCERE.
SOMEHOW I DOUBT THAT.
HOW ARE THINGS AT CHECKMATE, BY THE WAY?
THAT AMBASSADOR I WAS SPYING ON KILLED MY BOSS. HER LOVE DIDN'T SEEM TO HELP HIM MUCH, DID IT?
SURE IT DID...
...SHE MADE IT QUICK.
WHAT DO YOU WANT?
I WAS SHOT BY SOMEONE IN CHECKMATE. I WANT TO KNOW WHO.
NOT WHO GAVE THE ORDER, THAT HAD TO HAVE COME FROM THE TOP, FROM YOUR BLACK KING, MAX LORD.
I WANT TO KNOW WHO PULLED THE TRIGGER.
I WON'T TELL YOU.
SURE YOU WILL...
...AMBASSADOR I WAS SPYING ON KILLED MY BOSS...
...OR THE FACT THAT CHECKMATE'S BEEN SPYING ON A UNITED NATIONS AMBASSADOR IS GOING TO BE FRONT-PAGE NEWS...

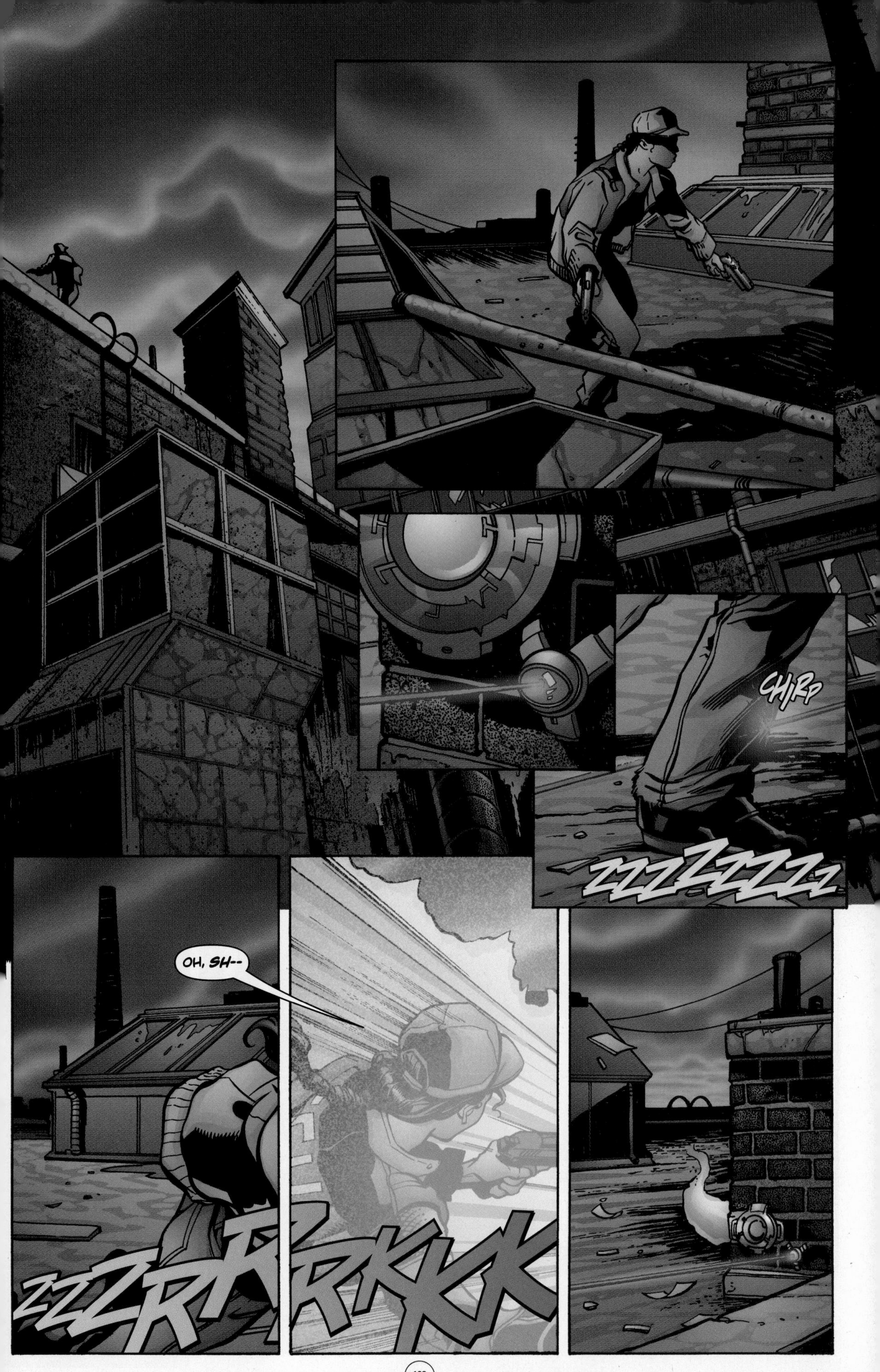
CHIRP
ZZZZZZZZz
OH, SH--
ZZZZRRRRKKK

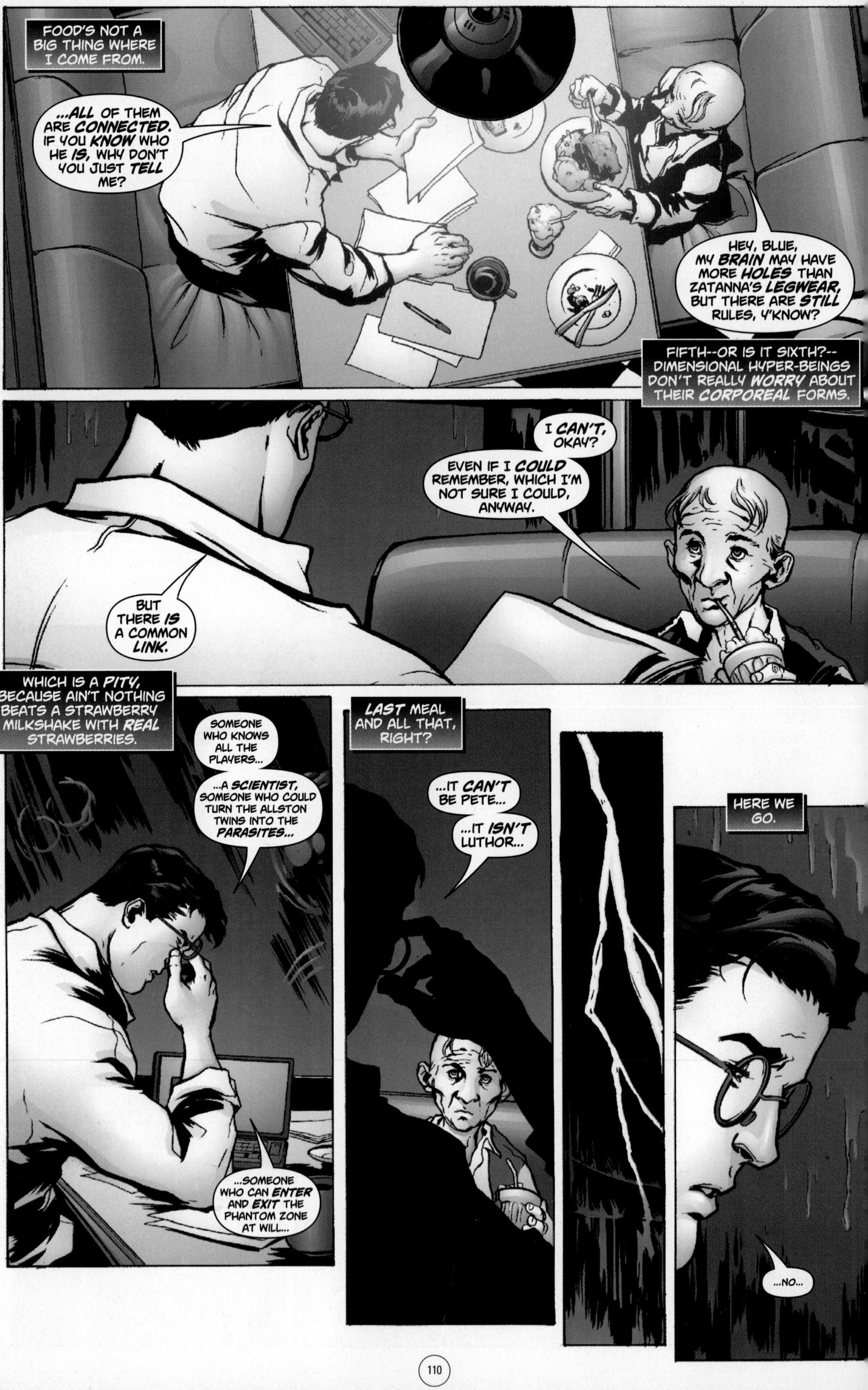

FOOD'S NOT A BIG THING WHERE I COME FROM.
...ALL OF THEM ARE CONNECTED. IF YOU KNOW WHO HE IS, WHY DON'T YOU JUST TELL ME?
HEY, BLUE, MY BRAIN MAY HAVE MORE HOLES THAN ZATANNA'S LEGWEAR, BUT THERE ARE STILL RULES, Y'KNOW?
FIFTH--OR IS IT SIXTH?--DIMENSIONAL HYPER-BEINGS DON'T REALLY WORRY ABOUT THEIR CORPOREAL FORMS.
I CAN'T, OKAY?
EVEN IF I COULD REMEMBER, WHICH I'M NOT SURE I COULD, ANYWAY.
BUT THERE IS A COMMON LINK.
WHICH IS A PITY, BECAUSE AIN'T NOTHING BEATS A STRAWBERRY MILKSHAKE WITH REAL STRAWBERRIES.
SOMEONE WHO KNOWS ALL THE PLAYERS...
...A SCIENTIST, SOMEONE WHO COULD TURN THE ALLSTON TWINS INTO THE PARASITES...
...SOMEONE WHO CAN ENTER AND EXIT THE PHANTOM ZONE AT WILL...
LAST MEAL AND ALL THAT, RIGHT?
...IT CAN'T BE PETE...
...IT ISN'T LUTHOR...
HERE WE GO.
...NO...

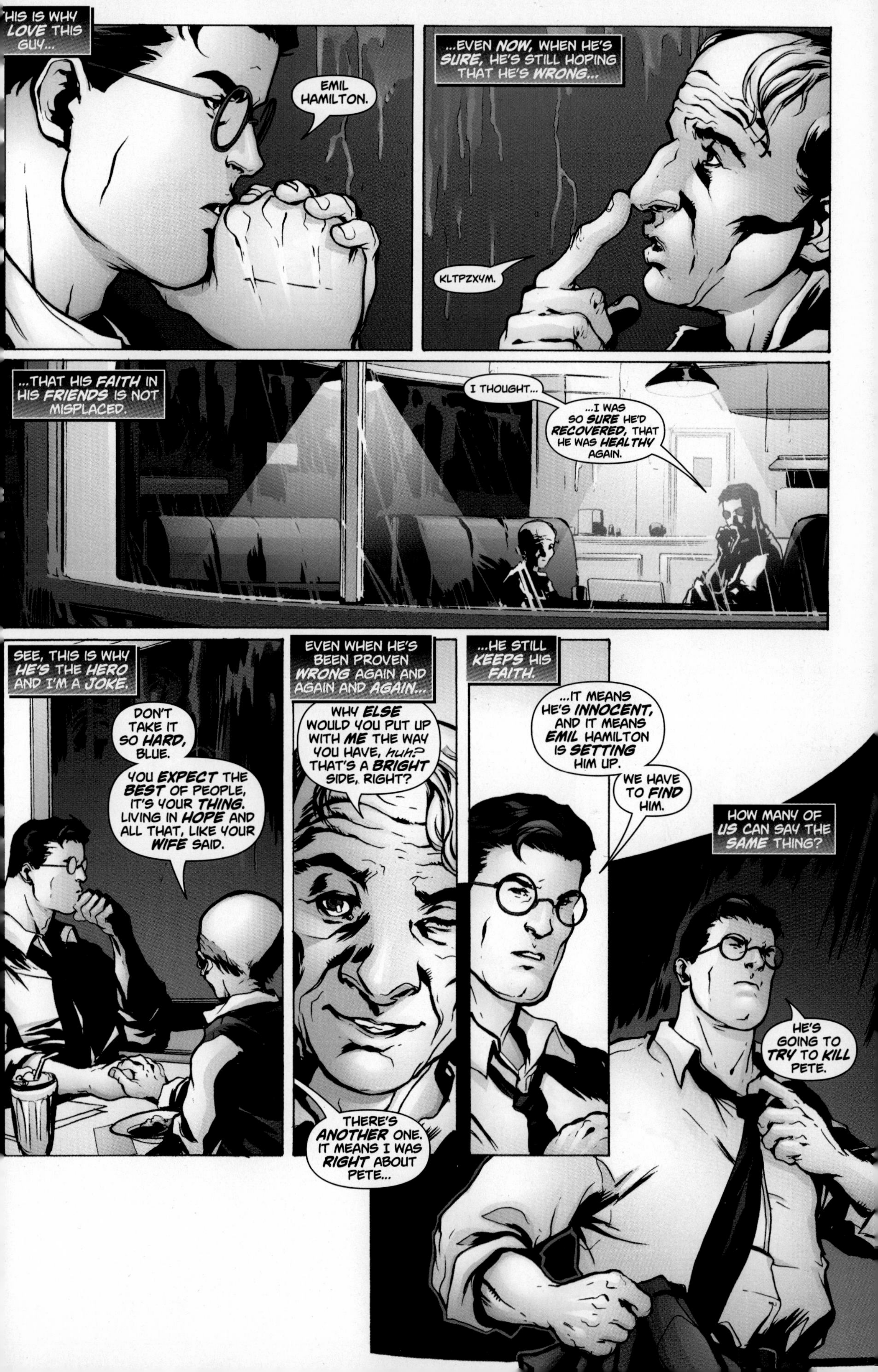

HIS IS WHY LOVE THIS GUY...
EMIL HAMILTON.
...EVEN NOW, WHEN HE'S SURE, HE'S STILL HOPING THAT HE'S WRONG...
KLTPZXYM.
...THAT HIS FAITH IN HIS FRIENDS IS NOT MISPLACED.
I THOUGHT...
...I WAS SO SURE HE'D RECOVERED, THAT HE WAS HEALTHY AGAIN.
SEE, THIS IS WHY HE'S THE HERO AND I'M A JOKE.
DON'T TAKE IT SO HARD, BLUE.
YOU EXPECT THE BEST OF PEOPLE, IT'S YOUR THING. LIVING IN HOPE AND ALL THAT, LIKE YOUR WIFE SAID.
EVEN WHEN HE'S BEEN PROVEN WRONG AGAIN AND AGAIN AND AGAIN...
WHY ELSE WOULD YOU PUT UP WITH ME THE WAY YOU HAVE, huh? THAT'S A BRIGHT SIDE, RIGHT?
THERE'S ANOTHER ONE. IT MEANS I WAS RIGHT ABOUT PETE...
...HE STILL KEEPS HIS FAITH.
...IT MEANS HE'S INNOCENT, AND IT MEANS EMIL HAMILTON IS SETTING HIM UP.
WE HAVE TO FIND HIM.
HOW MANY OF US CAN SAY THE SAME THING?
HE'S GOING TO TRY TO KILL PETE.

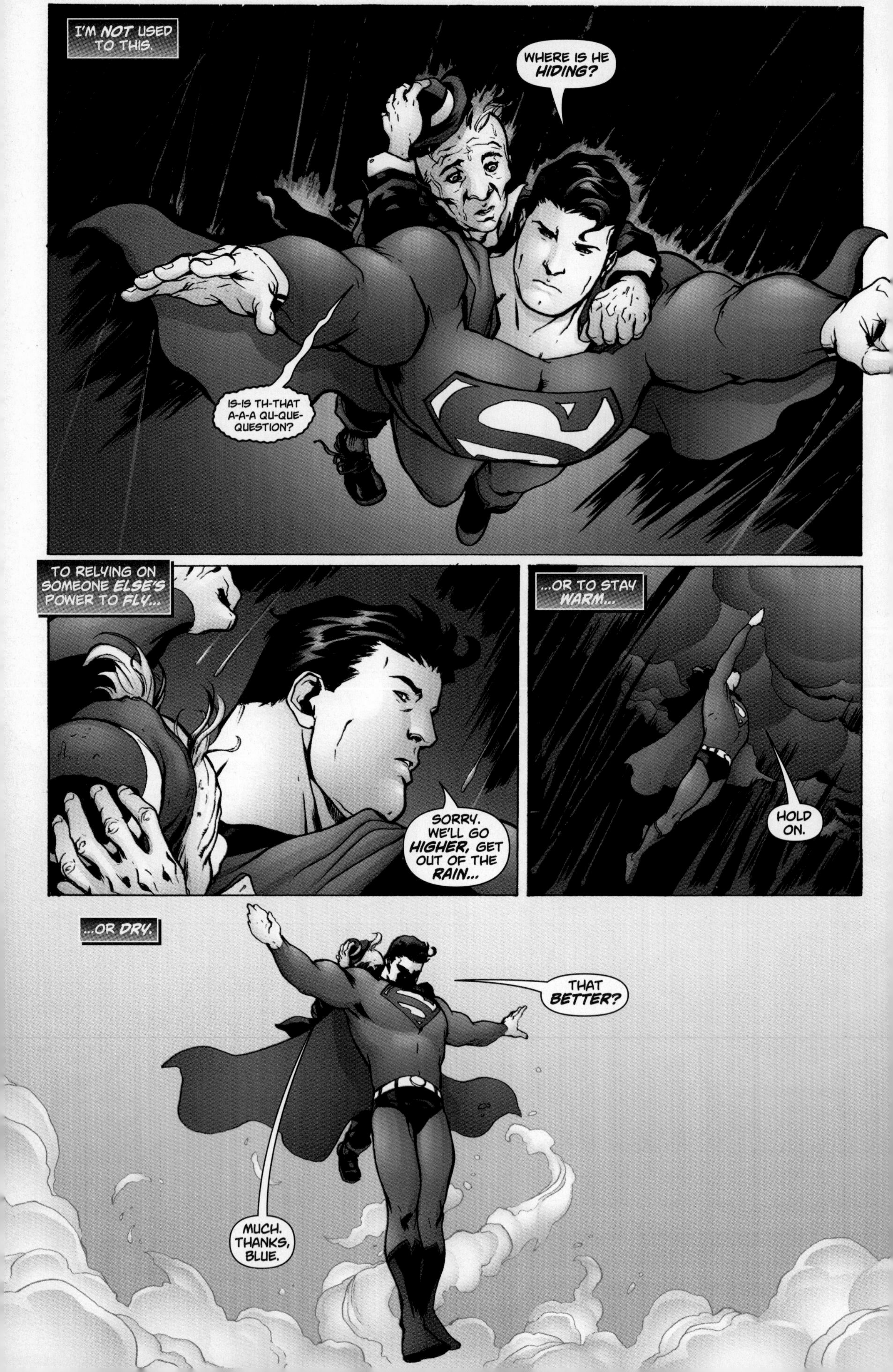
I'M NOT USED TO THIS.
WHERE IS HE HIDING?
IS-IS TH-THAT A-A-A QU-QUE-QUESTION?
TO RELYING ON SOMEONE ELSE'S POWER TO FLY...
SORRY. WE'LL GO HIGHER, GET OUT OF THE RAIN...
...OR TO STAY WARM...
HOLD ON.
...OR DRY.
THAT BETTER?
MUCH. THANKS, BLUE.

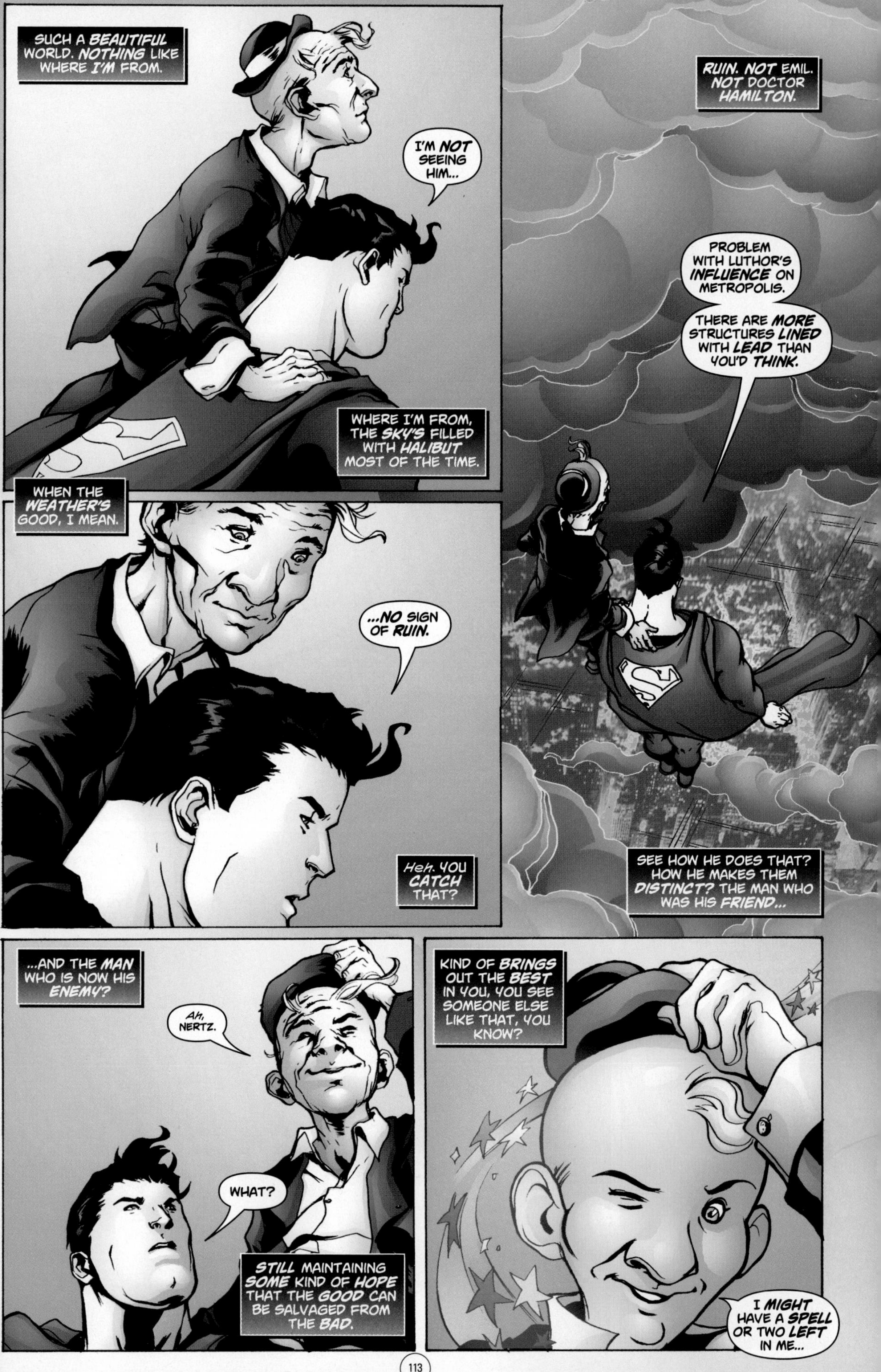
SUCH A BEAUTIFUL WORLD. NOTHING LIKE WHERE I'M FROM.
I'M NOT SEEING HIM...
WHERE I'M FROM, THE SKY'S FILLED WITH HALIBUT MOST OF THE TIME.
RUIN. NOT EMIL. NOT DOCTOR HAMILTON.
PROBLEM WITH LUTHOR'S INFLUENCE ON METROPOLIS.
THERE ARE MORE STRUCTURES LINED WITH LEAD THAN YOU'D THINK.
WHEN THE WEATHER'S GOOD, I MEAN.
...NO SIGN OF RUIN.
Heh. YOU CATCH THAT?
SEE HOW HE DOES THAT? HOW HE MAKES THEM DISTINCT? THE MAN WHO WAS HIS FRIEND...
...AND THE MAN WHO IS NOW HIS ENEMY?
Ah, NERTZ.
WHAT?
STILL MAINTAINING SOME KIND OF HOPE THAT THE GOOD CAN BE SALVAGED FROM THE BAD.
KIND OF BRINGS OUT THE BEST IN YOU, YOU SEE SOMEONE ELSE LIKE THAT, YOU KNOW?
I MIGHT HAVE A SPELL OR TWO LEFT IN ME...

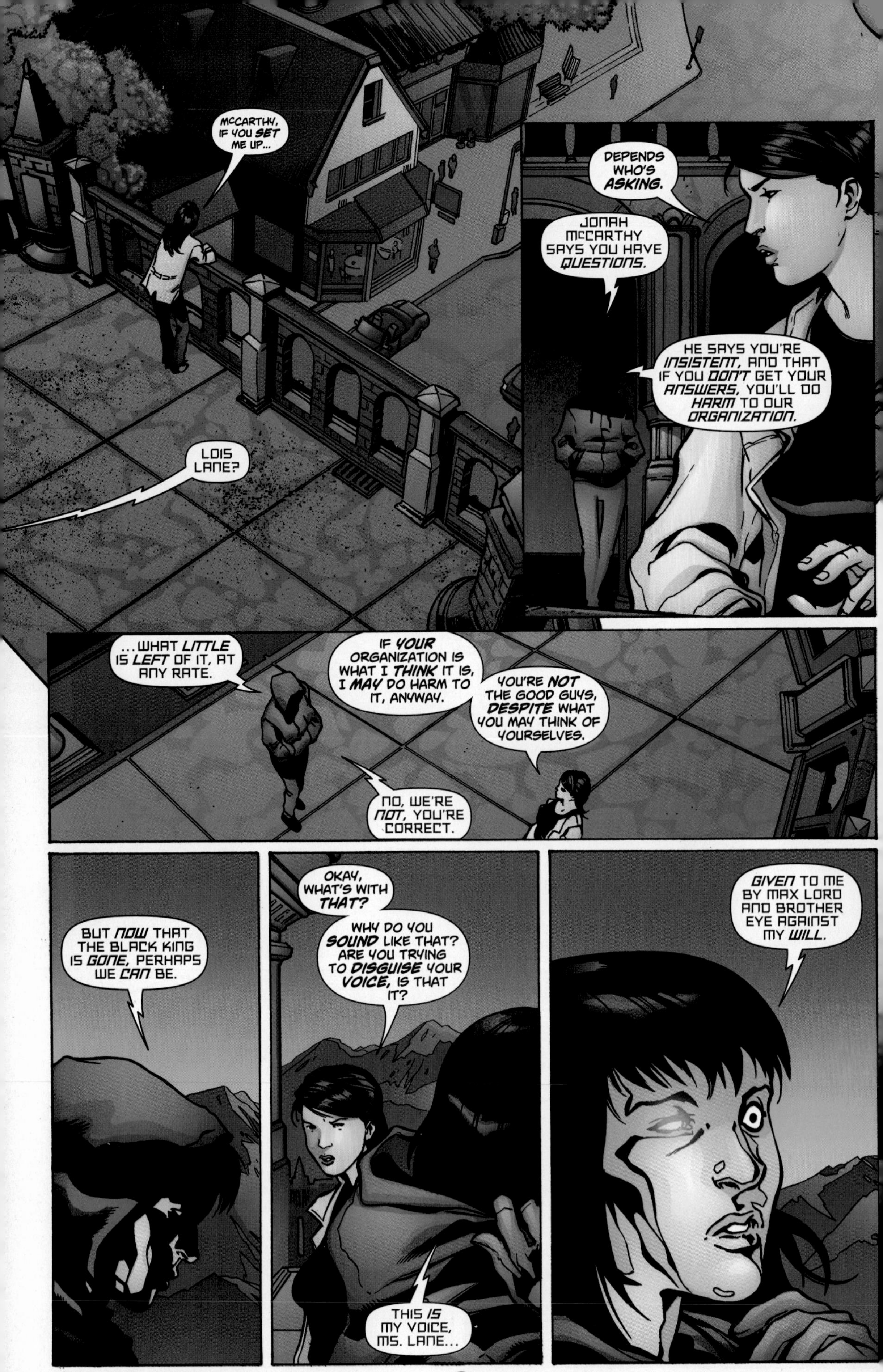
McCARTHY, IF YOU SET ME UP...
LOIS LANE?
DEPENDS WHO'S ASKING.
JONAH McCARTHY SAYS YOU HAVE QUESTIONS.
HE SAYS YOU'RE INSISTENT, AND THAT IF YOU DON'T GET YOUR ANSWERS, YOU'LL DO HARM TO OUR ORGANIZATION.
...WHAT LITTLE IS LEFT OF IT, AT ANY RATE.
IF YOUR ORGANIZATION IS WHAT I THINK IT IS, I MAY DO HARM TO IT, ANYWAY.
YOU'RE NOT THE GOOD GUYS, DESPITE WHAT YOU MAY THINK OF YOURSELVES.
NO, WE'RE NOT, YOU'RE CORRECT.
BUT NOW THAT THE BLACK KING IS GONE, PERHAPS WE CAN BE.
OKAY, WHAT'S WITH THAT?
WHY DO YOU SOUND LIKE THAT? ARE YOU TRYING TO DISGUISE YOUR VOICE, IS THAT IT?
THIS IS MY VOICE, MS. LANE...
GIVEN TO ME BY MAX LORD AND BROTHER EYE AGAINST MY WILL.

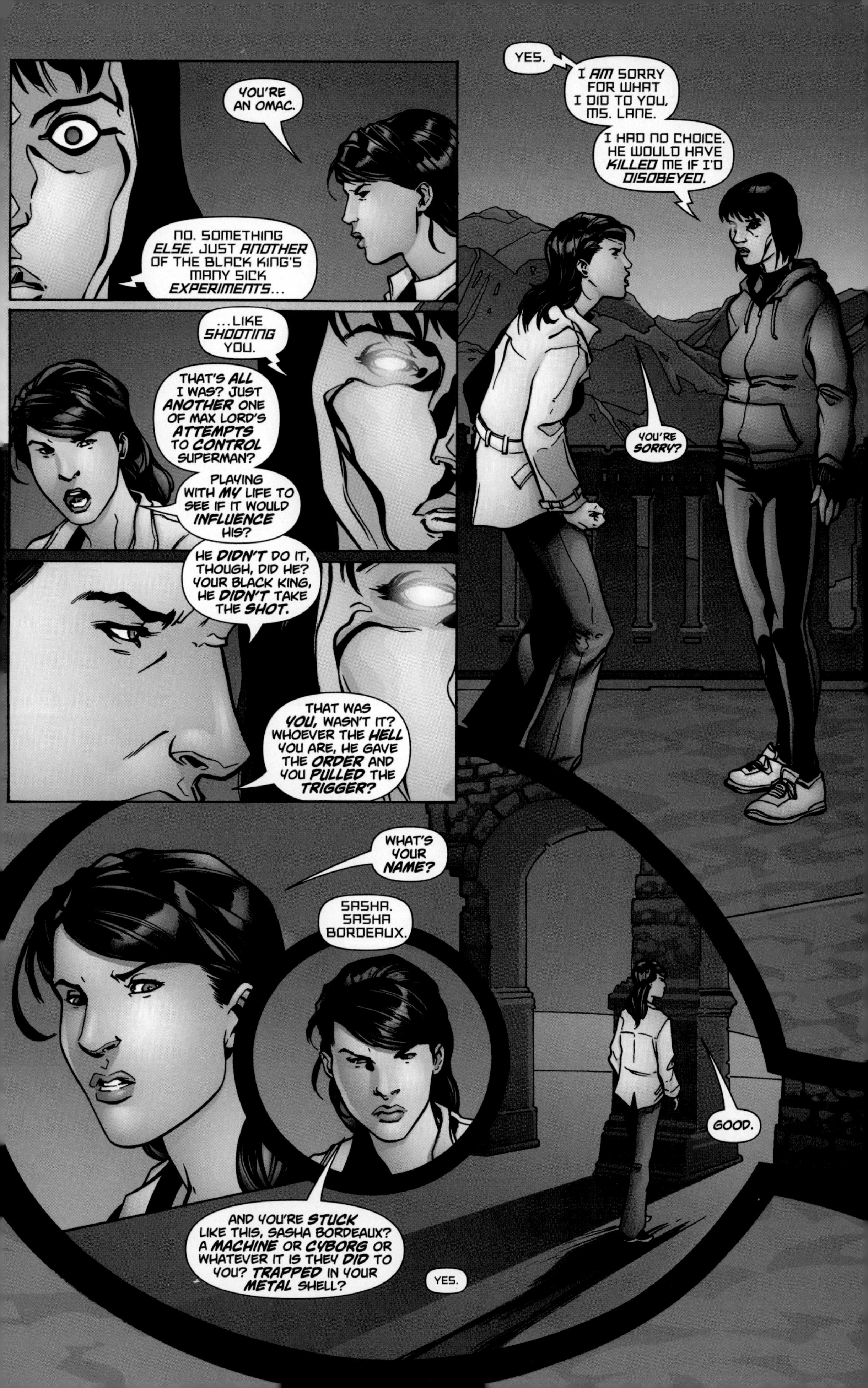
YOU'RE AN OMAC.
NO. SOMETHING ELSE. JUST ANOTHER OF THE BLACK KING'S MANY SICK EXPERIMENTS...
...LIKE SHOOTING YOU.
THAT'S ALL I WAS? JUST ANOTHER ONE OF MAX LORD'S ATTEMPTS TO CONTROL SUPERMAN?
PLAYING WITH MY LIFE TO SEE IF IT WOULD INFLUENCE HIS?
HE DIDN'T DO IT, THOUGH, DID HE? YOUR BLACK KING, HE DIDN'T TAKE THE SHOT.
THAT WAS YOU, WASN'T IT? WHOEVER THE HELL YOU ARE, HE GAVE THE ORDER AND YOU PULLED THE TRIGGER?
YES.
I AM SORRY FOR WHAT I DID TO YOU, MS. LANE.
I HAD NO CHOICE. HE WOULD HAVE KILLED ME IF I'D DISOBEYED.
YOU'RE SORRY?
WHAT'S YOUR NAME?
SASHA. SASHA BORDEAUX.
AND YOU'RE STUCK LIKE THIS, SASHA BORDEAUX? A MACHINE OR CYBORG OR WHATEVER IT IS THEY DID TO YOU? TRAPPED IN YOUR METAL SHELL?
YES.
GOOD.

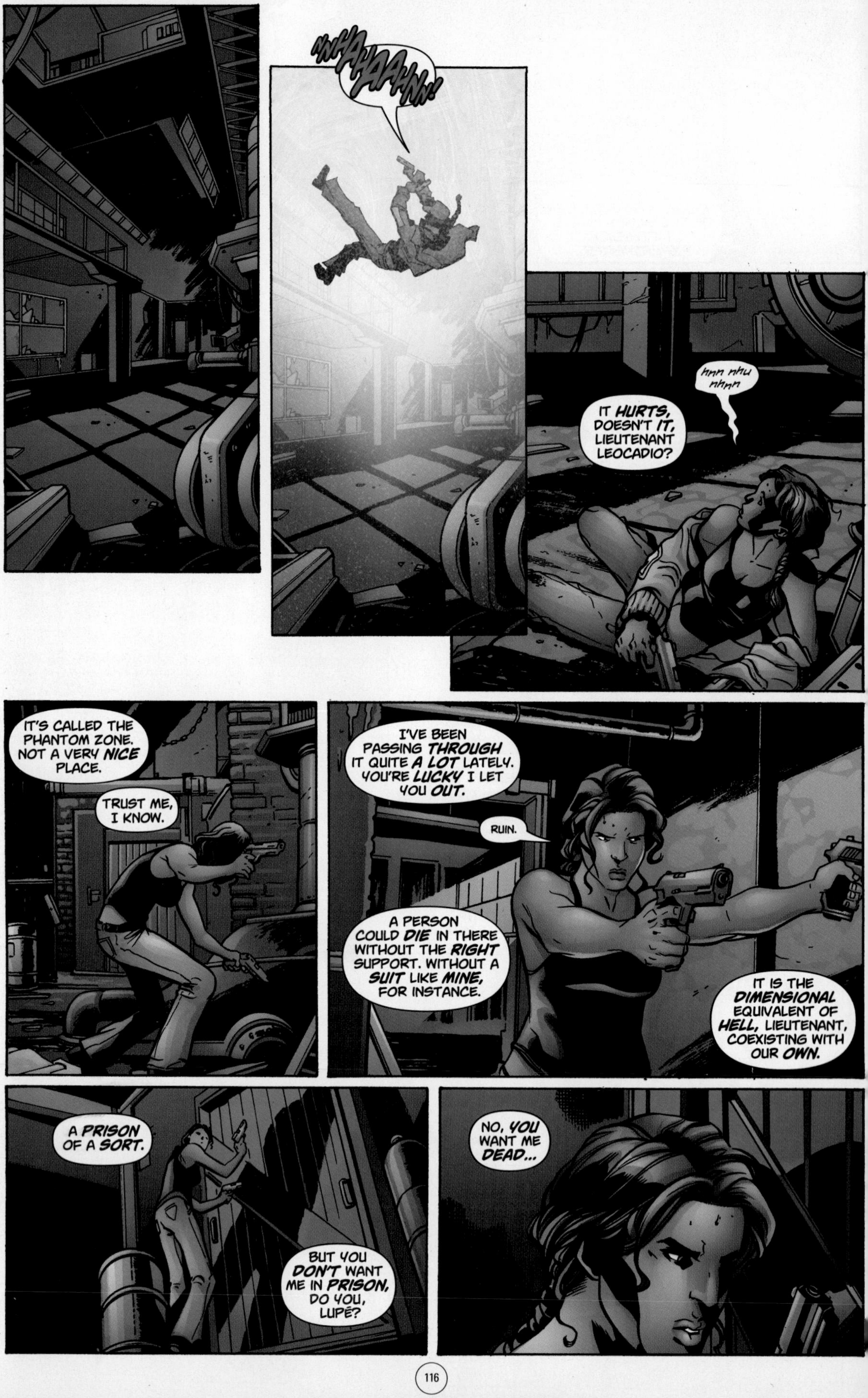
NNHAAAAAHNN!
IT HURTS, DOESN'T IT, LIEUTENANT LEOCADIO?
hnn nhu nhnn
IT'S CALLED THE PHANTOM ZONE. NOT A VERY NICE PLACE.
TRUST ME, I KNOW.
I'VE BEEN PASSING THROUGH IT QUITE A LOT LATELY. YOU'RE LUCKY I LET YOU OUT.
RUIN.
A PERSON COULD DIE IN THERE WITHOUT THE RIGHT SUPPORT. WITHOUT A SUIT LIKE MINE, FOR INSTANCE.
IT IS THE DIMENSIONAL EQUIVALENT OF HELL, LIEUTENANT, COEXISTING WITH OUR OWN.
A PRISON OF A SORT.
BUT YOU DON'T WANT ME IN PRISON, DO YOU, LUPÉ?
NO, YOU WANT ME DEAD...

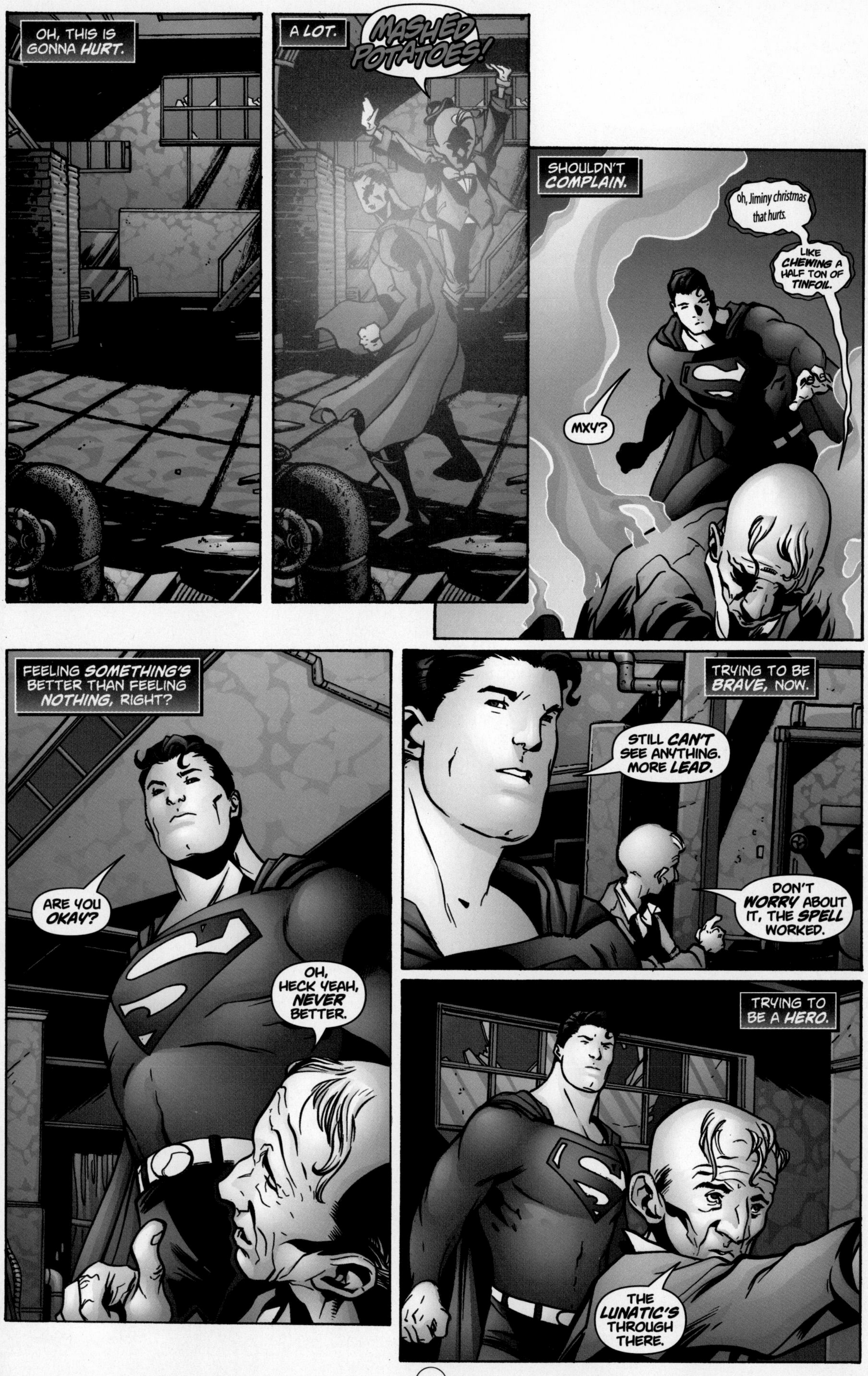
OH, THIS IS GONNA HURT.
A LOT.
MASHED POTATOES!
SHOULDN'T COMPLAIN.
Oh, Jiminy christmas that hurts.
LIKE CHEWING A HALF TON OF TINFOIL.
MXY?
FEELING SOMETHING'S BETTER THAN FEELING NOTHING, RIGHT?
ARE YOU OKAY?
OH, HECK YEAH, NEVER BETTER.
TRYING TO BE BRAVE, NOW.
STILL CAN'T SEE ANYTHING. MORE LEAD.
DON'T WORRY ABOUT IT, THE SPELL WORKED.
TRYING TO BE A HERO.
THE LUNATIC'S THROUGH THERE.

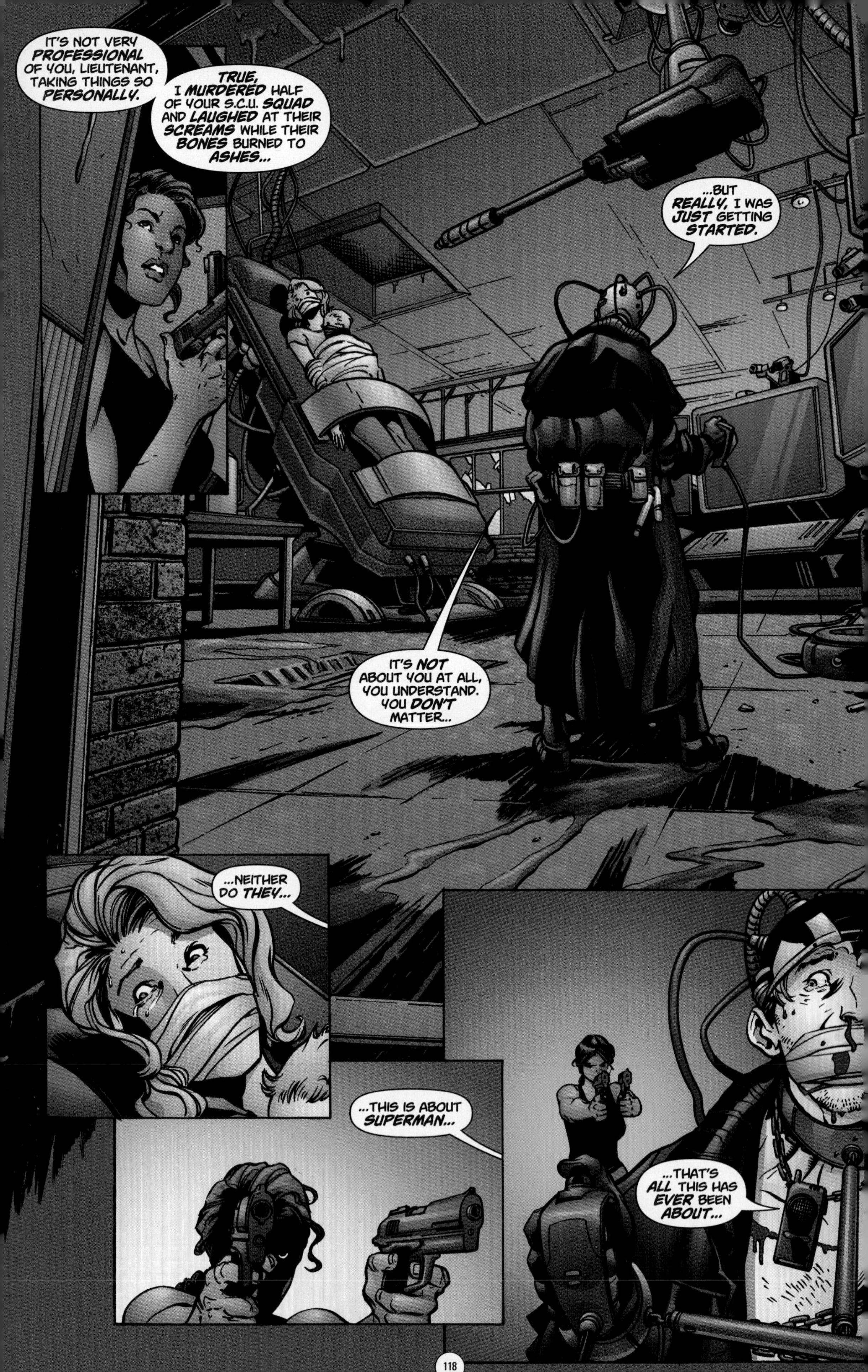
IT'S NOT VERY PROFESSIONAL OF YOU, LIEUTENANT, TAKING THINGS SO PERSONALLY.
TRUE, I MURDERED HALF OF YOUR S.C.U. SQUAD AND LAUGHED AT THEIR SCREAMS WHILE THEIR BONES BURNED TO ASHES...
...BUT REALLY, I WAS JUST GETTING STARTED.
IT'S NOT ABOUT YOU AT ALL, YOU UNDERSTAND. YOU DON'T MATTER...
...NEITHER DO THEY...
...THIS IS ABOUT SUPERMAN...
...THAT'S ALL THIS HAS EVER BEEN ABOUT...

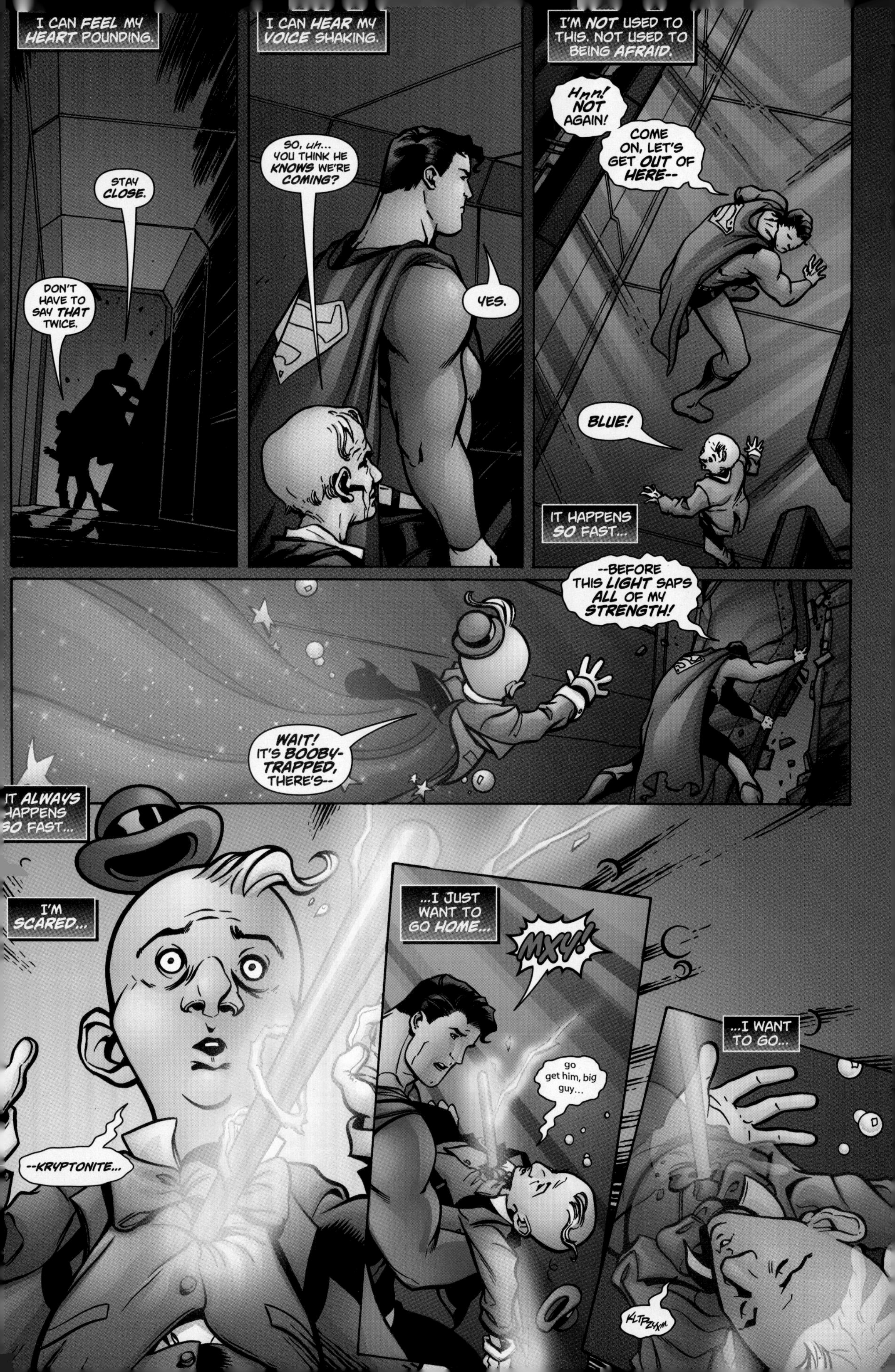
I CAN FEEL MY HEART POUNDING.
STAY CLOSE.
DON'T HAVE TO SAY THAT TWICE.
I CAN HEAR MY VOICE SHAKING.
SO, uh... YOU THINK HE KNOWS WE'RE COMING?
YES.
I'M NOT USED TO THIS. NOT USED TO BEING AFRAID.
Hnn! NOT AGAIN!
COME ON, LET'S GET OUT OF HERE--
BLUE!
IT HAPPENS SO FAST...
--BEFORE THIS LIGHT SAPS ALL OF MY STRENGTH!
WAIT! IT'S BOOBY-TRAPPED, THERE'S--
IT ALWAYS HAPPENS SO FAST...
I'M SCARED...
--KRYPTONITE...
...I JUST WANT TO GO HOME...
MXY!
go get him, big guy...
...I WANT TO GO...
KLTPZYXM.

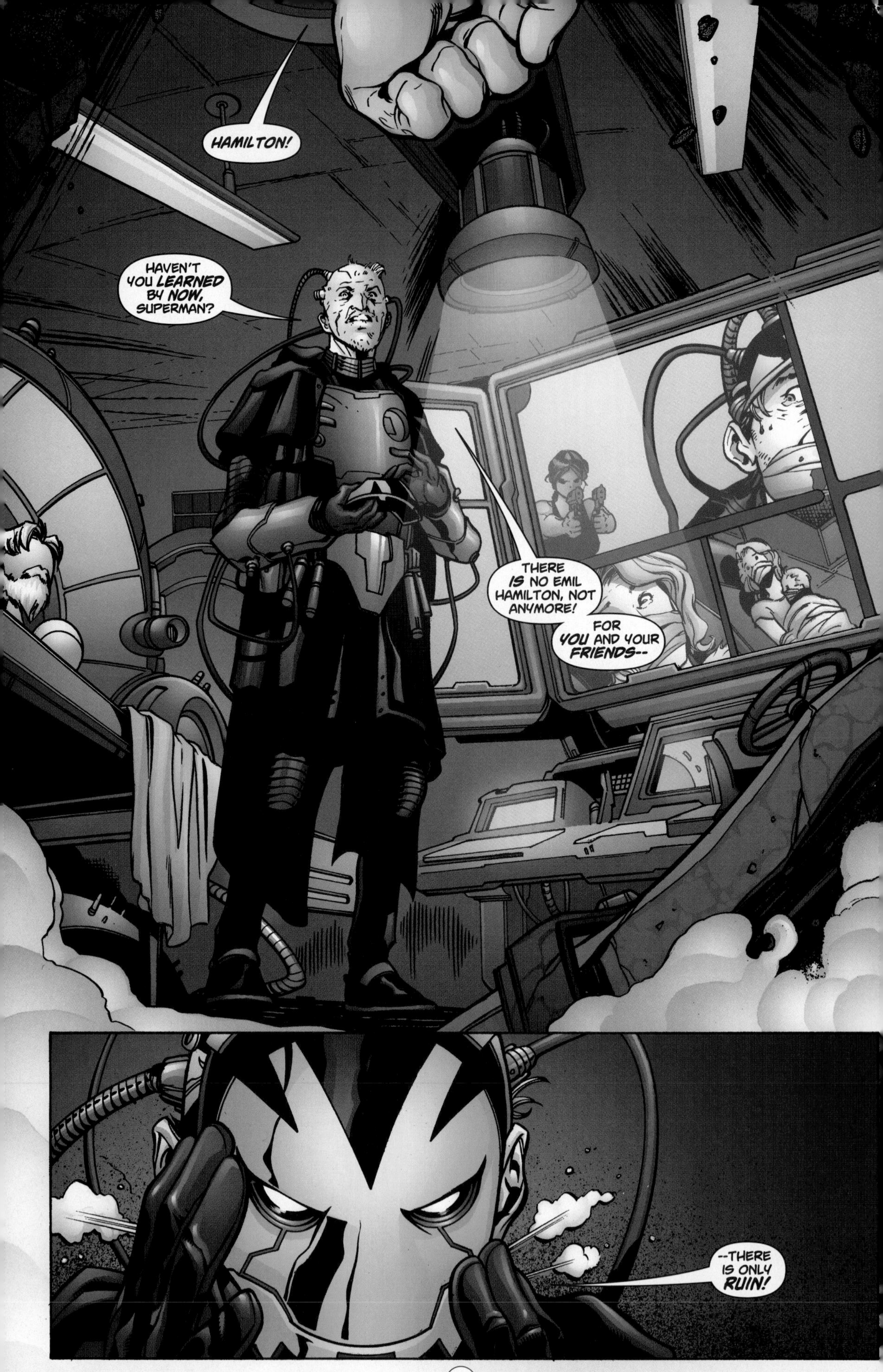
HAMILTON!
HAVEN'T YOU LEARNED BY NOW, SUPERMAN?
THERE IS NO EMIL HAMILTON, NOT ANYMORE!
FOR YOU AND YOUR FRIENDS--
--THERE IS ONLY RUIN!

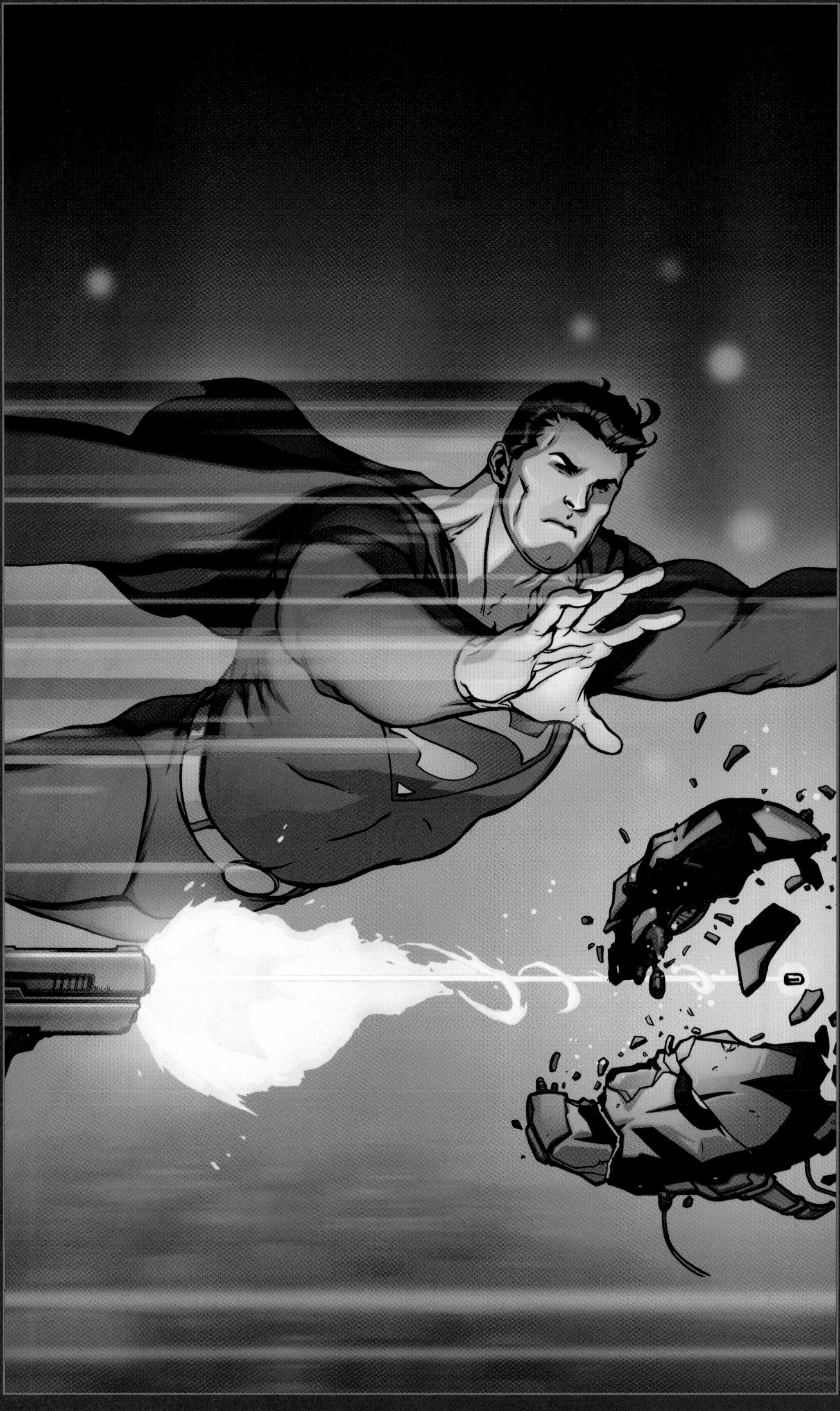

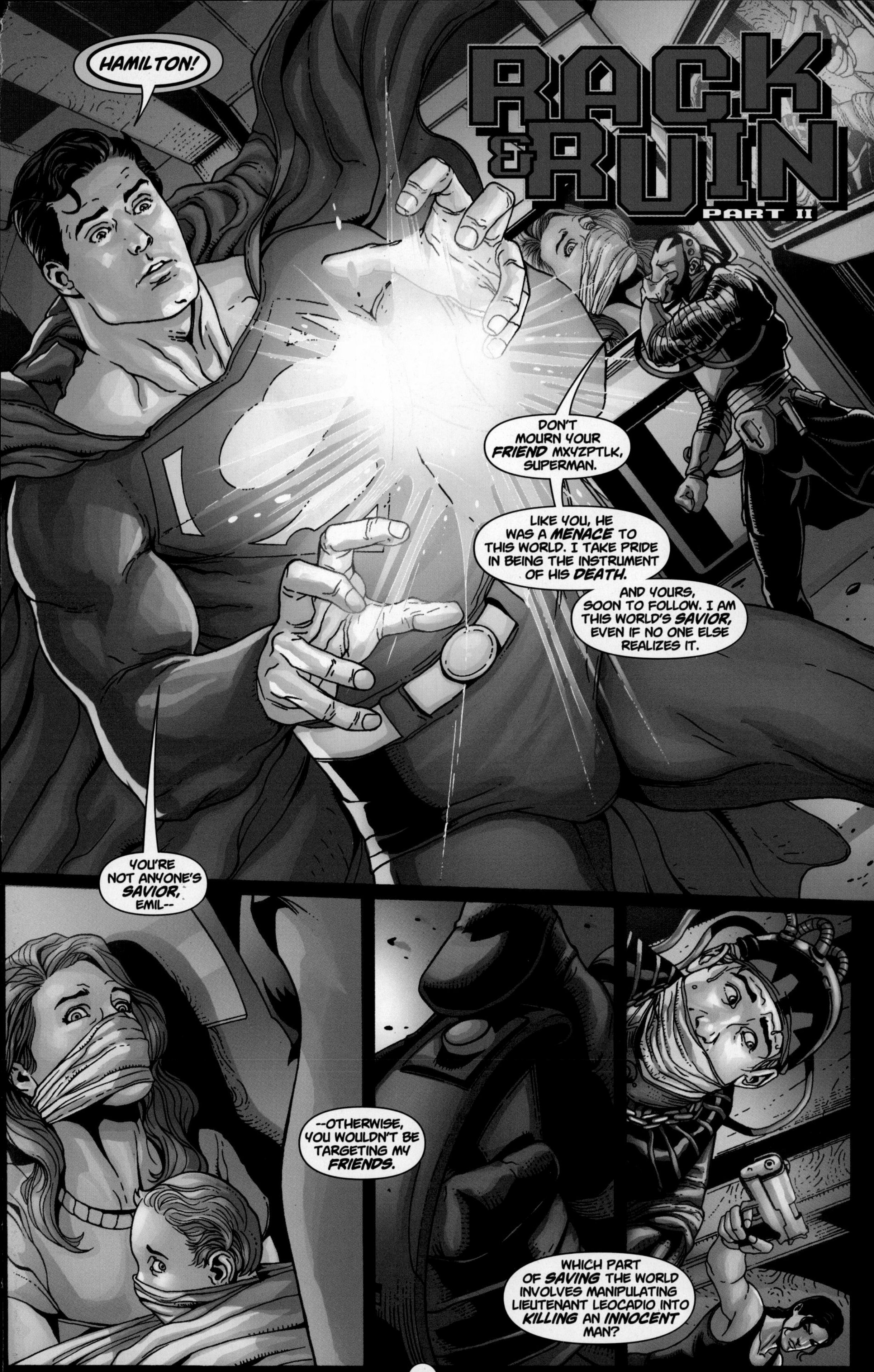
RACK & RUIN
PART II
HAMILTON!
DON'T MOURN YOUR FRIEND MXYZPTLK, SUPERMAN.
LIKE YOU, HE WAS A MENACE TO THIS WORLD. I TAKE PRIDE IN BEING THE INSTRUMENT OF HIS DEATH.
AND YOURS, SOON TO FOLLOW. I AM THIS WORLD'S SAVIOR, EVEN IF NO ONE ELSE REALIZES IT.
YOU'RE NOT ANYONE'S SAVIOR, EMIL--
--OTHERWISE, YOU WOULDN'T BE TARGETING MY FRIENDS.
WHICH PART OF SAVING THE WORLD INVOLVES MANIPULATING LIEUTENANT LEOCADIO INTO KILLING AN INNOCENT MAN?

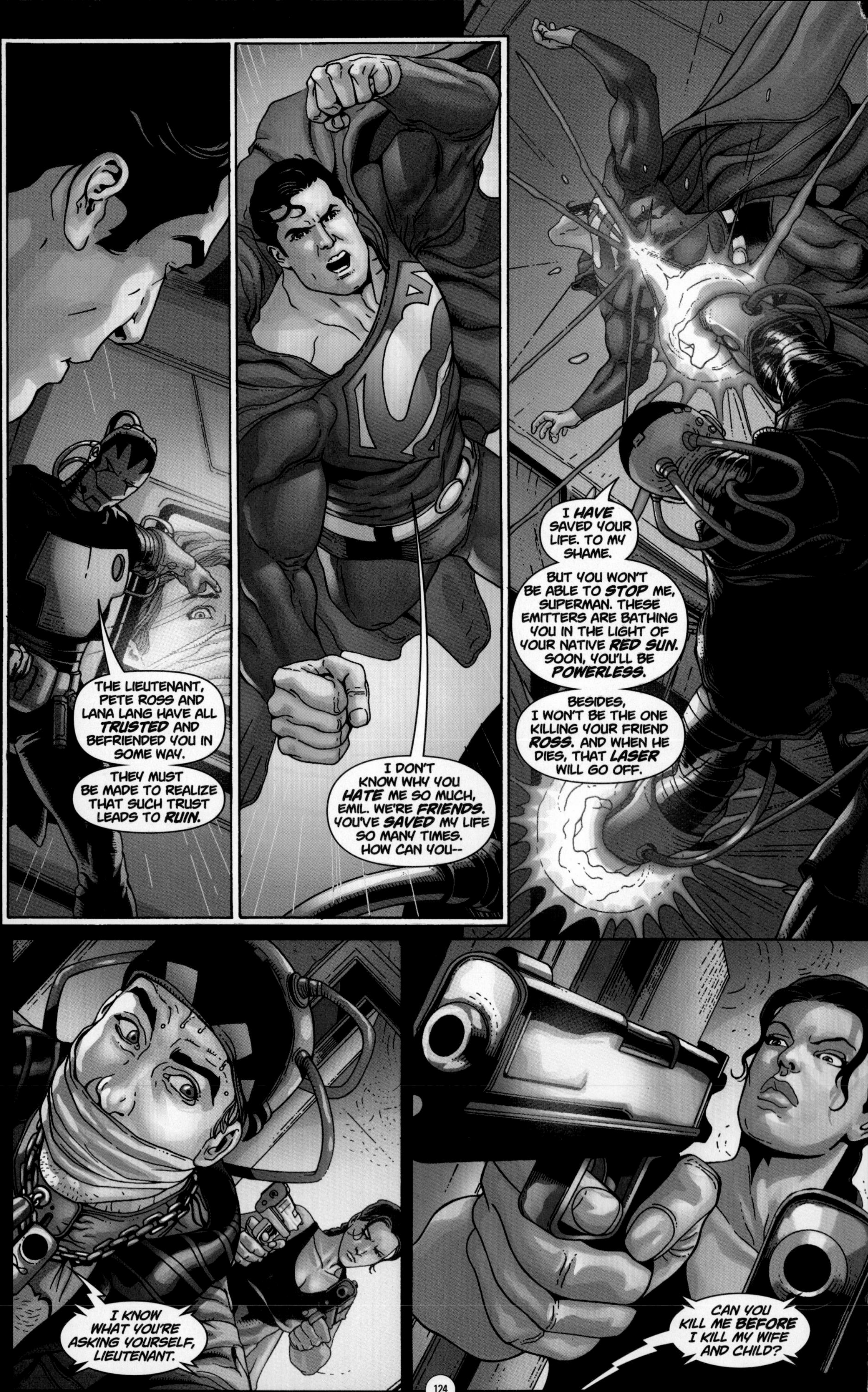
THE LIEUTENANT, PETE ROSS AND LANA LANG HAVE ALL TRUSTED AND BEFRIENDED YOU IN SOME WAY.
THEY MUST BE MADE TO REALIZE THAT SUCH TRUST LEADS TO RUIN.
I DON'T KNOW WHY YOU HATE ME SO MUCH, EMIL. WE'RE FRIENDS. YOU'VE SAVED MY LIFE SO MANY TIMES. HOW CAN YOU--
I HAVE SAVED YOUR LIFE. TO MY SHAME.
BUT YOU WON'T BE ABLE TO STOP ME, SUPERMAN. THESE EMITTERS ARE BATHING YOU IN THE LIGHT OF YOUR NATIVE RED SUN. SOON, YOU'LL BE POWERLESS.
BESIDES, I WON'T BE THE ONE KILLING YOUR FRIEND ROSS. AND WHEN HE DIES, THAT LASER WILL GO OFF.
I KNOW WHAT YOU'RE ASKING YOURSELF, LIEUTENANT.
CAN YOU KILL ME BEFORE I KILL MY WIFE AND CHILD?

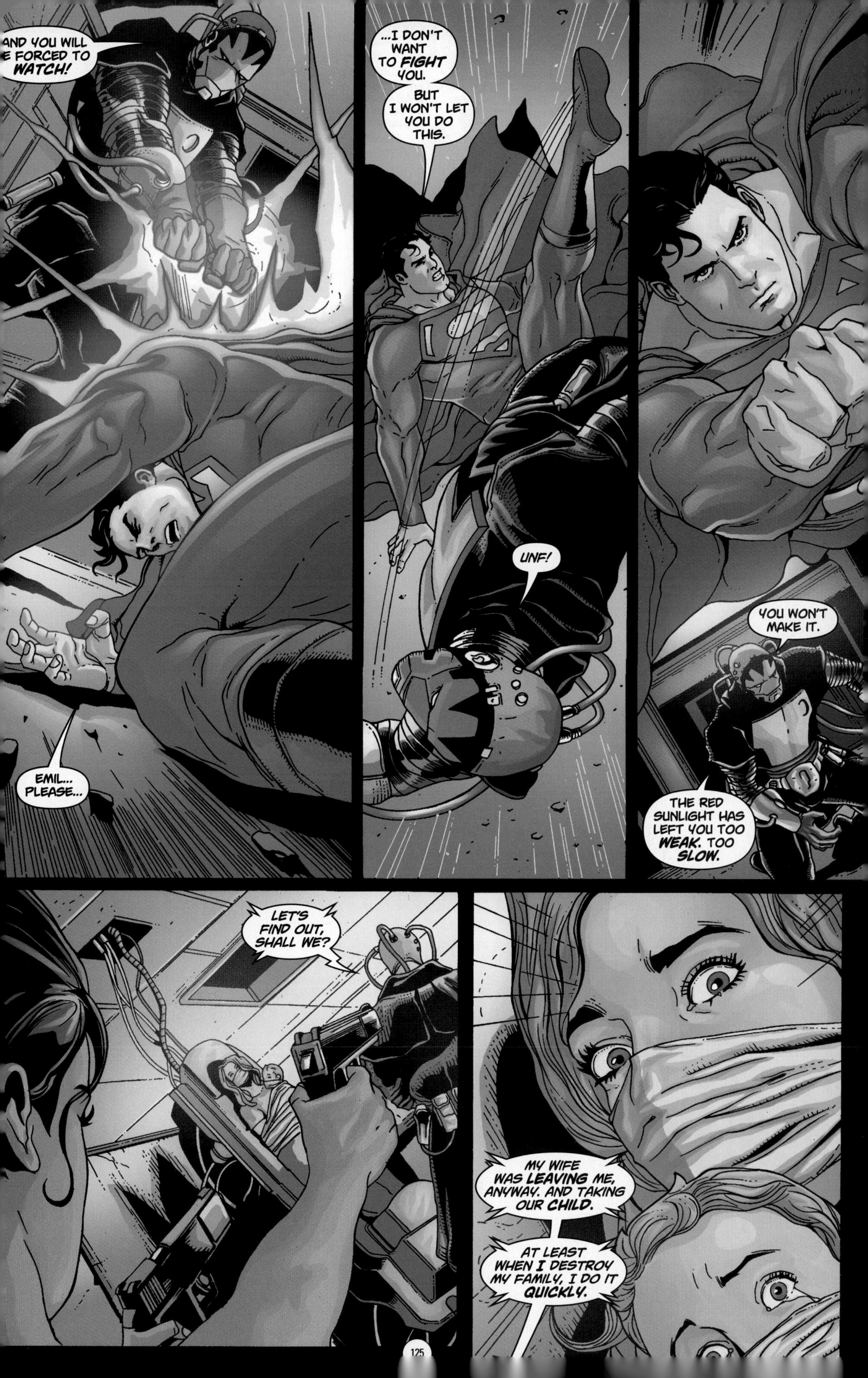
AND YOU WILL BE FORCED TO WATCH!
EMIL... PLEASE...
...I DON'T WANT TO FIGHT YOU.
BUT I WON'T LET YOU DO THIS.
UNF!
YOU WON'T MAKE IT.
THE RED SUNLIGHT HAS LEFT YOU TOO WEAK. TOO SLOW.
LET'S FIND OUT, SHALL WE?
MY WIFE WAS LEAVING ME, ANYWAY. AND TAKING OUR CHILD.
AT LEAST WHEN I DESTROY MY FAMILY, I DO IT QUICKLY.

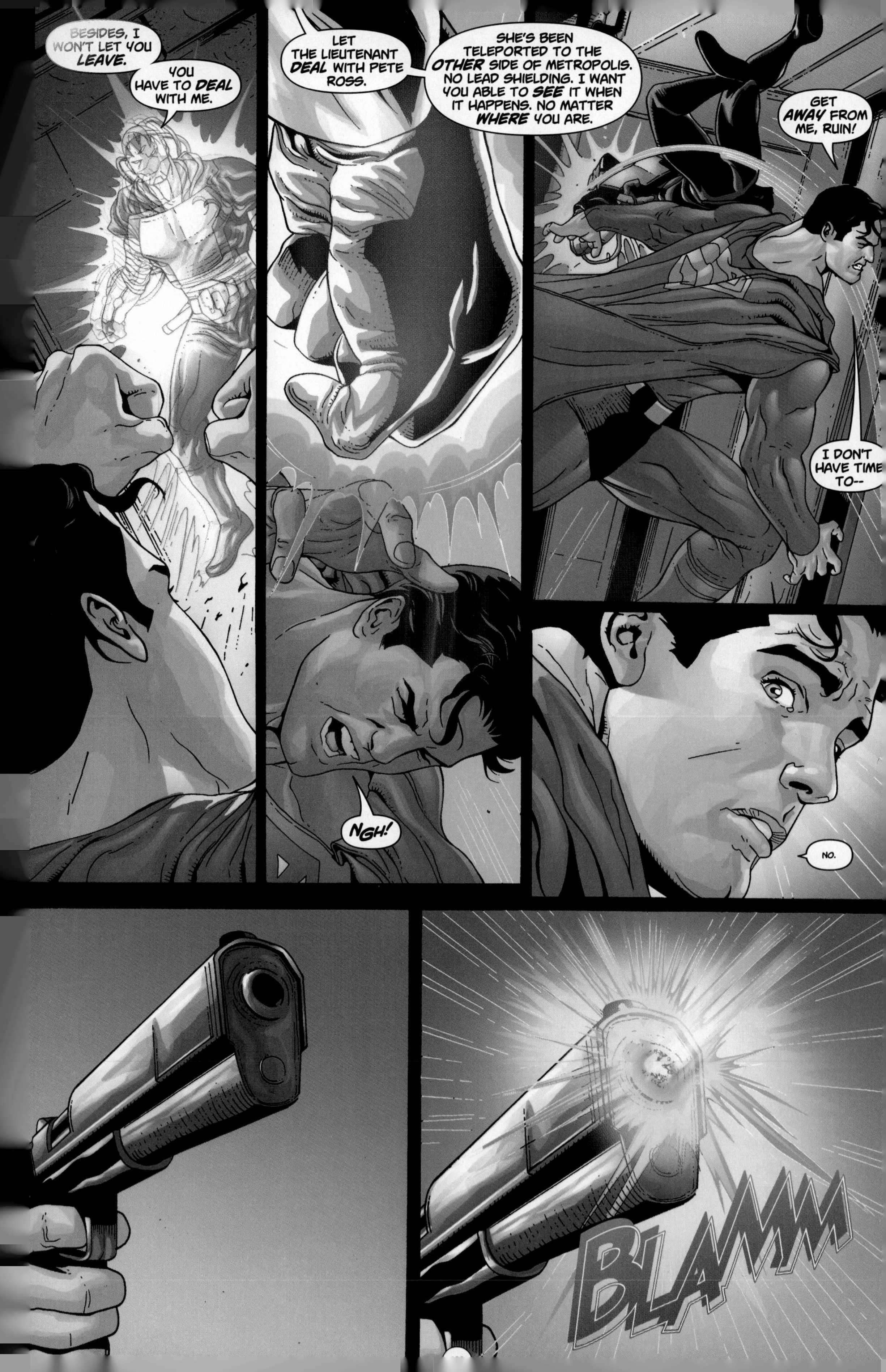
BESIDES, I WON'T LET YOU LEAVE.
YOU HAVE TO DEAL WITH ME.
LET THE LIEUTENANT DEAL WITH PETE ROSS.
SHE'S BEEN TELEPORTED TO THE OTHER SIDE OF METROPOLIS. NO LEAD SHIELDING. I WANT YOU ABLE TO SEE IT WHEN IT HAPPENS. NO MATTER WHERE YOU ARE.
NGH!
GET AWAY FROM ME, RUIN!
I DON'T HAVE TIME TO--
NO.
BLAMM

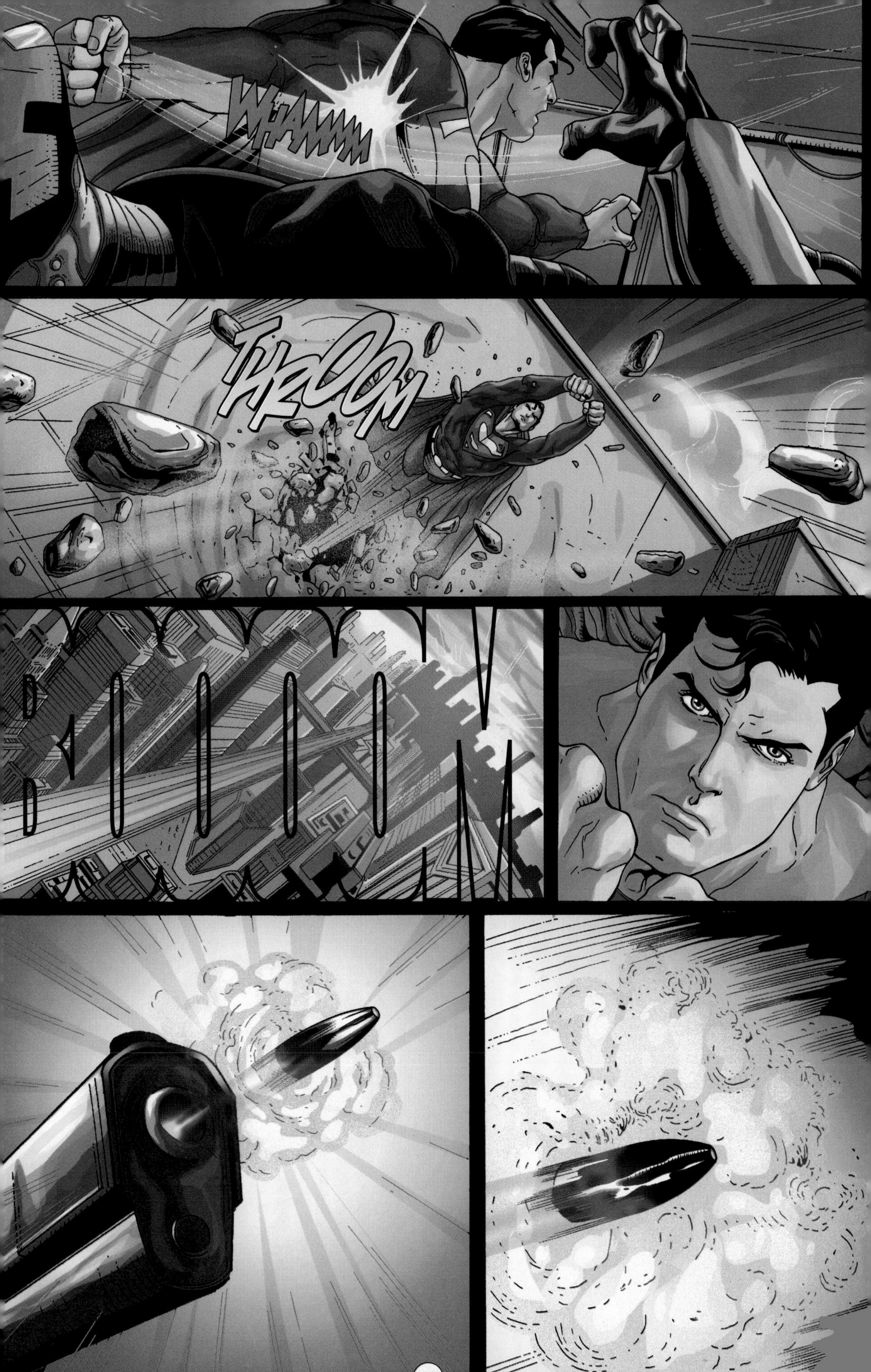
WHAMMM
THROOOM
BOOOOM

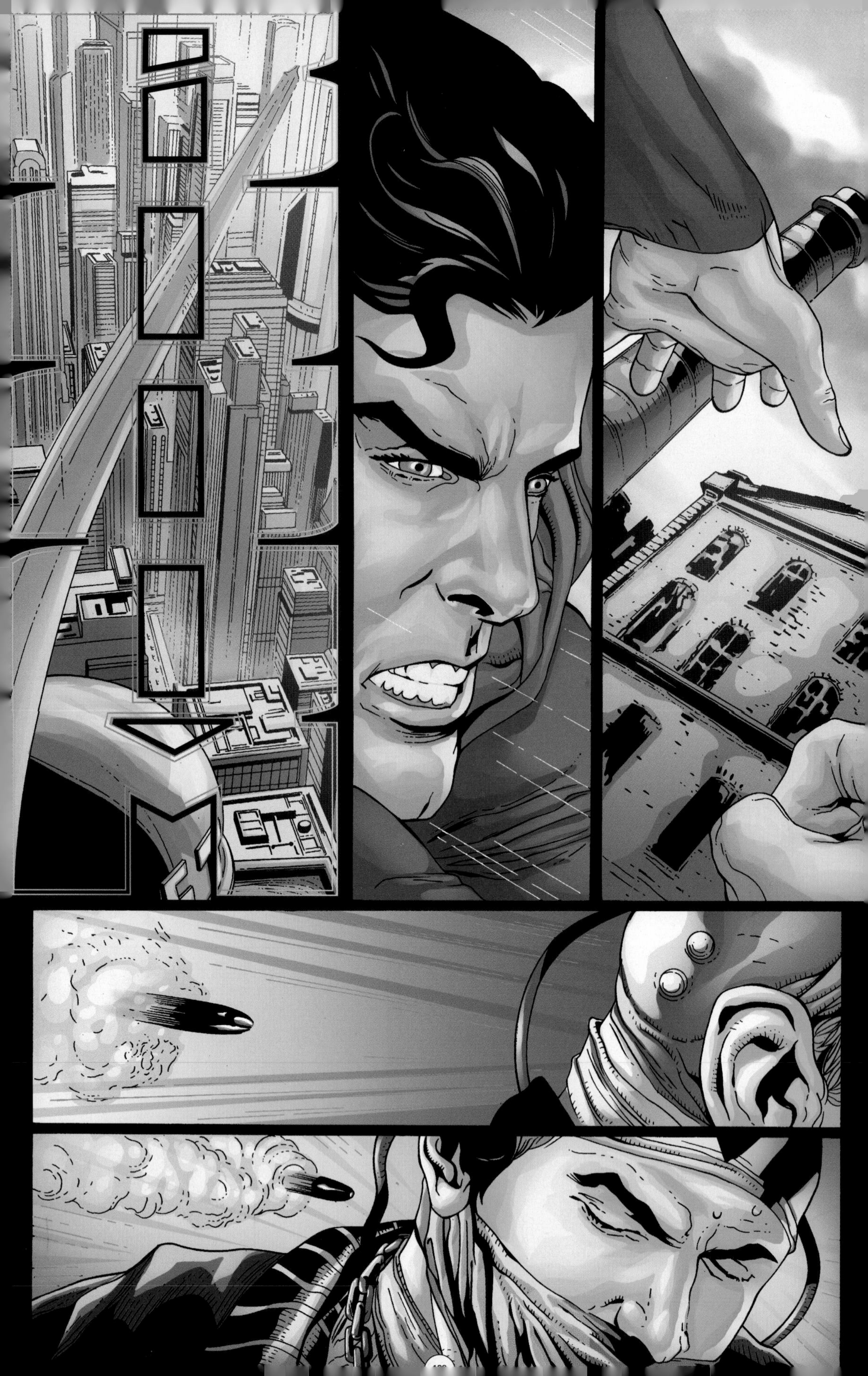

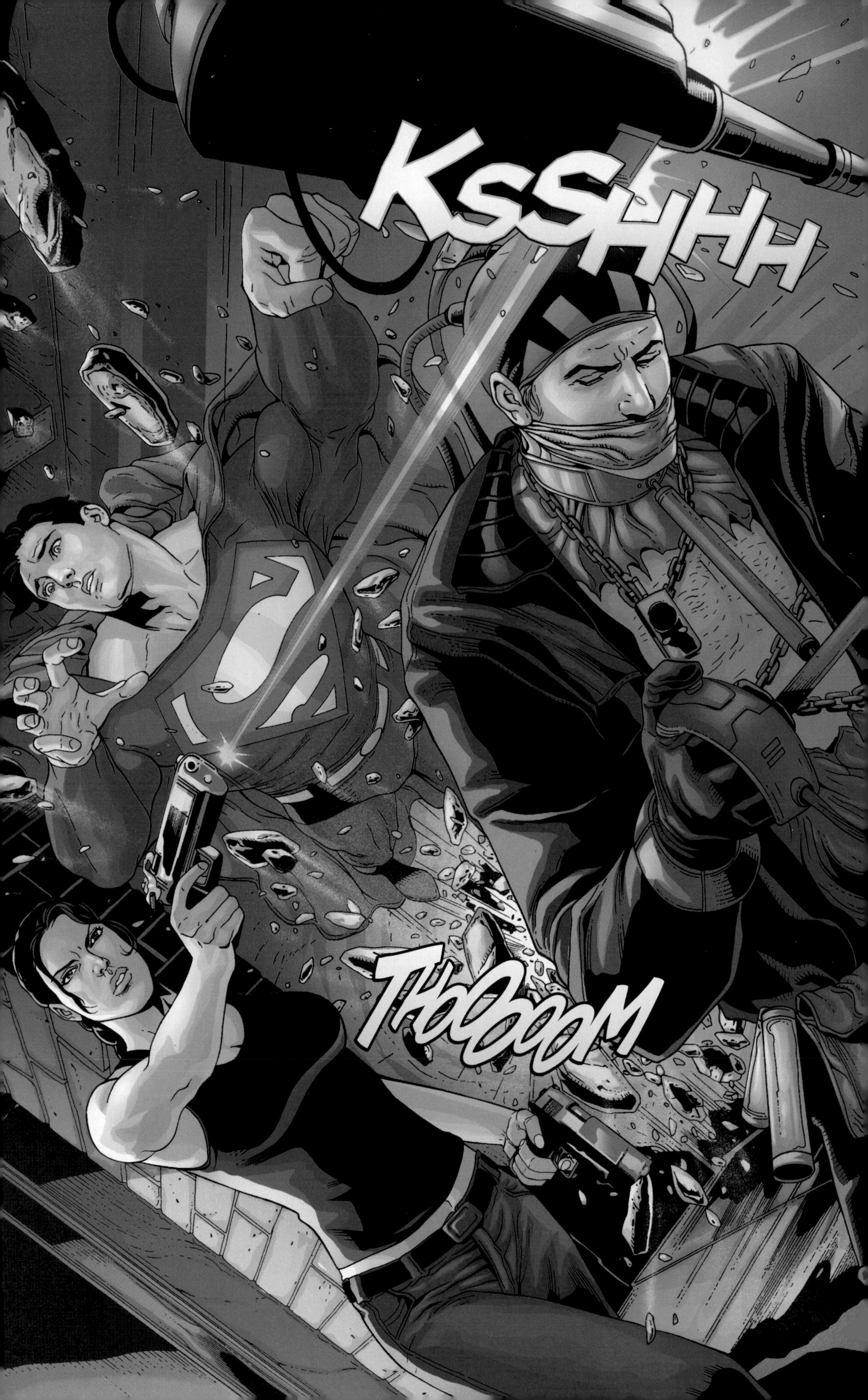
KSSHHH
THOOOOM

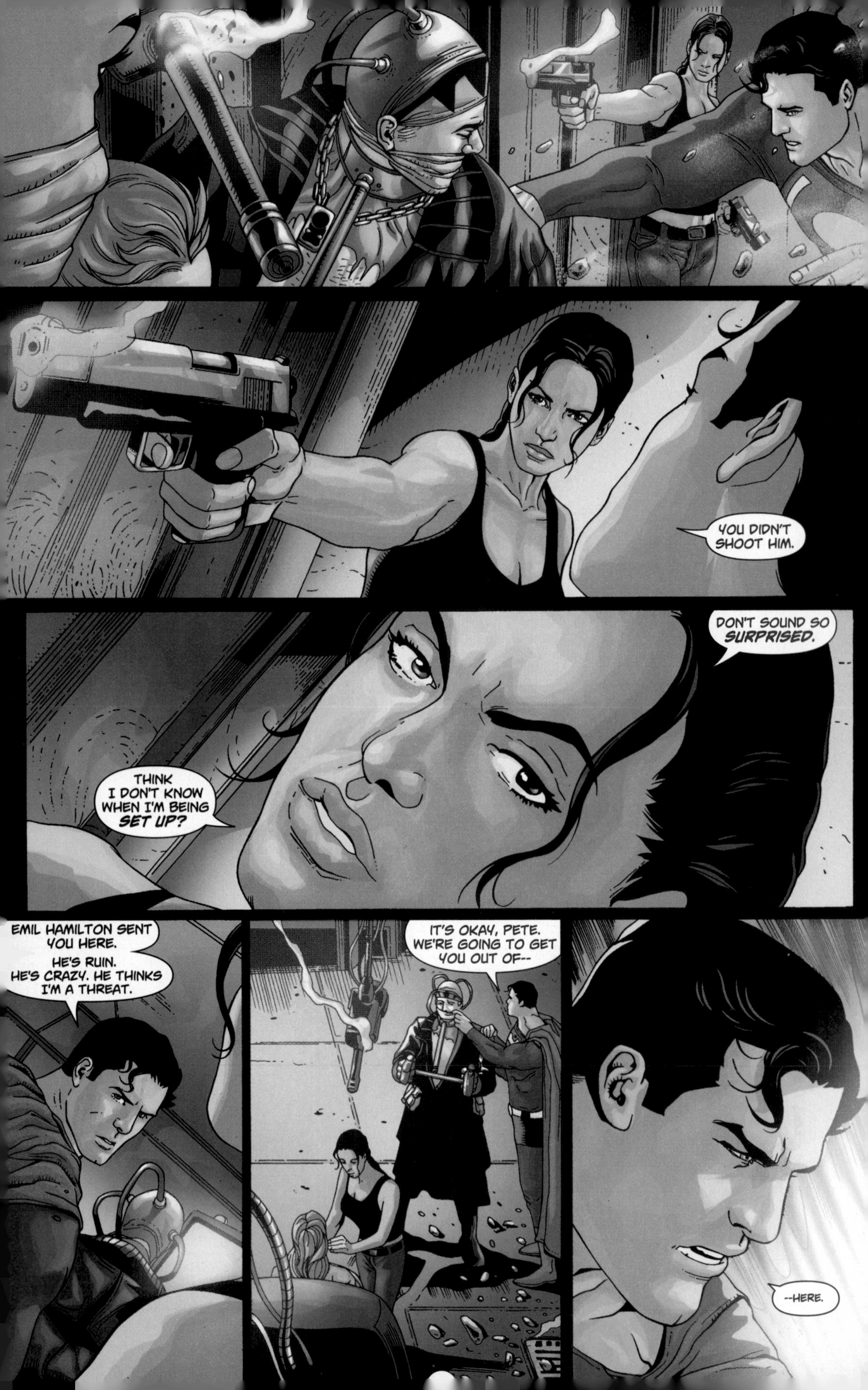
YOU DIDN'T SHOOT HIM.
DON'T SOUND SO SURPRISED.
THINK I DON'T KNOW WHEN I'M BEING SET UP?
EMIL HAMILTON SENT YOU HERE.
HE'S RUIN. HE'S CRAZY. HE THINKS I'M A THREAT.
IT'S OKAY, PETE. WE'RE GOING TO GET YOU OUT OF--
--HERE.

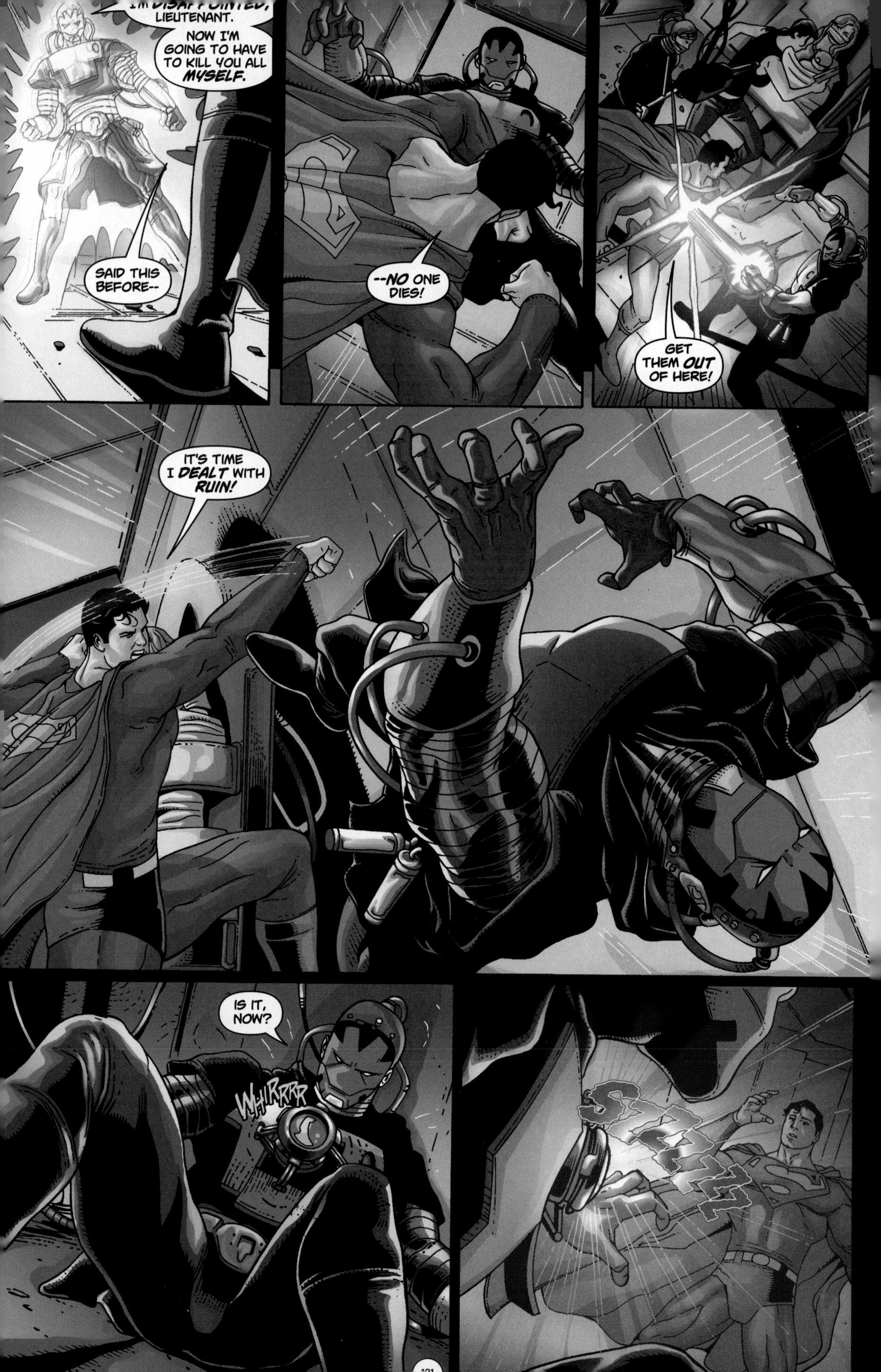
I'M DISAPPOINTED, LIEUTENANT.
NOW I'M GOING TO HAVE TO KILL YOU ALL MYSELF.
SAID THIS BEFORE--
--NO ONE DIES!
GET THEM OUT OF HERE!
IT'S TIME I DEALT WITH RUIN!
IS IT, NOW?
WHIRRRR

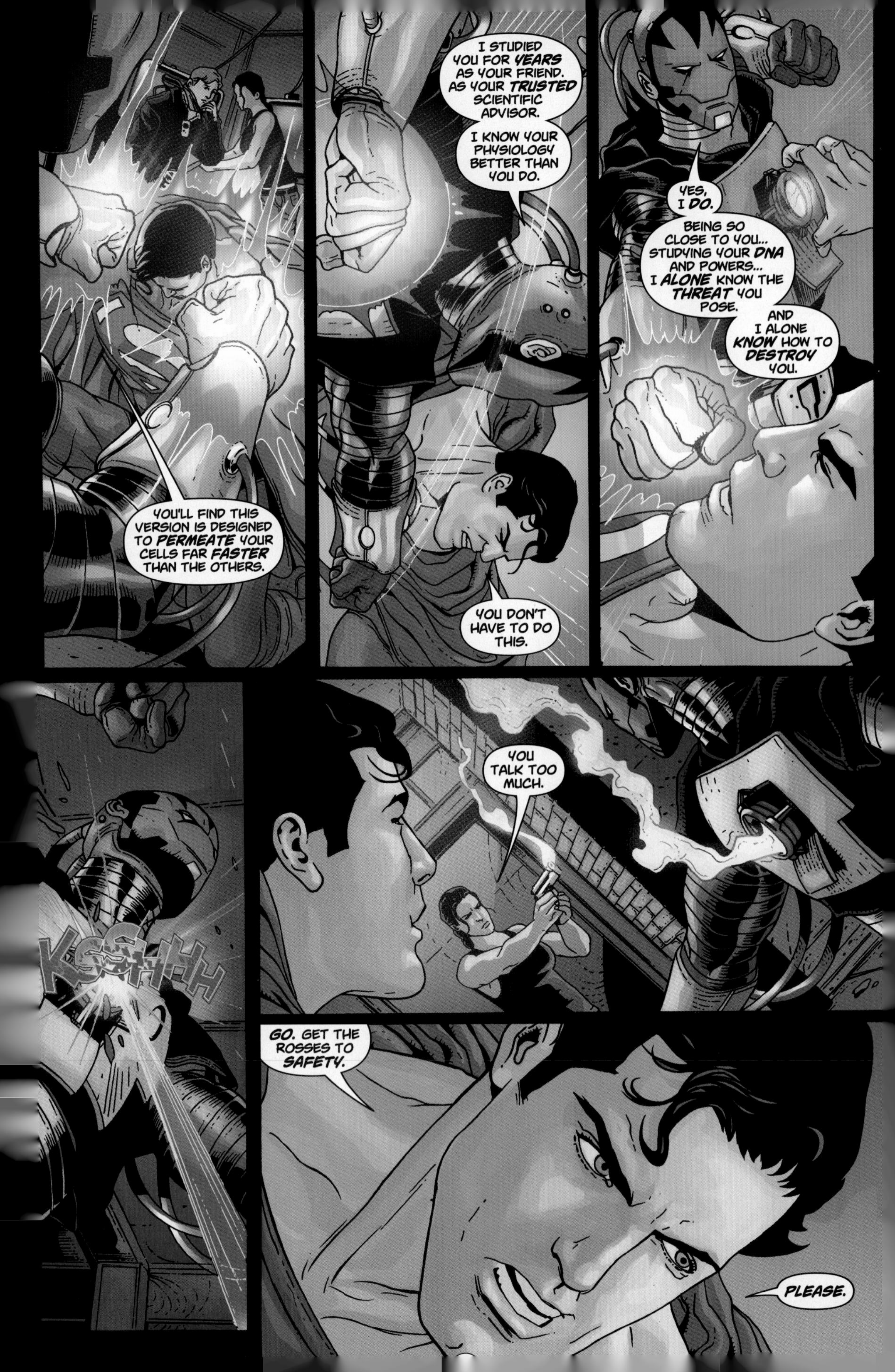
YOU'LL FIND THIS VERSION IS DESIGNED TO **PERMEATE** YOUR CELLS FAR **FASTER** THAN THE OTHERS.
I STUDIED YOU FOR **YEARS** AS YOUR FRIEND. AS YOUR **TRUSTED** SCIENTIFIC ADVISOR.
I KNOW YOUR PHYSIOLOGY BETTER THAN YOU DO.
YOU DON'T HAVE TO DO THIS.
YES, I **DO**.
BEING SO CLOSE TO YOU... STUDYING YOUR **DNA** AND POWERS... I **ALONE** KNOW THE **THREAT** YOU POSE.
AND I ALONE **KNOW** HOW TO **DESTROY** YOU.
KSHHH
YOU TALK TOO MUCH.
GO. GET THE ROSSES TO **SAFETY**.
PLEASE.

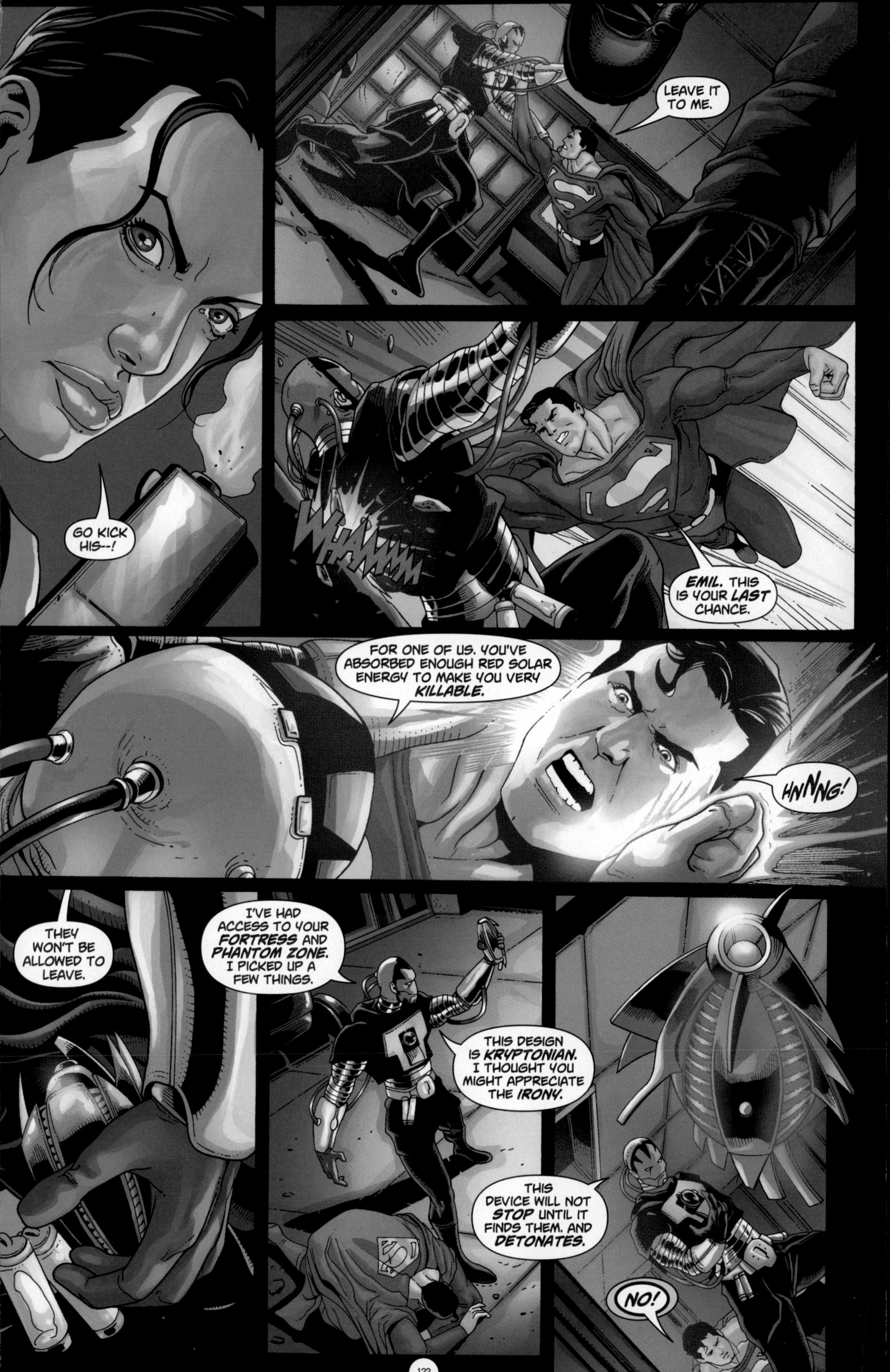

LEAVE IT TO ME.
GO KICK HIS--!
WHAMMM
EMIL. THIS IS YOUR LAST CHANCE.
FOR ONE OF US. YOU'VE ABSORBED ENOUGH RED SOLAR ENERGY TO MAKE YOU VERY KILLABLE.
HNNNG!
THEY WON'T BE ALLOWED TO LEAVE.
I'VE HAD ACCESS TO YOUR FORTRESS AND PHANTOM ZONE. I PICKED UP A FEW THINGS.
THIS DESIGN IS KRYPTONIAN. I THOUGHT YOU MIGHT APPRECIATE THE IRONY.
THIS DEVICE WILL NOT STOP UNTIL IT FINDS THEM. AND DETONATES.
NO!

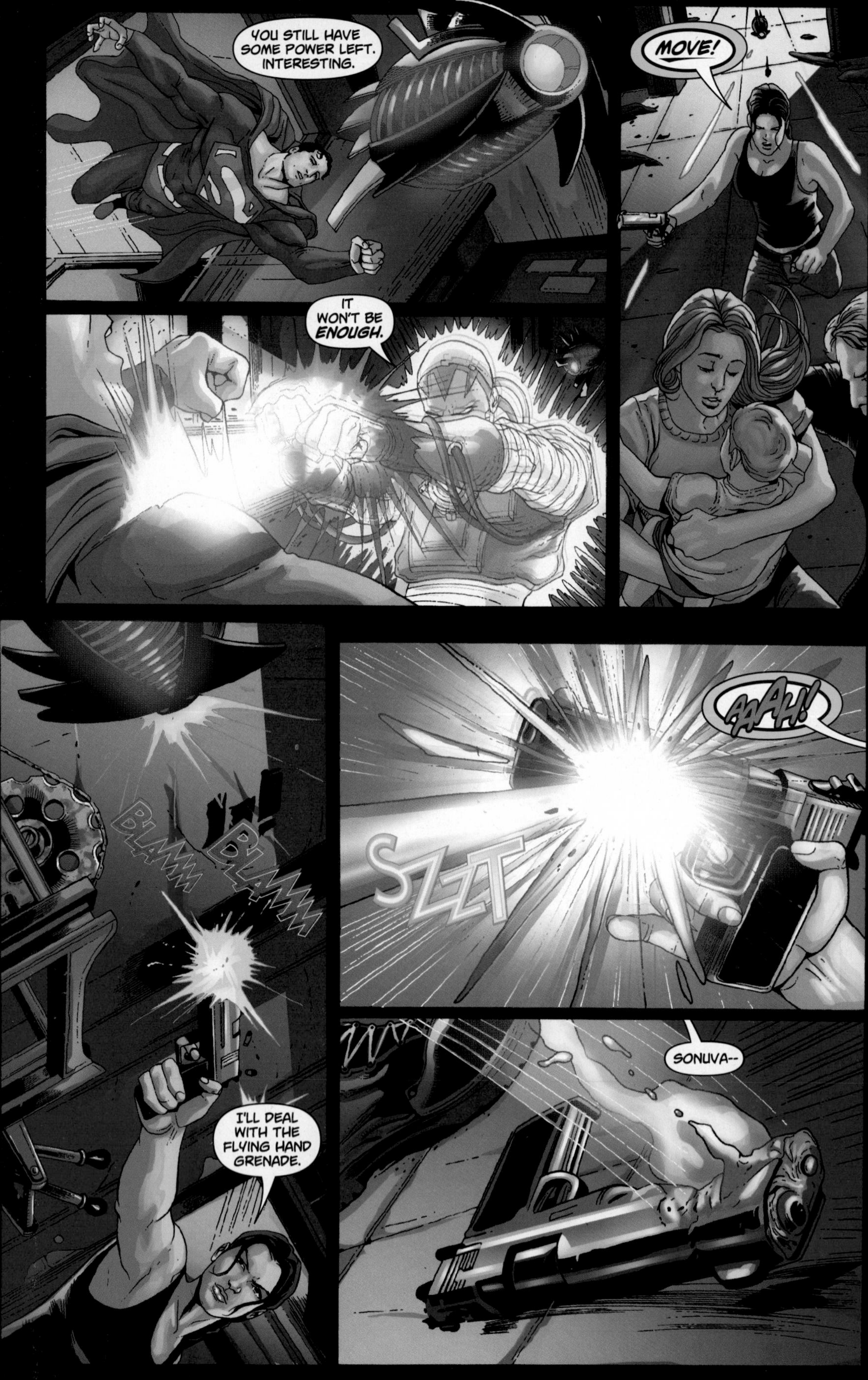
YOU STILL HAVE SOME POWER LEFT. INTERESTING.
MOVE!
IT WON'T BE ENOUGH.
BLAMM BLAMM
I'LL DEAL WITH THE FLYING HAND GRENADE.
AAAH!
SZZT
SONUVA--

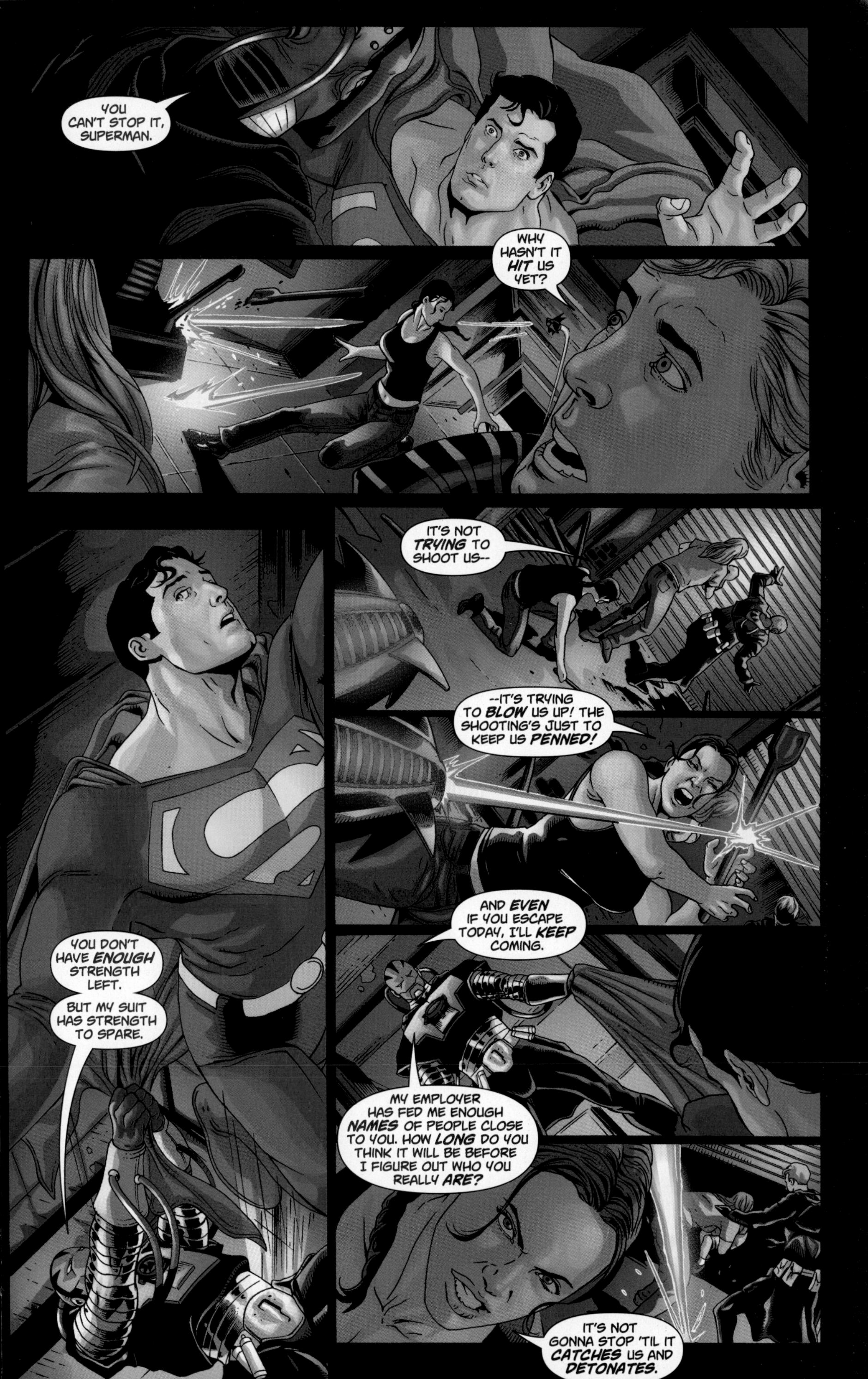
YOU CAN'T STOP IT, SUPERMAN.
WHY HASN'T IT HIT US YET?
IT'S NOT TRYING TO SHOOT US--
--IT'S TRYING TO BLOW US UP! THE SHOOTING'S JUST TO KEEP US PENNED!
YOU DON'T HAVE ENOUGH STRENGTH LEFT.
BUT MY SUIT HAS STRENGTH TO SPARE.
AND EVEN IF YOU ESCAPE TODAY, I'LL KEEP COMING.
MY EMPLOYER HAS FED ME ENOUGH NAMES OF PEOPLE CLOSE TO YOU. HOW LONG DO YOU THINK IT WILL BE BEFORE I FIGURE OUT WHO YOU REALLY ARE?
IT'S NOT GONNA STOP 'TIL IT CATCHES US AND DETONATES.

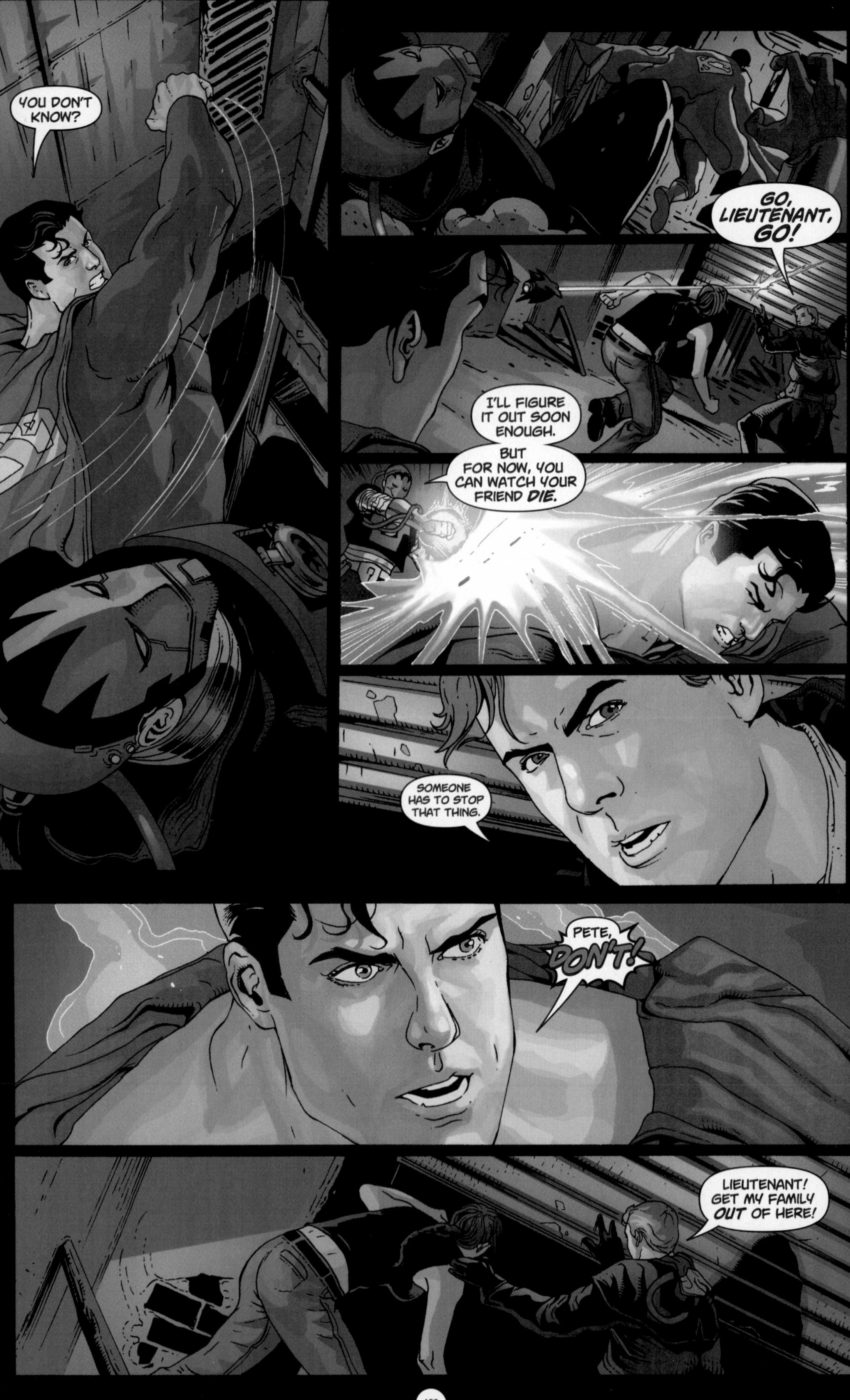
YOU DON'T KNOW?
GO, LIEUTENANT, GO!
I'LL FIGURE IT OUT SOON ENOUGH.
BUT FOR NOW, YOU CAN WATCH YOUR FRIEND DIE.
SOMEONE HAS TO STOP THAT THING.
PETE, DON'T!
LIEUTENANT! GET MY FAMILY OUT OF HERE!

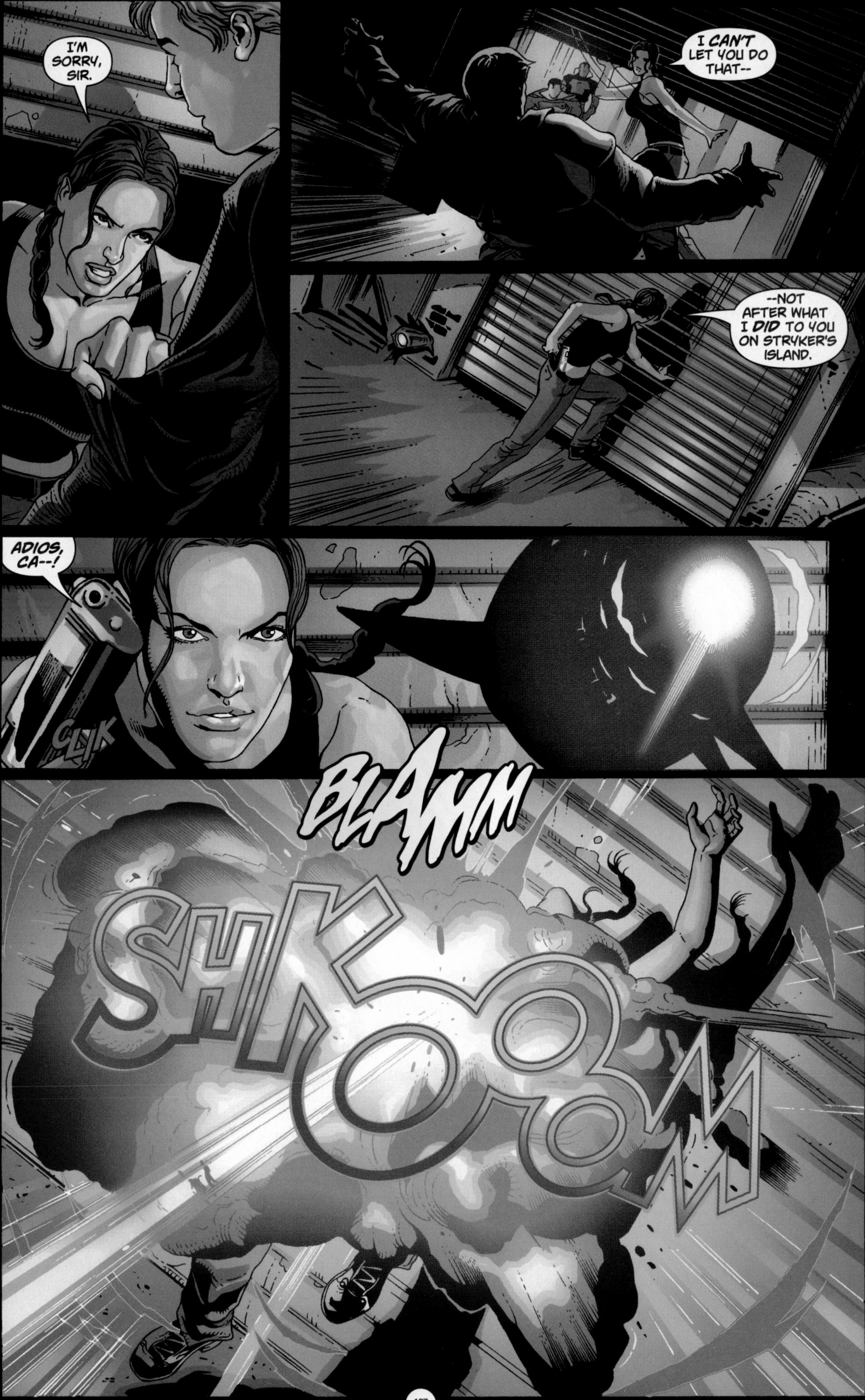
I'M SORRY, SIR.
I CAN'T LET YOU DO THAT--
--NOT AFTER WHAT I DID TO YOU ON STRYKER'S ISLAND.
ADIOS, CA--!
CLIK
BLAMM
SHKOOOM

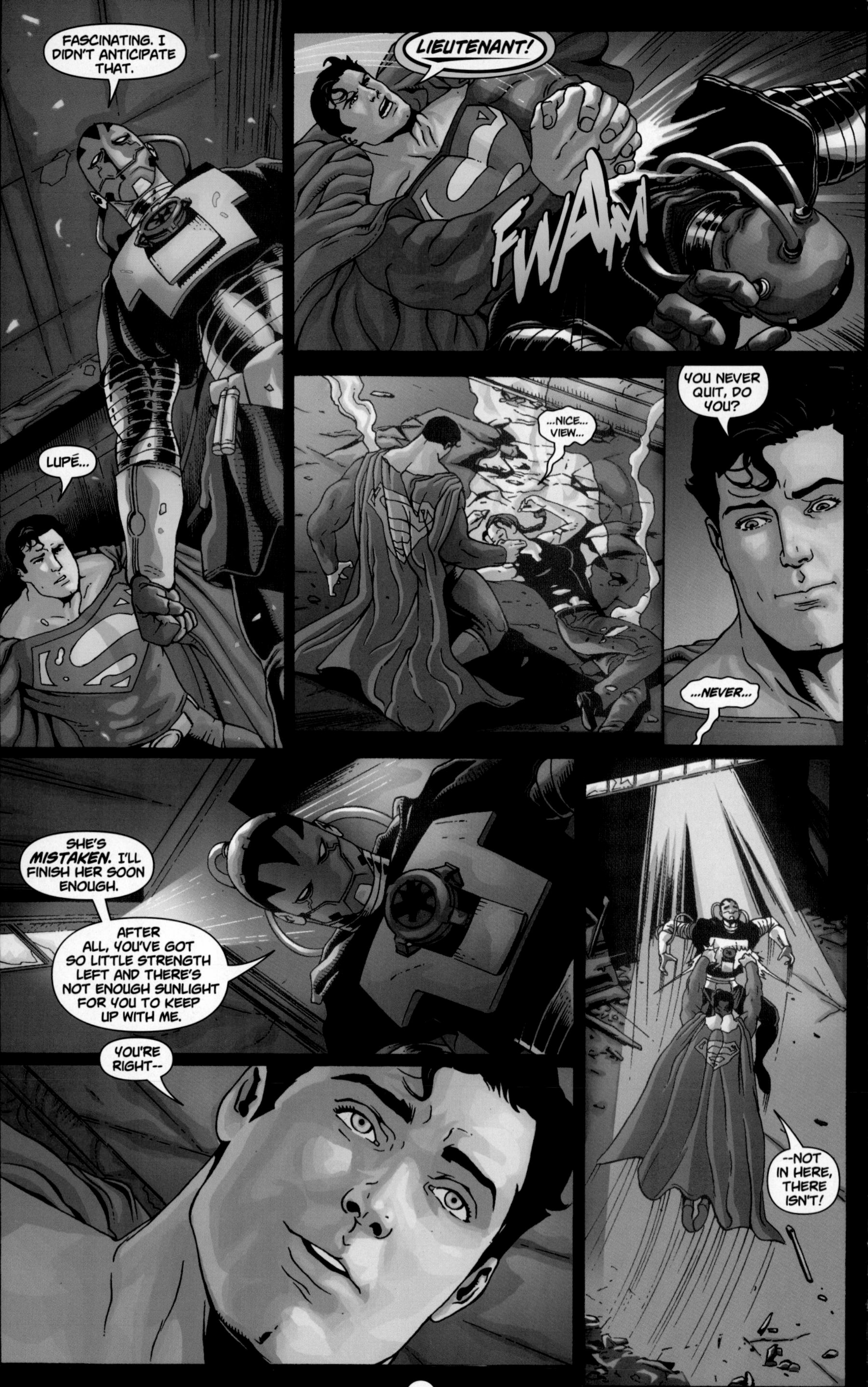
FASCINATING. I DIDN'T ANTICIPATE THAT.
LUPÉ...
LIEUTENANT!
FWAM
...NICE... VIEW...
YOU NEVER QUIT, DO YOU?
...NEVER...
SHE'S MISTAKEN. I'LL FINISH HER SOON ENOUGH.
AFTER ALL, YOU'VE GOT SO LITTLE STRENGTH LEFT AND THERE'S NOT ENOUGH SUNLIGHT FOR YOU TO KEEP UP WITH ME.
YOU'RE RIGHT--
--NOT IN HERE, THERE ISN'T!

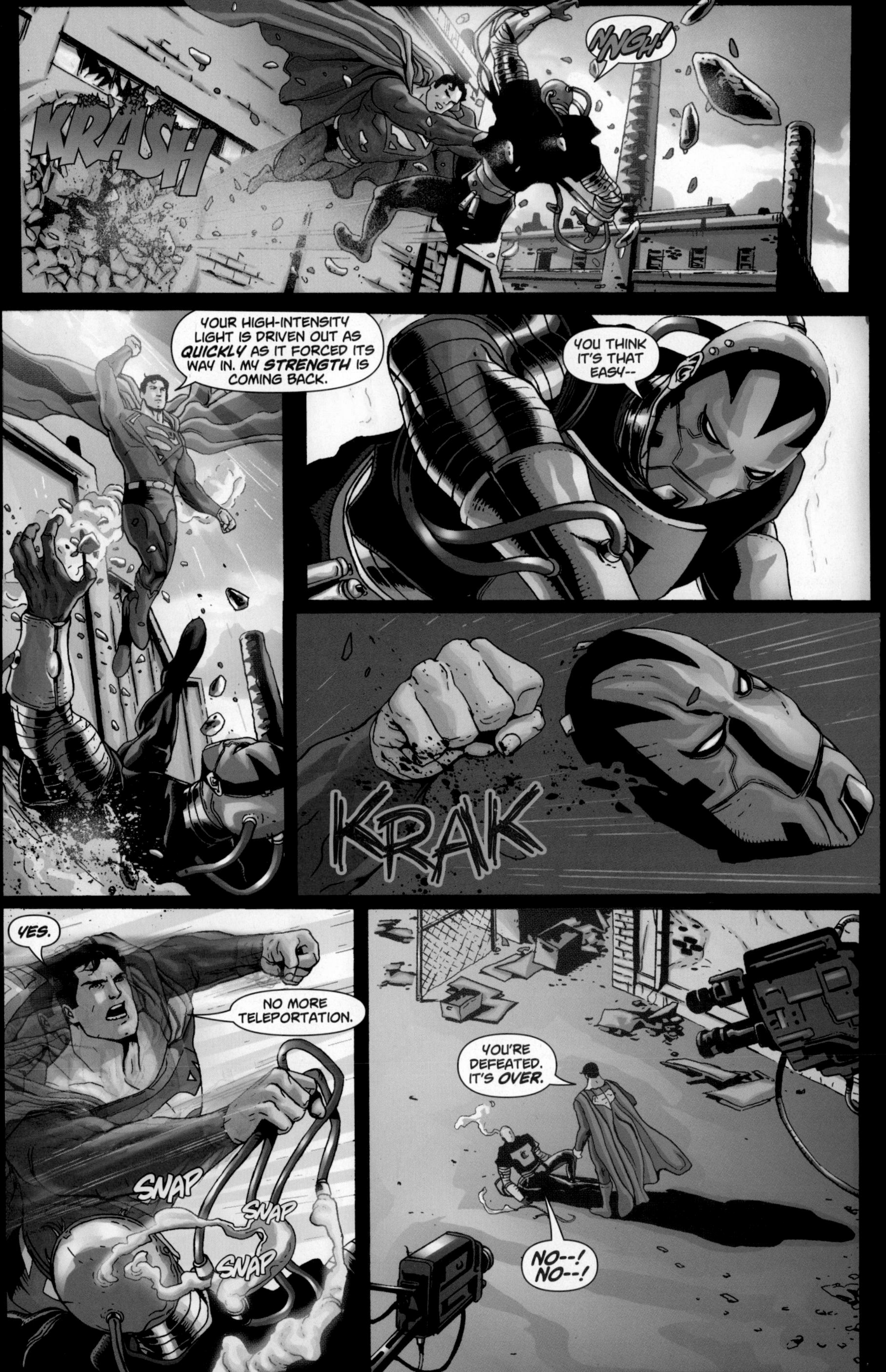
KRASH
N'NGH!
YOUR HIGH-INTENSITY LIGHT IS DRIVEN OUT AS QUICKLY AS IT FORCED ITS WAY IN. MY STRENGTH IS COMING BACK.
YOU THINK IT'S THAT EASY--
KRAK
YES.
NO MORE TELEPORTATION.
SNAP
SNAP
SNAP
YOU'RE DEFEATED. IT'S OVER.
NO--! NO--!

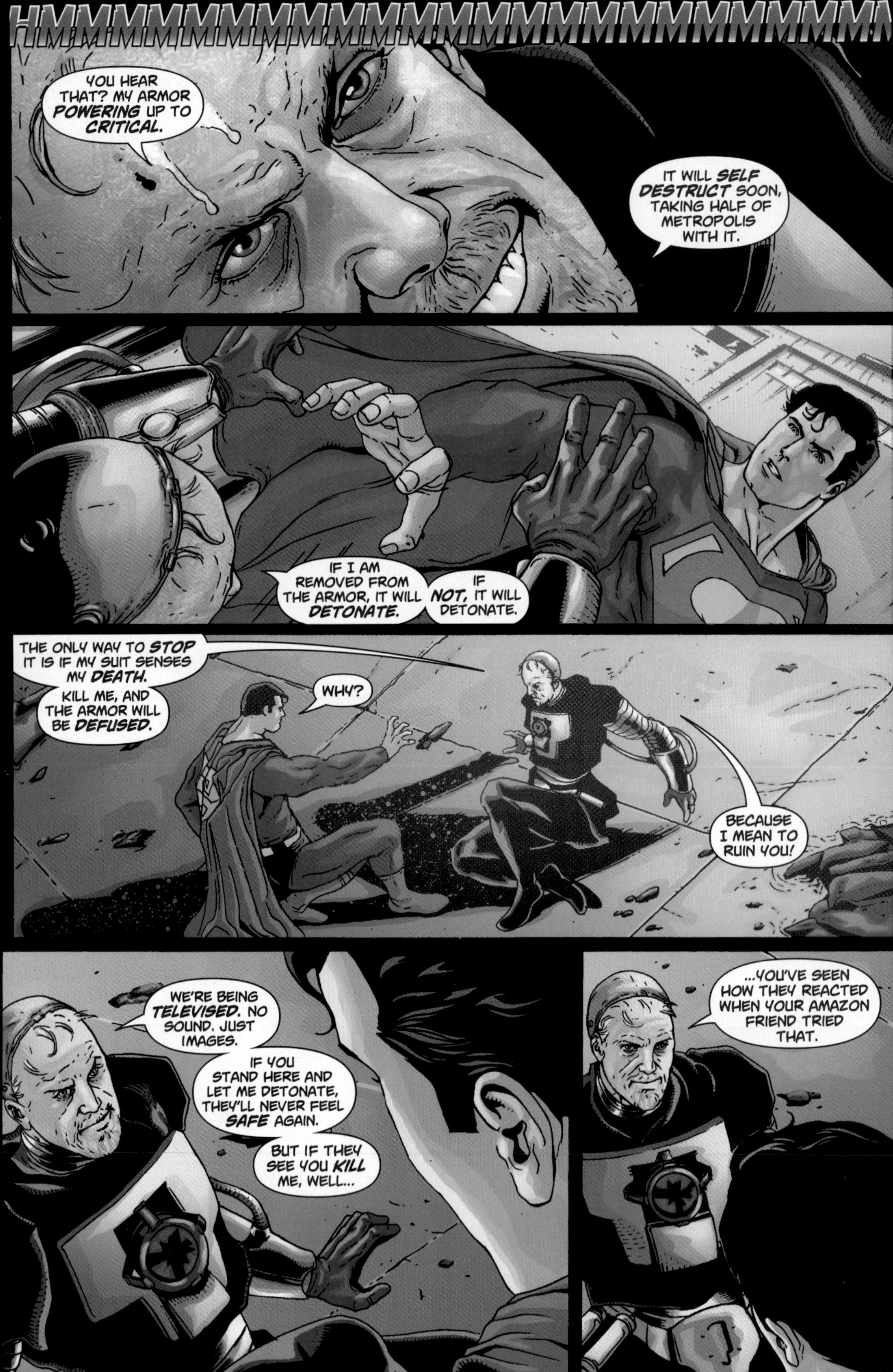
HMMMMMMMMMMMMMMMMMMMMMMMMM
YOU HEAR THAT? MY ARMOR POWERING UP TO CRITICAL.
IT WILL SELF DESTRUCT SOON, TAKING HALF OF METROPOLIS WITH IT.
IF I AM REMOVED FROM THE ARMOR, IT WILL DETONATE.
IF NOT, IT WILL DETONATE.
THE ONLY WAY TO STOP IT IS IF MY SUIT SENSES MY DEATH.
KILL ME, AND THE ARMOR WILL BE DEFUSED.
WHY?
BECAUSE I MEAN TO RUIN YOU!
WE'RE BEING TELEVISED. NO SOUND. JUST IMAGES.
IF YOU STAND HERE AND LET ME DETONATE, THEY'LL NEVER FEEL SAFE AGAIN.
BUT IF THEY SEE YOU KILL ME, WELL...
...YOU'VE SEEN HOW THEY REACTED WHEN YOUR AMAZON FRIEND TRIED THAT.

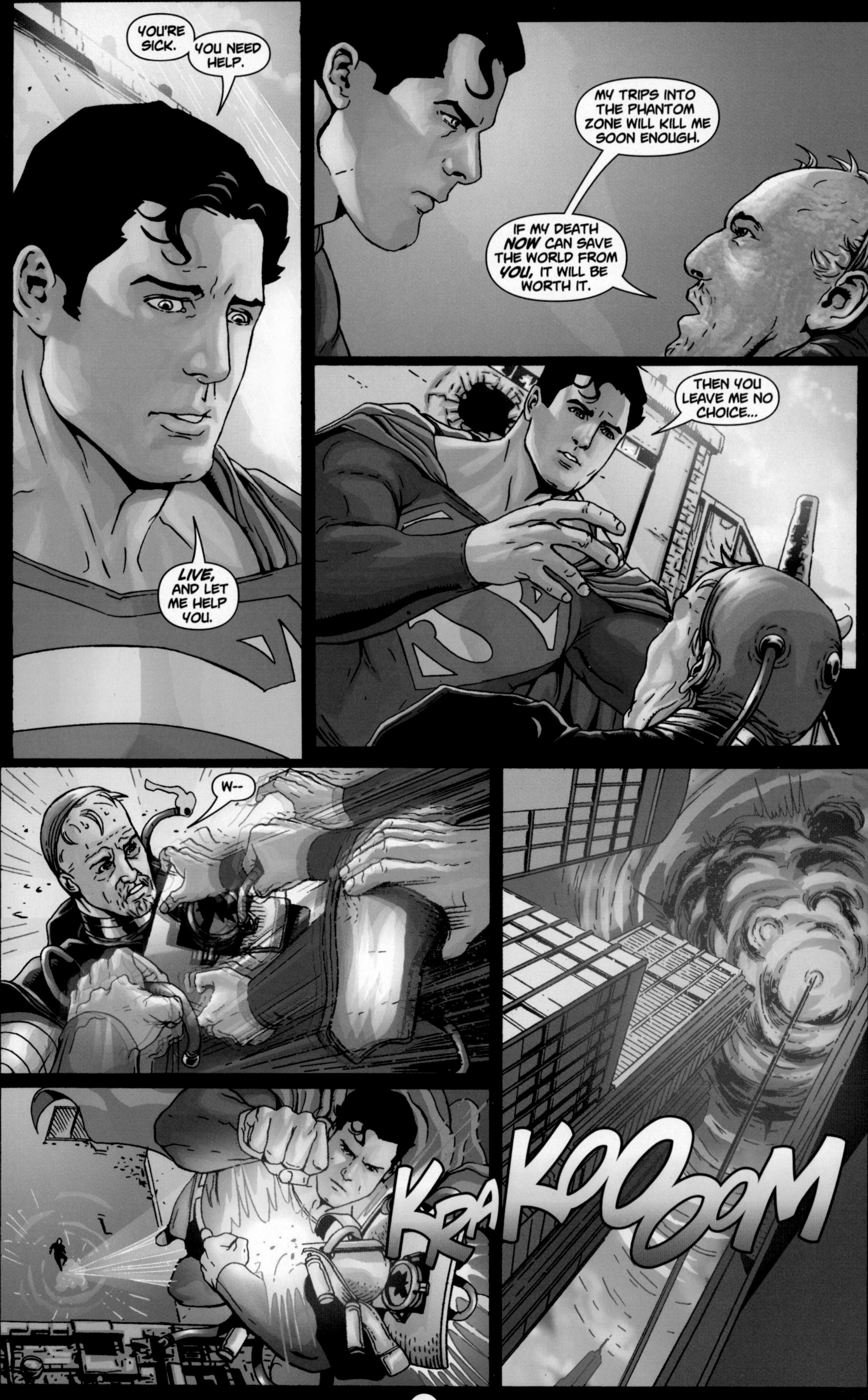
YOU'RE SICK.
YOU NEED HELP.
LIVE, AND LET ME HELP YOU.
MY TRIPS INTO THE PHANTOM ZONE WILL KILL ME SOON ENOUGH.
IF MY DEATH NOW CAN SAVE THE WORLD FROM YOU, IT WILL BE WORTH IT.
THEN YOU LEAVE ME NO CHOICE...
W--
KRAKOOOOOM

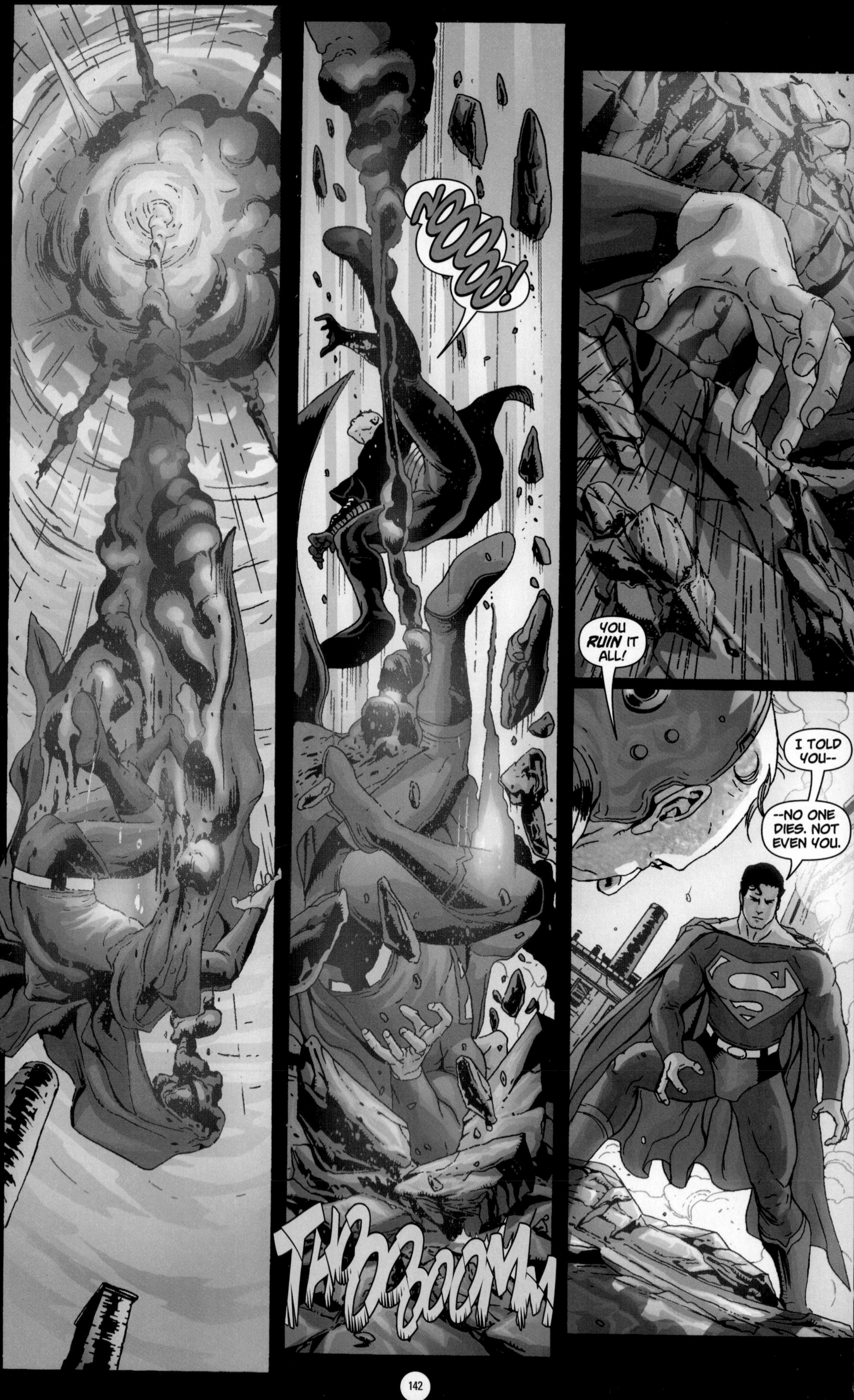
NOOOOO!
THOOOOOOMM
YOU RUIN IT ALL!
I TOLD YOU--
--NO ONE DIES. NOT EVEN YOU.

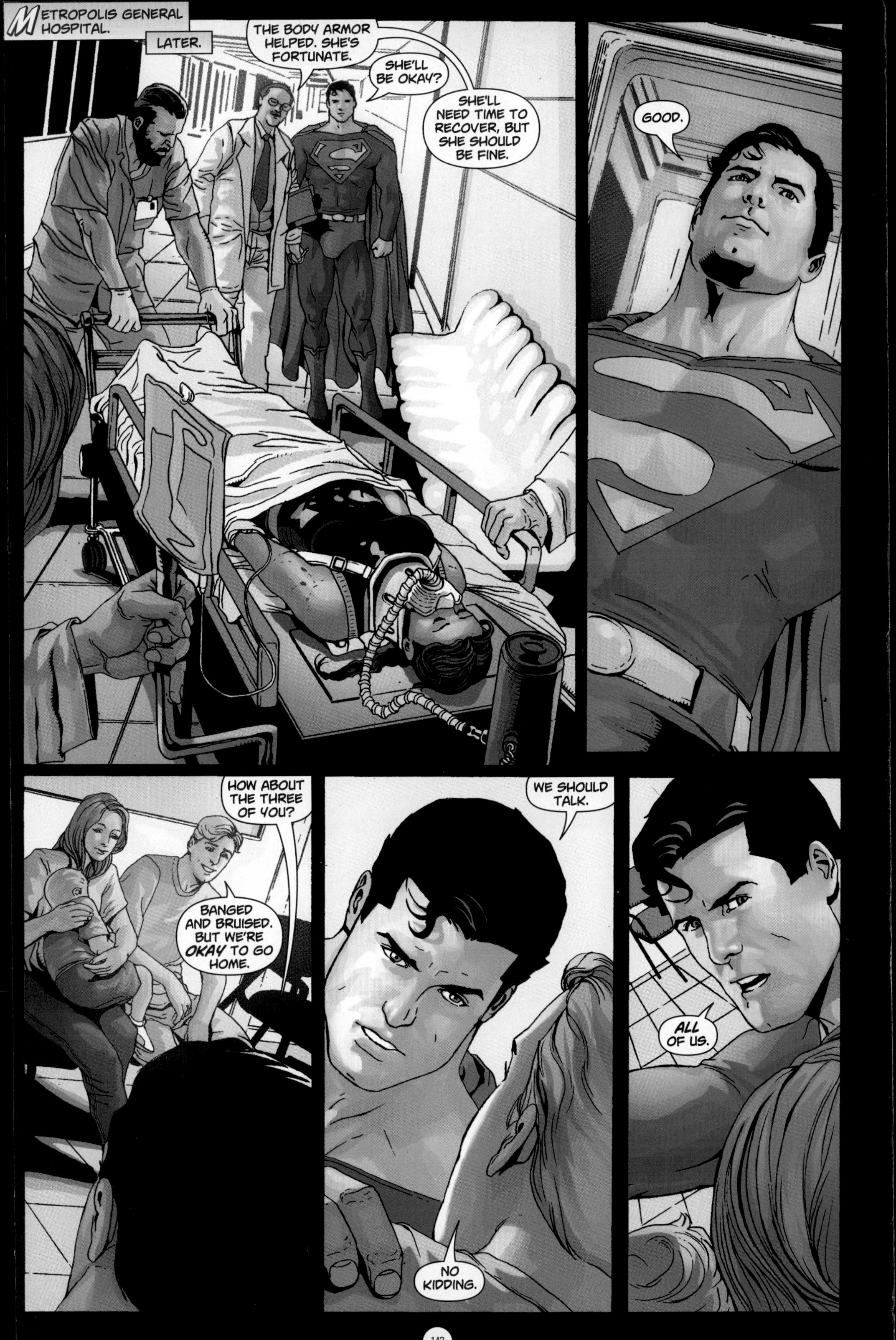
METROPOLIS GENERAL HOSPITAL.
LATER.
THE BODY ARMOR HELPED. SHE'S FORTUNATE.
SHE'LL BE OKAY?
SHE'LL NEED TIME TO RECOVER, BUT SHE SHOULD BE FINE.
GOOD.
HOW ABOUT THE THREE OF YOU?
BANGED AND BRUISED. BUT WE'RE *OKAY* TO GO HOME.
WE SHOULD TALK.
NO KIDDING.
ALL OF US.

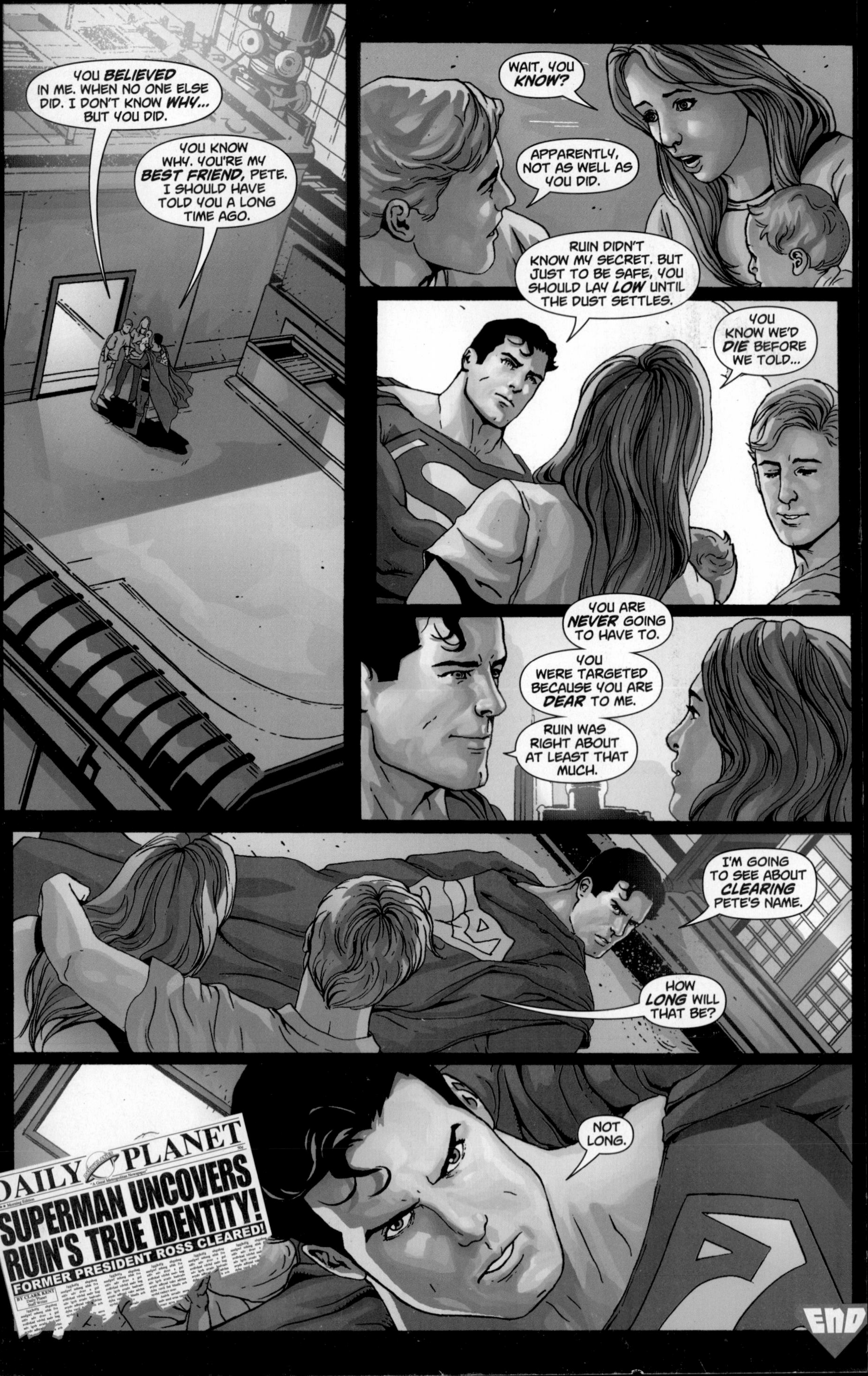
YOU BELIEVED IN ME. WHEN NO ONE ELSE DID. I DON'T KNOW WHY... BUT YOU DID.
YOU KNOW WHY. YOU'RE MY BEST FRIEND, PETE. I SHOULD HAVE TOLD YOU A LONG TIME AGO.
WAIT, YOU KNOW?
APPARENTLY, NOT AS WELL AS YOU DID.
RUIN DIDN'T KNOW MY SECRET. BUT JUST TO BE SAFE, YOU SHOULD LAY LOW UNTIL THE DUST SETTLES.
YOU KNOW WE'D DIE BEFORE WE TOLD...
YOU ARE NEVER GOING TO HAVE TO.
YOU WERE TARGETED BECAUSE YOU ARE DEAR TO ME.
RUIN WAS RIGHT ABOUT AT LEAST THAT MUCH.
I'M GOING TO SEE ABOUT CLEARING PETE'S NAME.
HOW LONG WILL THAT BE?
NOT LONG.
DAILY PLANET
SUPERMAN UNCOVERS RUIN'S TRUE IDENTITY!
FORMER PRESIDENT ROSS CLEARED!
BY CLARK KENT
END